Walking on Fire

Walking on Fire

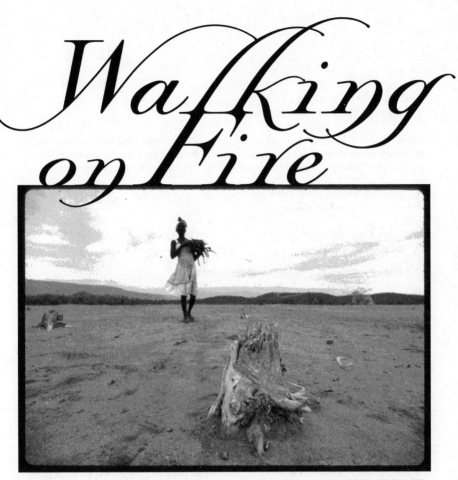

HAITIAN WOMEN'S STORIES OF SURVIVAL AND RESISTANCE

BEVERLY BELL

FOREWORD BY EDWIDGE DANTICAT

CORNELL UNIVERSITY PRESS

ITHACA AND LONDON

Copyright © 2001 by Beverly Bell
Foreword copyright © 2001 Cornell University

First published 2001 by Cornell University Press
First printing, Cornell Paperbacks, 2001

Printed in the United States of America

Library of Congress Cataloging-in-Publication Data

Bell, Beverly, 1962–
  Walking on fire : Haitian women's stories of survival and resistance
/ Beverly Bell.
    p. cm.
  Includes bibliographical references.
  ISBN 0-8014-3951-5 (cloth : alk. paper) — ISBN 0-8014-8748-X (pbk.
: alk. paper)
  1. Women—Haiti—Social conditions.   2. Women—Haiti—Interviews.
I. Title.
  HQ1511 .B45 2002
  305.42'097294—dc21
                                  2001004057

Cornell University Press strives to use environmentally responsible suppliers and materials to the fullest extent possible in the publishing of its books. Such materials include vegetable-based, low-VOC inks and acid-free papers that are recycled, totally chlorine-free, or partly composed of non-wood fibers. For further information, visit our website at www.cornellpress.cornell.edu.

Cloth printing   10 9 8 7 6 5 4 3 2 1
Paperback printing   10 9 8 7 6 5 4 3 2 1

To Rev. Jean-Marie Vincent,
who fell so others might rise,
and the fanm vanyan,
the valiant women,
aspiring to rise in Haiti
and everywhere.

CONTENTS

Foreword, by Edwidge Danticat ix

Preface: Beat Back the Darkness xiii

Acknowledgments xix

Introduction: The Women of Millet Mountain 1

1 Resistance in Survival 23
  YOLANDE MEVS *My Head Burning with the Burden* 36
  ALINA "TIBEBE" CAJUSTE *A Baby Left on the Doorstep in a Rotten Basket* 39
  LOVLY JOSAPHAT *I Always Live That Hope* 45
  ROSELIE JEAN-JUSTE *A Woman Named Roselie Who Fought Back* 50
  VENANTE DUPLAN *I Don't Have the Call, I Don't Have the Response* 55
  MARIE SONIA PANTAL *School* 57

2 Resistance as Expression 61
  LELENNE GILLES *I'll Die with the Words on My Lips* 68
  MARCELINE YRELIEN *Singing a Woman's Misery* 73
  ALINA "TIBEBE" CAJUSTE *Getting the Poetry* 76
  YANIQUE GUITEAU DANDIN *The Struggle for Creole* 82
  GRACITA OSIAS *Chaleron's Lesson* 83
  FLORENCIA PIERRE *The Cultural Soul* 86
  MARTINE FOURCAND *Expanding the Space of Expression* 90

3 Resistance for Political and Economic Change 93
  ALERTE BELANCE *My Blood and My Breath* 104
  YANNICK ETIENNE *A Grain of Sand* 110
  CLAUDETTE PHENE *A Little Light* 115
  YOLETTE ETIENNE *Jumping over the Fire* 120

LOUISE MONFILS *The Samaritan* 127
VITA TELCY *Five Cans of Corn* 131
MARIE JOSEE ST. FIRMIN *Sharing the Dream* 136
SELITANE JOSEPH *Chunk of Gold* 142
ROSEMIE BELVIUS *Reshuffling the Cards* 145

4 Resistance for Gender Justice 149
LISE-MARIE DEJEAN *Minister of the Status and Rights of Women* 157
GRACITA OSIAS *The Marriage Question* 163
LOUISE MONFILS *Walking with My Little Coffin* 166
CLAUDETTE WERLEIGH *Women's Business* 171
YOLANDE MEVS *Support for the Children* 176
YANIQUE GUITEAU DANDIN *A Country's Problems, A Woman's Problems* 178
MARIE JOSEE ST. FIRMIN *Deciding My Life* 182
OLGA BENOIT *Assuming the Title "Feminist"* 184
JOSETTE PERARD *The Carriage Is Leaving* 187

5 Resistance Transforming Power 193
CLAUDETTE WERLEIGH *Lighting Candles of Hope* 213
MARIE SONIA DELY *Sharing the Breadfruit* 214
LISE-MARIE DEJEAN *The People Say Jump* 216
MYRIAM MERLET *The More People Dream* 217
YANNICK ETIENNE *You Can't Eat Gumbo with One Finger* 221
MYRTO CELESTIN SAUREL *Rocks in the River* 223
KESTA OCCIDENT *A Stubborn Hope* 228

Epilogue: Resistance as Solidarity 231
ALERTE BELANCE *Get Up, Shake Your Bodies* 233

Notes 235

Glossary 243

For Further Research and Involvement 247

Bibliography 251

FOREWORD

EDWIDGE DANTICAT

"Walking on Fire," this is exactly what many Haitian women do everyday. Whether they are pounding pots and pans against the walls of their homes to protest the latest injustice, carrying heavy baskets on their heads for miles to the marketplace, singing by the river as they pound stones on the family wash, running a ministry dedicated to the status and rights of women, heading a grass-roots organization, or advising the government on financial matters, they always seem to have one foot over burning coals and the other aimed at solid ground.

In this book, you will meet many of those women as they try to avoid the flames and reach the other side. You will hear their stories in their own voices—or as close to their own voices as possible. You will meet Alina "Tibebe" Cajuste, who even though she was denied her own name as a child, reclaimed her voice by reciting poetry. You will meet Yanique Guiteau Daudin, whose life passion is to elevate her native language, Creole, for an entire section of the population that is silenced each time the language is repressed. You will meet Alerte Belance, who was left for dead in a ditch by the paramilitary henchmen who abducted and assaulted her, thinking they could take her life, never imagining that her spirit was strong enough to endure beyond suffering to witness, beyond despair to hope, beyond silence to testimony. You will meet Claudette Werleigh, once a cabinet member, who now sees her work, and the work of women like her, as "lighting candles of hope." Hope that thrives against all odds in women like Rosemie Belvius, who even after running naked from a burning house, returns to her hometown to continue to organize women to fight against the same kinds of attacks that had nearly taken her life.

Though these women have been forced to be more than heroic by the turbulent period covered by this book, the point is not to mythologize them. As they recount their survival, their resistance, their joy, their pride, their pains, the tone is almost matter-of-fact, as if they are simultaneously asking themselves, their interviewers, and now their readers, "What would you do if you were in my place?" Though one is almost tempted to stand up and cheer, find them and embrace them, beg them for their secrets, the answer always seems to be, "I would wish to do as well as you have." "I would hope to have been able to survive." "I would pray to have lived to testify." And testify is what each of them does, valiantly, eloquently, often modestly, while giving us not too commonly gendered lessons about Haiti, its history, its beauty, and its heartaches.

As we follow these women, they lead us to the sources of their inspiration: the women who came before them, the heroines of Haitian lore—Anacaona, and the goddess of love, Erzulie—their protest songs, their lost loved ones, their mothers, their children, and even Jesus Christ. No shred of hope is too near or too far to contemplate, no ounce of optimism overlooked. No person, no country is beyond redemption, especially their own, where hope is like a transient treasure that must be discovered again and again.

Like Yolette Etienne, a grassroots women's groups organizer, I kept thinking of the bamboo tree as I read and reread these testimonies. The bamboo, which before broader and more towering trees might appear brittle and frail, is able to bend against strong winds so that it is neither uprooted nor broken. The same bamboo, which if placed over fire, sounds like a gun barrel as its inner layers explode.

"What I have witnessed, I have no tongue to tell," explains Michaelle Jean-Louis, a vendor in Haiti's street markets. However, what makes these narratives so exceptional and their telling so valuable is their attempt at defining the undefinable, their recounting, in a few sentences, phrases, and paragraphs, experiences that are not only segments of individual lives but also indispensable sections of the larger fabric of Haitian history.

These testimonials are instructive and cathartic, for a nation that due to a series of continuous struggles has never really had time to pause and grieve any single tragedy for long. These women are not only brave, but they are also vulnerable, some battle-weary at times from losses of homes, families, and in a few cases, even country. However, their telling their stories is in itself an act of renewal, a celebration of survival, a moment of witness, for both the speakers and the listeners. The reader gains privileged entry into this intimate circle in part because the author and interviewer places these voices in context—in the context of Haitian history, the history of women's rights, the encroachment of globalization, migration, and the consequent efforts to mitigate their scars.

"Haitian women's history is such a long story," says Vita Telcy, a community health worker. "If we started talking about it, we'd have to stop midstream because otherwise we'd be talking all night."

Haitian women's history, women's history in general, has just gotten even longer and more interesting with the addition of these incredible women's voices. Let us gather around and listen to them. For after every night must come the dawn, a dawn that will take us not only midstream but all the way to the other side, away from the fires and the coals and hopefully toward more solid ground.

PREFACE

BEAT BACK THE DARKNESS

Bat tenèb, to beat back the darkness, is one of the many traditions in which Haitians turn their meager tools of survival—in this case, cooking spoons and pots—into a mighty form of power. In a daring and deafening act, women in the slums beat against metal to raise their voices against repression.

This book is a *bat tenèb*.

Walking on Fire began during the bleak years of a military dictatorship, 1991–1994. It did not take off, though, until the elected government was restored to Haiti in October 1994, when women were—at least for the time—free to speak out publicly. Although Haiti was relatively secure when most of the narratives were offered, everyone knew that insecurity and reprisals lurked around every corner. Still, Haiti was a nation whose people had just been gagged for three years by rape, disappearance, and murder. Women yearned to tell what they had suffered and survived, both for catharsis from the horror and for relief from a lengthy enforced silence.

Many of the women who speak on these pages have been my friends and colleagues for years, the relationships forged during our long collaboration for political and economic rights. To find other participants, I sought recommendations from key organizations of women, peasants, factory workers, and Christian base communities.

I recorded most of the narratives after President Aristide was restored to Haiti, while codirecting his International Liaison Office. Even if I had been able to work on the project full-time, it would have been impossible to meet the demand of all the women who wanted to give their stories. As word of the book spread, women I had never heard of began showing up in my office and home. Once, I was invited to an afternoon meeting of rape survivors where the organizer asked the packed room for one or two volunteers. Hours later, I ran out of cassettes as the last four women patiently awaited their turn to speak.

It is a tribute to the women and men who created the recent political changes in Haiti that this text could be written at all. At no other time in Haiti's history would large numbers of women have been able to speak so openly. Though several individuals raised questions about safety, and women's groups sometimes engaged in long discussions before deciding it was wise to participate, everyone I consulted, without exception, chose to do so. While each participant was given the option of using a *nom de guerre*, all decided to use their true name except two who always used a pseudonym in their public lives.

Even released from political constraints, the project was far from easy. As few Haitians have phones or street addresses, making contact with a particular woman often required going through elaborate chains of intermediaries in what Haitians call *teledjòl*, tele-jaw. In other instances, weeks would pass while I waited for my security clearance to come through. Often to meet the women, I traveled for hours in a battered Toyota on tracks barely resembling roads, sometimes on convoluted reconnaissance missions covering vast expanses of bush. Or I journeyed in *tap-taps*, converted flatbeds, emblazoned with *Bondye si bon*, God is so good, or *Non Jezebel*, where I held on my lap an elderly man, a soaked toddler, or two guinea fowl tied together by their feet. On occasion, the women walked for miles on narrow paths down steep mountains to meet me. During the rainy season in Cité Soleil, either the collaborators or I would slosh through green, ankle-deep, open sewers to find each other.

Women told their stories in sweltering tin shacks with flies buzzing around our sweat-covered bodies, in dirt yards with goats or chickens, and in an underground organizing center scarred with the broken windows and battered doors of a recent military attack. One woman recounted her story on a rooftop in a raging thunderstorm, another in a vodou temple, a third in a busy coffin-manufacturing workshop. The women and I sat on cement floors or lumpy beds or chairs with no seats. Often it was a strain to hear the women over the noise of children and roosters and car horns. Over and over, meetings took place in the pitch darkness of a *blakaout*, blackout, when whole parts of town—more often than not, the poor parts—lost electricity.

Interviews always took place in Creole, the first language of all Haitians and the only language of the majority. All interviews were open-ended and unstructured so as not to skew the outcome. They began with my holding a small tape recorder and saying, "Tell me anything you want about your life, about what it's like to be a Haitian woman." Invariably, within moments each woman had taken the recorder into her own hands as she began to recount her past and envision her country's future.

Help in transcribing and translating the 100-plus cassettes came from a large and wonderful team of Haitians and Americans. By then, Haiti had completed its first-ever transition from one democratically elected president to another, my colleagues and I had closed down Aristide's International Liaison Office, and I had moved to a mountain village in New Mexico to concentrate on this book. In my apartment in a dilapidated hacienda, sandwiched between a buffalo pasture and an Indian pueblo, I repeatedly answered the phone to hear this: the voice of a Haitian woman in Brooklyn or Boston or rural Florida, whom I didn't know, saying, "I *must* be involved with the book."

After completing a first round of editing, I again traveled south to meet with each storyteller and read back the text that had been created from her words. We worked together, correcting what I had misheard; adding what she had forgotten the first time; deleting what she realized, in retrospect, was dangerous to print. By the time the text had been reshaped to her specifications, every woman was in accord with both the content of her testimony and with how it would fit within *Walking on Fire*'s thematic structure.

None of the terms that normally characterize narratives of this sort—story, oral history, life history, ethnography, testimony—accurately reflect the nature of what is told here. Beyond their own experiences and analyses, almost all of the women weave in their interpretation of Haitian life, moving back and forth between personal anecdotes and macropolitical discussion. The best description of these narratives is the Creole word *istwa*, meaning both story and history.[1]

Borrowing on the tradition of the venerated storyteller, which stretches back to Africa and extends across Haiti, those who give their *istwa* here are termed *griyo*. Throughout Haiti, *griyo* are the repositories and transmitters of wisdom and knowledge. At all-night wakes, around evening cooking fires, in travels from hamlet to hamlet, and amidst circles of children, the *griyo* pass on the stories of the family, the village, and the country. In this predominantly oral culture, the *griyo* guard the word and determine how the word is spoken. The women in *Walking on Fire* are far younger than traditional *griyo* elders, and to my knowledge none holds this honor in her own family or village. Yet in this book, they are the keepers and recounters of history, truth, and wisdom.

The women's diverse responses to their realities call for expansive analyses, challenging monolithic assumptions often made about people in poor and black countries. Through their *istwa*, the *griyo* defy cultural and gender essentialism and implicitly rebuff any attempt to create a paradigm or symbol of "Haitian woman."

Walking on Fire is intended to pay homage to the vision, resistance, and daily triumphs of the women who speak within it but without minimizing the anguish of devastating poverty and repression. It would be impossible to present only one or the other, the ongoing victories or the ongoing pain; they exist simultaneously, heads and tails of the same coin.

There are many omissions from this set of *istwa*. Absent are the voices of those who were defeated—the thousands of women killed by military regimes, unalleviated hunger, or illness. In the interest of putting manageable borders around this project, the voices of women in exile are also excluded. Nor are the wealthy represented here, and the only middle-class women included are those who have chosen to stand with the marginalized majority. In this way I hope to offset the distortions of commonly presented history, in which the poor are underrepresented or missing altogether.

It is critical to acknowledge the power differentials reflected within the production and consumption of this book. There is, first, the matter of the disparity between this author—a white, middle-class American—and the black Haitian peasants who are the focus of this book. There exist, too, sizable contradictions in the consumption, by a largely Western, educated audience, of a text based on the lives of poor women from the global South. For one thing, the book is not written in the Haitians' language. Even if it were, most Haitian women do not read. Even if they did, most would not have the money to buy the book nor the time to read it.

Still, we Americans and Haitians from various classes who have been involved in creating this text hope that its contributions will outweigh the limitations of a lack of fully egalitarian or feminist process. For my part, I echo the words of anthropologist Lila Abu-Lughod: "The world from which I write still has tremendous discursive, military, and economic power. My writing can either sustain it or work against its grain."[2]

It is my hope that poor Haitian women will soon become empowered enough to write their own life stories, in their original words. *Walking on Fire* has already propelled that goal forward. One woman, Marie Josée St. Firmin, announced decisively, "Now that I've gotten started, I'm just going to have to write my autobiography!" The aforementioned group of rape survivors, after participating in this work, decided to launch their own oral history project. Many *griyo* declared their self-worth magnified. Lenyse Oscar and several others told me they had never before considered that their personal stories might be of interest to anyone, and Ginette Joseph reported, "I never realized my life was this important."

We who collaborated on this book also hope that it will strengthen solidarity between Haitian women and readers in the United States. We view that solidarity as bidirectional. On the one hand, the vision and experience of the movement for social change in Haiti have much to offer American efforts for a more compassionate, humane, and democratic society. On the other hand, we hope that American readers will be moved to support the Haitian people in their quest for justice, especially when barriers to that justice lie within U.S. spheres of power, as with the policies of the U.S. government, the World Bank, the International Monetary Fund, and the World Trade Organization.

In these ways, perhaps *Walking on Fire* can serve as a small contribution toward diminishing the harsh inequalities and contradictions so that Haitian women—and their sisters and brothers everywhere—can ultimately attain the better lives and better world they seek.

ACKNOWLEDGMENTS

The number of people who have been involved in turning this dream into a book is literally countless. I am grateful for their collaboration and humbled by their profound commitment to the cause *Walking on Fire* seeks to further.

Chapo ba, hats off, to all the women who gave their *istwa*, including those whose narratives were not included here due to space constraints: Claude Ambroise, RoseAnne Auguste, Jacqueline "Sè Fritz" Desir, Therese Desir, Marie Carme Eulice, Matylia Fleurvil, Bebe Ilopsi, Ginette Joseph, Maria Joseph, Mesinette Louis, Lenyse Oscar, Ghislaine Payen, Estella Rejuste, Freda St. Juste, Clairedora St. Vil, and Edèle Thébaud.

Numerous individuals deserve my deep thanks for their invaluable assistance with translation, transcription, editing, and research: Bina Agarwal, Candace Akins, Marie Simone Alexandre, Larissa Annoual, Myriam Augustin, Max Blanchet, Carla Blunschley, Caroline Butler, Dorothy Chavannes, Andrea Clardy, Gina Constant, Marie Andrine Constant, Peggy Dadaille, Courtney Fell, Danielle Georges, Bee Gosnell, Anne Hastings, Mika Hilbers, Mona Jean and the association of rape survivors of Martissant, Mara Kaufman, Hershe Michele Kramer, Sabine Mattar, Myriam Merlet, Gina Moïse, Josette Pérard, Marie M. B. Racine, Guitele Rahill, Laurie Richardson, Jennie Smith, Emmanuel Vedrine, Joan Wade, Anna Wardenburg, and Claudette Werleigh. Six people merit profound thanks for their dedication of so much time, talent, and heart: Gabrielle Civil, Edwidge Danticat, Cynthia Green, Tara Hefferan, John Nichols, and Suzanne Phillips.

For generous financial and in-kind support, I am deeply appreciative of

Robin Lloyd, as well as Jacques Bartoli, the Bay Area Haitian-American Coalition, Ann Garvin, Leah Gordon, Bishop Tom Gumbleton, the Lambi Fund of Haiti, Rev. Joseph Lapauw and Missionhurst-CICM, the Money for Women/Barbara Deming Memorial Fund, Maggie Steber, and the Women's Peacepower Foundation.

Finally, five people deserve special recognition. Catherine Maternowska, sister, editor, and one-woman pep squad. Frances Benson, editor at Cornell University Press, who believed in these stories. Rev. Antoine Adrien, my premier mentor. And most of all, Bryan and Rubie Crosby Bell, unconditional supporters of this book project and its author from day one. To you all, *mèsi anpil.* Thank you very, very much.

Walking on Fire

INTRODUCTION

THE WOMEN OF MILLET MOUNTAIN

Many years ago, under the fecund mango trees on Mòn Pitimi, Millet Mountain, and around the embers of the fires on which they had cooked their suppers of corn porridge, Josie, Nana, Micheline, Dieusil, Rosianne, and Marie Maude told their stories.

Josie always told the same story, but no one minded. All eyes focused intently on her as she slowly brought her knees up closer to her chest and, with long narrow fingers, drew the edges of her skirt more tightly under her lean calves. Though years have passed, I can almost remember her every word. "The courage of Haitian women has a background. It didn't begin now, no. It began with Anacaona, an Indian queen."

Josie continued in a deep voice. "You know Haiti was peopled by Indians before the Spanish came. There were several zones, with a king for each zone. Anacaona was the wife of one of those kings. Near Leogane, close to here. Now what was the name of that king? I can never remember his name. Anyway, when the Spanish disembarked in Haiti, the Indians received them with open arms. But the Spanish wanted gold. They made the Indians do hard labor for that gold. Oh, it was brutal."

The women sitting on rocks in the small circle were still. "The Indians began to revolt. Anacaona's husband was one of the kings struggling against the Spanish. Anacaona herself was a poetess and singer. But still she was supporting her husband shoulder-to-shoulder. When the Spanish killed him, Anacaona carried on the fight. She was courageous. I tell you: courageous! She rallied others to challenge the Spanish; she organized and plotted to save their land. But the

Spanish had sophisticated weapons; Anacaona had none. They captured her and killed her too.

"From Anacaona we were born. When you take our history—the struggle against the invaders, the war of independence, and everything that came after—there were women there standing strong, right next to the men. But they're rarely told about in history. Only their husbands—unless a woman does the telling."

"Mm!" Old, toothless Nana made a sharp sound in her throat, then said, "*Eben.*" Oh well. The look on her wizened face managed to express both smug satisfaction and resignation—a common expression when Haitians take in their proud past and painful present at once. The only sounds for some moments, as each woman stared reflectively at the fire, were the popping of embers and the shuffling of stiff legs rearranging themselves in the dust. Then Rosianne sighed heavily.

It would be years before I realized the significance of what the women pondered that thick damp night. The story of Anacaona, especially as juxtaposed to late-twentieth-century Haiti, spoke worlds about matters essential to Haitian women. It addressed fundamental questions of power, resistance, history, and women's roles therein. Those four issues are the subjects of this introduction. As any poor Haitian woman knows, to leave out any one of those areas is to render the story incomplete.

POWER AND RESISTANCE ON MILLET MOUNTAIN

It was within that *lakou,* the packed-earth courtyard at the center of the circle of mud-and-thatch huts beside the sugarcane fields, where I first began listening to Haitian women. And I have been listening to them, in the slim domains where they are able to speak and be heard, ever since those evenings in 1977. Through the decades I have been consistently struck by the dissonance between how Haitian women experience and understand their lives, and how those lives are presented and perceived in the larger world.

The portrayals of people in the global South that circulate in the North rarely come from Southerners themselves, especially the poorest ones. Perhaps nowhere is this phenomenon more true than in the case of poor Haitian women. They are virtually absent as recorders of history and as actors in that history. The routine muffling of their voices has expunged the lives of millions of Haitian citizens. It has also crippled the breadth, depth, and accuracy of depictions of Haiti, its history, and its women. At best, women are portrayed peripherally, as helpless victims or exotic folklore.

Anacaona's tale, as presented by Josie, is something altogether different. Both the account and how it was told reveal a great deal about power dynamics. Most Haitians in the largely illiterate society learn their history through stories shared around a cooking fire or in an open-air marketplace, a community washing hole at a bend in a river, or a thatched-roof church on a rocky field. Oral storytelling is how people transfer cultural memory. It is also one tool with which to challenge domination by the elite. The tradition gives those denied power in other domains the space to speak within their community. And it lets them memorialize their history of resistance, a history that is largely absent from the official transcript. For women, it allows them to put a gender perspective on the story.

In the same vein, the *griyo* in *Walking on Fire* are challenging control of the production of information and knowledge. Like Anacaona, all are freedom fighters in one way or another. Some do not read or write. Few have had the opportunity to influence the public record. Thus, if not for the oral tradition, most of their acts, like those of Anacaona, would be lost from memory. Yet in this text, women become the chroniclers and interpreters of history. Their own feats, struggles, and legacies, which otherwise would be written out of history, are instead written into it.

Simply changing dominant ways of seeing and of canonizing history cannot transform the forces and structures that threaten or thwart the survival of poor Haitian women. Knowledge and belief systems alone cannot match the strength of rubber truncheons, AIDS, and an unequal global economy; the women who speak in this book are poor and violated no matter how the world understands them. Their problems are rooted in entrenched systems—Haitian and international—that have systematically robbed them of land, resources, viable incomes, and social enfranchisement. Yet altering the way these women, and others in similar positions, are viewed and understood in the world is a first step toward changing the relations of power that determine the conditions of their lives.

Each evening on Millet Mountain, old Nana would light her pipe—that is, if she had the money to buy tobacco that day. Someone else would stir the charcoal embers with a stick. And the women would begin their *istwa*. Most of the stories were decidedly more quotidian than that of Anacaona. They were about how Micheline's husband had left her and their four children to go cut sugarcane in the Dominican Republic last week because he couldn't find any work at home. And how one-eyed Maïlene's hut had been torn down by white missionaries who, armed with a paper from President-for-Life François Duvalier, claimed that her tiny plot of land belonged to them. Together the women around the fire filled in details about the death of Shabim's baby boy on Tuesday after Shabim hadn't been able to find the twenty cents in bus fare to get him to the hospital in time.

The stories followed themes of suffering, survival, and transcendence. Underlying them all were the women's dismal poverty and the constraints on their power—defined here as the ability of a social class or group to realize its own interests.[1] Transversing the words—and perhaps more importantly, the silences—were the themes of coercion and domination by a brutal dictatorship, the local landowner, and their husbands.

The *istwa* also revealed the women's strong wills, fierce pride, and creativity in making their lives more sustainable. One week after the missionaries had robbed her land, Maïlene had her nephew slice a steak off the flank of the white couple's cow as a small act of retribution. After years of silently observing her man Fanfan having affairs, Simone finally took her case to the community, trashing the scoundrel to anyone who would listen. Brazen Giselle spoke out, as was her habit, this time cursing the Tonton Macoute—the member of the state terror gang—who demanded payment of forty gourdes, lying that her old cow had strayed into his Congo pea garden. And she was locked up in the Leogane jail as a result.

Resistance, or the negotiation of power by the weaker against the strong, was a dominant element. As the *istwa* from Millet Mountain demonstrated, if the outcomes of power serve the interests of the powerful, then the outcomes of resistance, when effective, serve the interests of the powerless.[2]

Traditionally, analysts have used four criteria to identify resistance: The action must be collective and organized; it must be principled and selfless; it must have a revolutionary impact; and it must negate the basis of domination.[3] As a nation, Haiti boasts many historical cases that fit these criteria. They include uprisings against the French, with protracted battles and *mawonaj*, the escape and guerrilla tactics practiced by underground communities of slaves; the total emancipation from slavery in 1804; the defeat of Napoleon Bonaparte's army and of colonial rule, also in 1804; an armed insurrection against the U.S. occupation of 1915–1934; the peaceful overthrow of a thirty-year dictatorship in 1986; and the reversal of a coup d'etat in 1994.

These feats notwithstanding, standard criteria are far too narrow to encapsulate the breadth of Haitian resistance. The *istwa* recounted in this book bring to light some of the many challenges to domination that are usually overlooked. The narratives also expand in two ways—one general and one particular to Haiti—how resistance is normally perceived and measured.

In the first instance, the definition of resistance is expanded to include any act that keeps the margins of power from being further encroached upon, even where the protagonist cannot expand those margins. Given the forces arrayed against a Haitian woman, simply to *kenbe la,* hold the line—even without making any advance—is a victory. If she does no more than maintain her resources and rights—in the face of attempts by other people, institutions, or systems to deny her them—then she practices resistance.

This element is notable in the case of survival, as stated time and again in the *istwa*. Survival can be a purposeful act of defiance against the many components of life in Haiti, from assassination to disease to despair, that impel the destruction of body and spirit. For example, the preservation of something as seemingly intrinsic as moral integrity or dignity—given the exertions of will required—can be a triumph.

Haitian resistance, in particular, is also reexamined here to incorporate a wide range of forms where domination is rejected in implied, covert, or daily ways. Resistance does not arise only from those who are political in a traditional sense, such as leaders of prodemocracy groups, organizers of cooperatives, and radical cultural workers. The *griyo* demonstrate, in the case of Haiti, what James Scott and others have argued elsewhere: resistance is often subtle or imperceptible. It bubbles beneath the surface, outside obvious public domains. Even where the women appear to be quiescent or the margins of maneuverability seem to be completely constrained, they might be engaged in multilayered negotiations of power.

There are numerous reasons why resistance may go unseen or underreported. Many gestures in the unremarkable, quotidian realms of Haitian women's lives are overlooked, and challenges to power often occur in just those domains. An outsider might miss the intentionality or significance of small-scale, discrete dissent or fail to notice its occurrence at all. Too, acts of the poor generally are not recorded when they oppose the interests of the rich. Because elite sectors control the public transcript, and with rare exception the media, such actions are likely to disappear from the record except where they constitute exceptional rebellion or revolution.[4]

Of course, not everyone challenges the status quo. Protest does not occur at all times and in all places. At various points in their lives, individuals may give themselves over to their fate and go along with the system. This is evidenced by Haitian women gently slapping the back of one work-worn hand into the palm of the other and murmuring, *M reziyen m.* I resign myself.

Some observers might assume defeat, or worse: false consciousness, the concept that the women have bought into their own subjugation. But there is no way to know that the women have acquiesced out of weariness or that they have been won over ideologically. Instead, the necessary circumstances for protest—such as political awareness, leadership, social cohesion, and infrastructure for organizing—simply may not exist during that period. Rebellion may be latent or in quiet formation. Protest rarely bursts onto the scene full-blown; more often it forms the same way peasants make charcoal from sticks, smoldering below the surface, in development, for some time.

Alternatively, women may be engaged in a survival strategy based on the *appearance* of compliance. Defending the space to live, and protecting against the consequences of protest, may mean conciliatory activity and relations with their enemies.[5]

The main body of *Walking on Fire* looks at how one of the most disadvantaged populations in the world negotiates the circumstances of their everyday lives to access more personal, political, and socioeconomic control. Daily the women of Millet Mountain, and their compatriots throughout the island nation, climb over barriers and probe the tension between oppression and rebellion. Where their survival depends on their maintaining silence or acquiescence, they may do that. Where they find an opening, they may push—often gently, so no one will notice, but sometimes hard because they feel they have no other choice. Where there is no opening, they may seek to create one. Their exertions of will may mean, at certain times, simply refusing to despair, and at other times, refusing to die. How they mitigate the crippling impacts of their gender, class, and race is elaborated throughout these chapters. When their acts are multiplied by the thousands, these women have altered the larger society and political economy, changing the country's course.

The resistance takes different forms: covert and overt, individual and group, and combinations thereof. The zone of struggle is often material, against economic and political oppression. Yet as Scott noted, "Poverty is far more than a simple matter of not enough calories or cash."[6] The ideological issues that accompany poor Haitian women's social position, such as shame and disrespect, are key to their suffering. Thus, their dissent is also ideological in nature, challenging human degradation.

Each chapter focuses on a different form of resistance, including maintaining survival and psychological integrity (Chapter 1); enacting personal, political, and cultural expression (Chapter 2); battling for political and economic justice (Chapter 3); fighting gender oppression (Chapter 4); and transforming the nature and application of power to create a new civil society and polity (Chapter 5). This collection represents only a fraction of the strategies employed on a daily basis. Others have been omitted, at the hushed warnings of the book's collaborators, so as to remain effective.

At the same time, to overstate poor women's capacity to fight back is to exaggerate their ability to make choices and act upon them. Crediting them with social power they do not have can result, in turn, in assigning women responsibility for the desperate condition of their lives.[7] For example, "Third world" women are often blamed for "choosing" to have so many children. But the seven offspring of Celine Edgar, who live with her deep within a maze of alleyways so narrow the sun never penetrates, illustrate that many large families are the result of something other than free choice. Celine's lack of economic and gender power have constrained her options to short-term survival strategies. Financial desperation propelled her into the successive liaisons through which she repeatedly became pregnant. She was aware that every man would probably leave her life as quickly as he entered it—which all the men did. Still, she needed the small gifts of cash and food that the successive partners brought into her household so much that she felt her only option was to sleep with them. Moreover, gender relations in Haiti are such that Celine could not have gotten her partners to wear condoms—even if she could have afforded them and even though it meant increasing the risk of pregnancy.

On a larger scale, underestimating the impact of national and international forces in Haitian history and politics has erroneously led to ascribing the imperiled state of Haiti to a failure of Haitians themselves. "What could we possibly do to help Haiti?" a high-level official in the Bush *Père* administration asked me. "Haven't they just made a basket case of their country?" To understand that land's dire domestic situation and its peripheral location in the world system, it is necessary to recall that for centuries, Haiti has been exploited by more powerful international actors. In other words, the majority of Haitians have been excluded from the decisions that have resulted in their country's crises.

Still, the lives and actions described in this book demonstrate that there is no *absolute* line between power and powerlessness. How women challenge their constraints, or amass strength and resources *within* those constraints, is the focus of *Walking on Fire*.

A HISTORY OF POWER AND RESISTANCE

Haitians say, *Pou w konprann sa k pase joudi a, fòk ou konnen sa k pase anvan.* To understand today we must know the past. Most do. To wit: The vast majority of women on Millet Mountain do not know their age, sign their names with an X, and believe that Miami is a country. But ask them about their nation's history and they will reel off a dizzying litany of personages and events. And they will do so with an obvious pride over what their ancestors—Anacaona, and others more humble—accomplished.

This domestic pride stands in stark contrast to a dominant international perception of Haiti as an irredeemable country. "Haiti is the only country in the world with a last name. It is Haiti, the Poorest Country in the Western Hemisphere," says the poet Jean-Claude Martineau. The nation is often characterized, overtly or through inference, as a troubled, Godforsaken place, where troubling, Godforsaken things happen.[8]

Problems that occur elsewhere *are* often more extreme in Haiti, the causes found in age-old processes of domination and expropriation. But, hold the history up to a different light and another pattern becomes visible. This is a history in which the destitute majority has constantly vied with national and foreign states and elite sectors for control of Haiti's material resources and political voice. It is an interplay between exertions of power by the strong and of resistance by the weak.

The history is particularly compelling because of the determination and aggressiveness of each side. The iron might of successive Haitian rulers, on one side, is infamous. Yet on the other side, the poor citizenry has been equally obstinate. Two centuries of noncompliance, protest, and revolt have kept the economic and political rulers from ever fully consolidating their power.

Haiti's path toward becoming a sovereign nation of free women and men in 1804 reflects this interplay. When Spanish colonists arrived with Columbus in 1492, they quickly decimated the Arawak, Anacaona's people, and the Caribs. Within twenty-seven years of colonization, brutal labor practices and the spread of European diseases had taken the lives of roughly nine hundred thousand of the original one million Indians.[9] The Spanish then imported Africans to replenish the labor force and generate riches. In the early days of the slave trade, the number of Africans brought to the entire French West Indies was small relative to the number brought to many other parts of the Americas: one thousand to two thousand people annually at the end of the 1600s. Then came the introduction of sugarcane by the French, who had supplanted the Spanish in 1697. The cultivation and processing of cane required a large and diversified labor force; within a century, the average immigration of enslaved people to the region had grown to roughly thirty-seven thousand.[10] On the back of this labor, Haiti produced the most wealth of any colony in the Caribbean, earning it the sobriquet "Pearl of the Antilles." Indeed, Haiti became one of the most productive colonies in the world.

In the 1790s, the Africans and their descendants began a rebellion that merged subterfuge, violence, and *mawonaj*. Women played key roles throughout. In 1804, black and mulatto Haitians were able to declare themselves free from both slavery and colonialism. The victory marked the only successful slave revolution in world history. It made Haiti the first independent black republic in the world, and the second independent country in the Western Hemisphere, after the United States.

Though liberated from France and from official slavery, still poor women and men never became free. Self-proclaimed emperors and presidents-for-life, militaries and Tontons Macoutes all exploited the poor for the benefit of a small elite: the oligarchy and commercial sector, and the governments that served them.

Meanwhile, foreign nations and capital exerted their force over Haiti and its citizens. Nervous at the message the revolution would send to the slaves of other nations, the United States refused to recognize Haiti's sovereignty for fifty-eight years. It determined, moreover, to weaken Haiti's economy by spearheading an international embargo. Then from 1915 to 1934, the United States again imposed its authority on the restive nation through a military occupation. During this time, the United States reinforced its control by drafting a new Haitian constitution and creating a new security apparatus—an early precursor to the Tontons Macoutes. When Haitian civilians organized an armed guerrilla force, the Cacos, to repel the invaders, the U.S. Marines exterminated them and publicly displayed their dead leader, Charlemagne Peralte, in crucifixion position.

Among internal influences on Haiti, the Duvalier family regime has been one of the most damaging. First rising to power in a rigged 1957 election, the country doctor François "Papa Doc" Duvalier quickly consolidated his power into a vicious dictatorship. Duvalier's personal force, the Volunteers for National Security, was so named because the troops were unpaid; extortion, then, became their means of survival. The more common appellation was Tontons Macoutes, from the lore that good children get presents from Tonton Noel, Uncle Christmas, while bad children are carried away by Tonton Macoute, Uncle Sack, never to be seen again. The sunglass-wearing, Uzi-toting militia assassinated thousands of citizens, while imprisoning and torturing countless more.

Duvalier affected the persona of Baron Samedi, the vodou *lwa*, spirit, who controls all the souls of the graveyards. To a nation of faithful *vodouizan*, worshipers, the message was that opposition to his rule was futile since his control over his subjects' lives extended into eternity. Before his death in 1971, Duvalier turned the self-proclaimed title of president-for-life over to his rotund eighteen-year-old motorcyclist son, Jean-Claude or "Baby Doc."

The Duvalier reign was backed from the start by the American government. U.S. support for the anticommunist leader grew after Fidel Castro took power next door in Cuba in 1959,[11] and continued throughout the thirty-year rule of the Duvalier family, with only a brief interruption during the Kennedy administration.

Jean-Claude Duvalier's policies furthered what Haitians call the development of underdevelopment. Neglect, corruption, and mismanagement by the government and elite, coupled with U.S.-promoted economic policies bent on destroying peasant production and creating hordes of underpaid factory workers,[12] drove the majority of Haiti's population into ever-bleaker poverty.

Throughout this period, civil society maintained opposition, though most activities were conducted underground. But public revolt burst forth in the mid-1980s, sparked by the *tilegliz*, the liberation theology–inspired "little church" or church of the poor. The mobilization of Christians who believed that justice is God's will galvanized the population into action. Among the clergy and laity, women were more central and vociferous than ever before.

During a hot and angry summer in 1985, in the gritty town of Gonaïves, Tontons Macoutes gunned down three youths. The murders marked the boundary between pent-up rage and open fury, and years of covert organizing broke into a public declaration of opposition.

The uprisings crippled the country, and Jean-Claude Duvalier's power quickly eroded. Hastening his descent were two other factors: growing alienation by the wealthy, who were facing a declining economy, and withdrawal of U.S. government support. The latter was due to both growing pressures from an international human rights movement led by Haitian exiles and, as Duvalier's grip weakened, an interest in cultivating other, stronger political allies. Preempting the ascendance of a leftist government, the United States negotiated the erstwhile president-for-life's departure to France on February 7, 1986, then helped install a military-led junta the next day.

The so-called popular movement,[13] a loosely organized coalition of grassroots groups representing women, youth, peasants, workers, shantytown dwellers, and faith-based communities, together with progressive professional associations and intelligentsia, made itself ubiquitous. Through marches, strikes, free-speech radio, graffiti, and other fora, the movement demanded human and social rights, economic justice, and participatory democracy. Even though they faced obstacles to full participation, women came forward in large numbers to demand political rights for all, as well as gender-specific rights.

Mass organizing campaigns created new democratic structures—organizations that furthered the popular movement's objectives in both goal and process—and helped change the face of civil society. During this period activists stated often, *Yo debouche boutèy la. Yo pa kapab bouche l ankò.* The bottle has been uncorked. The cork can't be put back in now.

Yet though Duvalier had fled to France, Duvalierism remained. The country continued to be ruled by successive military juntas, supported by powerful civil sectors in Haiti and by the U.S. government. Repressive traditions of past dictators thrived. Nevertheless, strong grassroots rebellion forced the government to concede some important political reforms, civil liberties, and democratic openings, such as the popular ratification of a new constitution in March 1987.

A primary demand of the movement was free elections with full suffrage, something Haiti had never before experienced. The late 1980s witnessed one violently aborted and another fraudulent round of presidential elections. Then, for the vote in December 1990 in which citizens faced yet one more choice between corrupt and brutal candidates, grassroots organizations converged in raucous negotiations to select their own candidate: the radically populist Rev. Jean-Bertrand Aristide. As maddening to the Vatican, his own Catholic order of priests, and the elites as he was beloved by the poor, Aristide registered on the last day allowed by law and ran a candidacy without any money or technical support. Nevertheless, in every burg across the country, citizens waited in long lines under the hot sun to vote for the poet-activist-priest. Out of a field of fourteen candidates, Titid — Little 'Tide, as he was known to all— received 67 percent of the vote.

The election brought to power both a president and an agenda responsive to the majority's needs and priorities. The margins between the empowered and the disempowered shifted once again, as the people's movement known as *lavalas,* flash flood, began implementing a new political and economic program.

Using an array of tactics, *lavalas* launched offensives for land reform, new agricultural policies that benefited peasant producers, labor rights, increased government spending on social programs, a nonabusive army, a government ministry representing women, an end to corruption—in short, a panoply of demands related to full rights, equity, and dignity. Human rights activist Marie Josée St. Firmin captures the period experienced by many as euphoria: "What existed during the next seven months was hope, a people breathing the sweet air of night-blooming jasmine all day long."

Forces of the status quo ante immediately waged battle on *lavalas* and its leader. On September 30, 1991, only seven and a half months into the new presidency, sectors of the military, led by General Raoul Cédras, staged a coup d'etat. The coup was financed by some of Haiti's richest families, known to the black majority as the *zye vèt*, green-eyed. According to high-level officials of Aristide's government, the coup was also supported, at least tacitly, by the U.S. government.[14] In addition to sending the deposed leader off to Venezuela (from where he would relocate to Washington), soldiers went on a killing rampage. Morgue employees, after stacking bodies several levels high on the racks, lined the hallways with corpses. Staff at overflowing hospitals jammed two wounded, head to foot, on to each narrow bed. With the overthrow, forces of the old order finally succeeded in realizing the goal they had held since 1986: quashing popular voice and power.

For the next three years, a campaign known as the *machin enfènal,* hellish machine, repressed virtually all open dissent. Some of the leaders of terror squads known as *zenglendo* (the name derived from a term for shards of shattered glass) gave their men crack cocaine each morning and then encouraged them to bet as to who could kill the most people that day.[15] The most well-organized and active of these death squads was the Revolutionary Front for the Advancement and Progress of Haiti, or FRAPH—a play on the identical-sounding French word *frappe,* meaning to strike or hit. Some of the group's leaders, most notably Emmanuel "Toto" Constant, collaborated with and were financed by the CIA.[16] FRAPH's reign resulted in thousands of deaths; they proudly hung "trophy photographs" of some of the victims on their office walls.[17] A common tactic of FRAPH members—themselves largely recruited from slums and villages—was to slice off the faces of their victims before depositing them in open-field garbage dumps in Cité Soleil. Eyewitness Catherine Maternowska, an American anthropologist working in Cité Soleil at the time, described it: "Pigs feasted on corpses while people starved."

The terror forced hundreds of thousands into internal exile, where they rotated between safe houses in varying towns like pieces of a swirling kaleidoscope. Hundreds of thousands of others, in search of a more complete escape, chose to slip into flimsy wooden boats in the middle of the night, risking sharks and, if they made it that far, persecution in another country. During the George H. W. Bush administration, thousands of refuge seekers were interdicted on the high seas and delivered back to the hands of their oppressors. Human rights advocates likened this policy to firemen throwing those fleeing a burning house back inside it. Under Bush and then Bill Clinton, until popular outcry reversed the policy, those who arrived on U.S. shores were imprisoned, mostly in a squalid, overcrowded, make-shift prison on Guantánamo Base.

The Organization of American States, and later the United Nations, implemented an international embargo. But it was sporadically applied so that the rich and the army continued to prosper while the poor were squeezed harder. Though one woman complained that she could no longer dry-clean her clothes (laundries lacked the requisite chemicals) or get chlorine for her swimming pool, import records documented a continued flow of Beck's beer and Mercedes-Benz parts into the country. More important, the army's access to guns and gas was never jeopardized, while the embargo gave them a powerful business in contraband. Meanwhile, production dropped by 30 percent during the three coup-era years, while consumer prices increased between 20 and 50 percent each year.[18] Less calculable was the hardship on the population already living so close to the margins, such as market women who found no buyers for what they could scrounge up to sell—a comb, a used bra, five avocados—and thus had no money to spend. Attempts by the Aristide government-in-exile and allies to get the U.S. government, the United Nations, and the Organization of American States to tighten the porous embargo, so that it would weaken the military regime, yielded few results.

Yet grassroots groups continued their work covertly, refusing to admit defeat. They repeated over and over, *Nou te bite, nou pat tonbe.* We have stumbled, but we have not fallen. Haitians in their country and in the diaspora, aided by the Aristide government-in-exile and sympathizers in the Americas, Europe, Asia, and Africa, dedicated themselves to pressuring the coup regime and keeping the restoration of democracy central to the international agenda. Haitian human rights workers and women's advocates secretly collected and disseminated news of abuses out to a global network, faxing in the dark of night from a different secure location each week. Church workers housed and fed untold numbers of frightened citizens. Peasant associations sneaked their members out of the country to generate support from church and community groups throughout the world, while exiled journalists set up radio news programs in many foreign cities. Refugees forcibly interred at Guantánamo Base and in other immigration detention centers mounted hunger strikes.

Within the United States, as in many other countries, civil society's opposition to the coup and to the international community's lack of decisive action was as creative as it was sustained. California dock workers refused to unload shipments off of boats coming from Haiti. Hollywood actors and directors inundated President Clinton's office with letters and petitions. Students protested on campuses from the East to the West Coast. Trade union and civil rights leaders got themselves arrested in front of the White House. Journalists and activists collaborated on stories about the role of the U.S. government in abetting Haitian military-sponsored drug running.[19] Delegations ranging from

Jewish rabbis to Midwest high school students traveled to Haiti to provide accompaniment and try to deter violence.

The underground work of *lavalas* within the island nation, plus the fierce pressure from Haitians and their backers abroad, finally prompted definitive action from the international community. The U.S. government took the lead in sending to Haiti, first, a multinational invasion dominated by nearly twenty thousand U.S. soldiers, and then, on October 15, 1994, Aristide himself. Haitian activists invoked the analogy of David and Goliath, referring to their overpowering what they perceived was, at best, ineptitude, and at worst, collusion by the Goliath of the United States and other nations, the United Nations, and the Organization of American States.

Aristide was ushered in the same way Duvalier had been ushered out: aboard a U.S. government aircraft. Aristide emerged from an American helicopter onto the grounds of the National Palace, in front of which tens of thousands danced euphorically on that sweltering, chaotic day. The terms for the carefully orchestrated scenario, determined in tense negotiations in Washington and Paris, contained many preconditions for the United States, World Bank, and International Monetary Fund's future power over political, financial, and development policies and programs.[20] While among the population, opposition to the intervention and the subsequent occupation ran high, still the circumstances surrounding the president's return were viewed with a mixture of pragmatism and shrewd exploitation of opportunity. Repeatedly citizens expressed deep awareness of the high price for Aristide's plane ride home. Then they shrugged and expressed a variant of the following: "If the foreign presence can help provide security so we can start organizing and mobilizing, we'll use that."

For the first time in three years, Haitians could mention Aristide's name aloud, talk in the streets without fear, and dream openly of a future with democracy. For weeks after the elected government's restoration, girls and women hiked up their skirts as they walked down dusty streets, twitching their behinds defiantly as they chanted: *Viv Aristide! Men bounda m, vin ban m baton.* Long live Aristide! Here's my ass, *now* try to whip it.

All across the nation, civil society began testing out the possibilities for social change. Yet the second part of Aristide's term (December 1994–February 1996), during which his government shared power with U.S.-led occupational forces, little resembled the first. While the president made some dramatic achievements such as the dissolution of the army, his administration's prior pro-poor stance suffered under international pressure from without and a dissipated resolve from within. Its agenda no longer closely paralleled that of the popular movement. Indeed, some political circles asserted that the restored government was actually undermining the progressive agenda.

Too, the strength of grassroots organizations was not what it had been. Ranks were decimated by death and exile, while morale lagged under the losses of the coup years and the subsequent slow pace of change. And, since the multinational forces arrested or even disarmed very few of the death squads, the old terror apparatus lurked in the wings, occasionally coming out to stage violent reprisals.

Aristide was barred by the 1987 Haitian constitution from succeeding himself as president; his prime minister, René Préval, instead carried the 1995 elections. Aristide then returned to power five years later. Neither of these elections gained the momentum of the 1990 vote, nor has either of these administrations been backed by the same popular will as Aristide's first term. There exists a different relationship between government and populace than when the people's movement allied itself with formal power.

Despite the many obstacles, still activists are working to reclaim the democratic space lost since the coup. Another round of opposition has emerged, with a new hatch of community-based organizations engaging in public protest. Women form a stronger core of the movement, and their rights and status are more central to the agenda, than ever before. Their dissent, like those of other sectors of the movement, is augmented by new strategies to address new threats to the poor's power and sustenance.

These threats include, in addition to ongoing state-sponsored violence and repression, increasing hunger, landlessness, and unemployment. Under the development model now being imposed by the U.S. government, World Bank, and International Monetary Fund, in which Haiti is increasingly forced—without protection—into the global economy, poor women and men are experiencing a decreased ability to sustain peasant production, traditional culture, or local economic autonomy.[21]

Thus, the contestation continues, with the marginalized pushing to expand their portion of power from the sum held by opposing political and financial actors. As Mona Jean, a Haitian women's rights lawyer, puts it, "We know that no one can change our situation for us. After God, it's up to us."

THE STATUS OF HAITIAN WOMEN

Many times throughout the day on Millet Mountain, as throughout Haiti, one can see this: Two men lift a fifty-pound sack of rice or a ten-gallon bucket

of water. They place it on the head of a woman who squats between them. She then stands, her forehead crunched and backbone compressed from the weight, and walks away.

Women carry on their heads the family, household economy, local economy, and culture. While women assert that they are the *poto mitan,* central pillar, of society, they are also quick to point out that they are the most *defavorize,* marginalized, within the *klas defavorize,* marginalized class. Women's current socioeconomic status is the by-product of Haiti's history—especially how power has been apportioned and applied throughout.

A quick glance in villages throughout Haiti confirms that women, along with their children, suffer most under the weight of the injustices. Millet Mountain residents are illustrative. With rare exception, the women there are thin and clothed in raggedy skirts or dresses, one of which typically comprises a full wardrobe. Their faces are often pinched, giving the appearance of a far older age than their biological years. Most of the young children sucking on collapsed breasts are naked, their bodies covered with festering sores. The children's eyes are usually lackluster from hunger, while some have orange hair, an indicator of severe malnutrition. In the presence of an outsider or a group of men, most of the women and the children are silent. One notable exception is the short, feisty Giselle, who will say *anything* to *anybody.*

As women carry the rest of the country, so they carry the brunt of Haiti's exaggerated socioeconomic patterns. Women battle each day to ensure their own and their families' survival, and to do so with maximum dignity. They must continually defend themselves against landowners, bosses, and government, which together define so many aspects of their lives. They also must struggle with men for resources and power within the household.

While the daily defeats and losses caused by poverty cannot be grasped through figures, still a few statistics and indices are illuminating. According to the United Nations Development Program, Haitian women rank last in a gender development index of countries in the Western Hemisphere, while they rank 150 out of a total of 174 countries surveyed.[22] According to the Inter-American Development Bank, of women in twenty-five Latin American countries, Haitian women place at the absolute bottom in female-male life expectancy differential, incidence of teen marriage, contraceptive use, primary school enrollment, secondary school enrollment, and ratio of secondary school teachers. They tie for worst, or rank second worst, in the following: economic equality with men, political and legal equality, social equality, life expectancy, mortality in childbearing years, fertility, rate of widowhood/divorce/separation, university enrollment, female adult literacy, discrepancy between male and female literacy, percentage of paid employees, and percentage of professionals.[23] Female life expectancy is 56.4 years; the literacy rate among women is 45.6 percent; and their combined enrollment rate in primary, secondary, and tertiary schools is 24 percent.[24]

Relative poverty is worse now than at any time in recent history, while per capita income is U.S.$410.[25] Consumption of calories per capita dropped from 1,944 in 1970 to 1,869 in 1997,[26] and starvation is on the rise; marasmus and kwashiorkor are common among young children. Women swallow pebbles to fill the void, or wear a "hunger belt," which they tighten when the pangs become too strong.

In as many as 60 percent of families, women bear the sole responsibility of child support, stretching their meager financial resources far beyond their limits.[27] One reason for the high incidence of single mothers is the massive outflow of migrants over the past four decades. Roughly one million, out of a population of eight million, have gone *lòt bò dlo*, to the other side of the water. To leave is called *chèche lavi*, to search for life. But for women, that term is ironic. The search for life for women, who have much less flexibility to leave because of the need to care for their children and because of their lesser economic independence, becomes harder in the absence of their partners; women's labor grows while their income usually shrinks. (Others receive remittances from partners or relatives abroad.)

Even where a father is present, a woman's financial burden is not necessarily alleviated. While in one study, rural fathers generally were found to assume their financial responsibility,[28] according to other research, men use most of their personal earnings on their own needs and leisure.[29] What men do contribute to child care is most often divided among several homes, as it is common for men to have more than one family, leaving the overwhelming financial responsibility on the mothers' shoulders.

Given the circumstances in which most women live, bearing and raising children can have other grave consequences. Lack of food, clean water, and health services results in high infant and maternal mortality rates. The mortality rate of children under five is 130 per 1,000 live births,[30] the highest in the hemisphere. Along with poor women's lack of control over contraceptives, this has yielded a fertility rate of 4.4 percent,[31] since actual death or fear of death of children tends to increase childbearing rates.[32] Limited or no prenatal care, inadequate health care during labor, and high rates of malnutrition—compounded by multiple pregnancies—make motherhood a serious threat to women's health. So, too, does excessive work; for example, carrying heavy loads on the head can cause pelvic deformity, a prolapsed uterus, and complications during childbirth.[33] The combined result is a maternal mortality rate of 457 per 100,000 live births.[34]

The division of labor in rural areas runs rigidly along gender lines. Poor women work from long before the sun rises over the mountains to long after it has set, 365 days a year. In the home, they cook all meals, wash dishes, clean, do laundry, sew and mend clothing, and carry water. They also are obliged to earn a wage whenever they can, performing as many jobs as they can. Marketing and petty commerce comprise the largest productive activity in which women are engaged, with 78 percent involved. Along with the men, they also contribute substantially to animal husbandry and farming; almost 59 percent of women engage in some agricultural wage labor.[35] An estimated eighteen thousand to twenty thousand factory workers—most of them women—work in the multinational assembly factories, where the minimum wage for producing Pocahontas pajamas and computer chips at break-neck speed is thirty-six gourdes, or U.S.$1.44 per day[36]—though this legal floor often is not respected and workers receive far less. Moreover, the value of the minimum wage has fallen 81 percent since 1980.[37] Nevertheless, a woman's factory earnings support six people on the average.[38] Gnawing poverty under the international embargo imposed during the coup pushed many Haitian girls and women into prostitution, where unprotected sex sold for U.S.$1.75 and a virgin could bring in U.S.$5.00.[39]

Reflecting Haiti's status in the international economy, most income-generating work available to women garners very low wages and is insecure. Women's paid jobs depend precariously on the vagaries of international capital, in which factories may pull out of the country with a few day's notice and the jobs-creation schemes of international development agencies shift frequently. A weak market for agricultural produce and other local merchandise, due to competition with imported goods, further jeopardizes poor women's guarantees even to the minuscule incomes they may earn.

At the domestic level, women's powers are sharply circumscribed by their male partners. They lack control over reproduction, sexuality, personal earnings, land, and property. An indicator of their lack of social power is the astronomical incidence of domestic abuse. One study, a community sample taken over a ten-year period in Cité Soleil, reported a 100 percent incidence of battery among the women.[40] Another study found that 70 percent of women had been subjected to physical assault at the hands of a domestic partner at some point in their lives.[41]

Women also have suffered rampant and devastating state-sponsored violence. They have been subject to torture, abuse, illegal arrest, disappearance, and assassination since the time of "Papa Doc" Duvalier.

During the 1991–1994 coup period, women's bodies became domains for the regime to assert its power and authority, with rape regularly used as a weapon of war. Human rights reporting commonly understated the gender-specific focus of the violence, suggesting instead that rapes and other attacks against women were intended to punish their male relatives and partners. And the U.S. Embassy, in a cablegram to Washington, reported:

> The Haitian left, including President Aristide and his supporters in Washington and here, consistently manipulate or even fabricate human rights abuses as a propaganda tool. . . . A case in point is the sudden epidemic of rapes reported . . . by pro-Aristide human rights activists.[42]

Yet a 1995 survey by the Haitian Center for Research and Action for the Promotion of Women reported that 37 percent of 1,705 women admitted having been raped or otherwise sexually abused, or said they knew someone else who had been.[43] And the independent National Commission on Truth and Justice, after a lengthy investigation, characterized the raping as a "politically orchestrated campaign conducted in the context of intimidation and savage repression against opposition to the State."[44]

A brief survey of Haitian law reveals that women have been defined as daughters and wives legally, as well as socially.[45] Until 1915, women who married foreigners lost citizenship and property rights. Married women were legally minors until 1979. Women gained the right to vote in 1950, though only upper-class women were allowed to exercise this right, and then only when it could enhance the dictators' power—until 1990.

Property rights is another area in which women suffer the consequences of gender-biased legal and social systems. As agriculture is the backbone of the economy, control over land is critical to a peasant's survival. Much of the arable land has always been owned by the state, the latifundia, and the local functionaries—the triumvirate that has long ruled Haiti's peasantry. Now, between free market policies and environmental degradation, insecurity has become worse; many peasants have been forced from subsistence farming into landless day-labor or feudal-style sharecropping, often paying the landowner with half their crops plus rent. Others have been forced into Port-au-Prince, where they join the unemployed or underemployed or, if they're lucky, get a job in a sweatshop.

Poor peasant women are doubly vulnerable under this land tenure system. Wives in *plasaj*, common-law marriages, which constitute an estimated 85 percent of conjugal unions,[46] can work the land of their *plase*, common-law, husbands for years but be left with nothing upon their husbands' deaths. Though a wife may have invested half of the labor and capital, if the couple had no children the land passes to the man's parents and siblings, because land is almost always registered in the man's name, and *plase* wives have no inheritance protection. Only by having children can a common-law wife secure her position on her land, and then only through her children's holdings. Yet because men frequently have children with more than one woman, each heir, not only those of his common-law wife, inherits a portion of his land, diminishing her access to land-holdings even further.

Moreover, regardless of laws which stipulate that male and female children inherit equally, male offspring often inherit the agricultural plot while females inherit the house and only the land on which it stands, leaving them without control of agricultural subsistence holdings. Between expropriation by the government, brothers, and husbands, women have little security in the production of small crops for the household or for cash.

Women have faced staggering odds throughout the world's history. In Haiti, these challenges are compounded by the sheer challenge of living in the poorest country in the Western Hemisphere. Yet, despite all, as the *istwa* throughout this book graphically indicate, women continually *degaje*, innovate as best they can, to *kenbe fèm*, hold strong. Haitian women are slowly but consistently changing their course and in the process are changing the course and discourse of power.

1 RESISTANCE IN SURVIVAL

*The bamboo symbolizes the Haitian people to a T, eh? We are a little
people. The bamboo is not a great big tree with a magnificent appearance. But when the strong winds come, well, even a great tree can be uprooted. The bamboo is really weak, but when the winds come, it bends
but it doesn't break. Bamboo takes whatever adversity comes along, but
afterwards it straightens itself back up. That's what resistance is for us
Haitians: we might get bent . . . but we're able to straighten up and
stand.*

—Yolette Etienne

*By resistance I mean the ingenuity we use that allows us to live. Resis-
tance is inside how we do the thing that lets us hold on and gives us a
better way. It's in the very manner in which we organize ourselves to survive our situation.*

—Vita Telcy

INSISTING ON LIFE

Marlene Larose is a woman with an indomitable spirit and a ferocious will.
She has a dozen pseudonyms, Marlene Larose being one, and underground af-
filiations. Her large body and deep voice assert themselves in any situation; her
dark eyes bore with disconcerting intensity. You would not want this woman as
your enemy.

The death squads didn't either, and they threatened to kill her. Undaunted,
she moved her husband and four children out of their home and onto a
rooftop. Taking advantage of the visibility afforded by their open-air residence,
they took up surveying and documenting the death squads' activities, even

sending for infrared film from human rights organizations in the United States, to photograph the killers on their nightly rounds.

Marlene's commitment to democracy has not come cheaply. Her eighty-three-year-old mother was assassinated and dismembered in 1983. In 1988, Marlene was shot twice—once in her neck and once between her lung and heart—when *zenglendo* stormed a mass she was attending.

Several years later, Marlene became pregnant. Doctors discovered that the bullet that had lodged near her heart had traveled down to her womb. They warned that her fetus and her own health were threatened. Marlene refused to abort her baby.

Her story echoes the themes of this book—survival, resistance, and occasional triumph by women with little formal power. It highlights Marlene's own resilience against the forces encroaching on her claim to life. Like all the *istwa* in this book, Marlene's story reveals how so-called private decisions and behavior can become willful acts against dehumanization or destruction.[1]

Despite the medical risks, Marlene survived. And somehow, sharing the womb with a bullet, her fetus did as well. Finally Tibi entered the world, healthy, pudgy, and cherubic. "They tried to kill that baby," Marlene said, "but he insisted on becoming life."

DAILY ACTS OF RESISTANCE

Popular snacks in Haiti are *peze souse,* squeeze and suck, frozen pops in plastic bags that are consumed by people sucking from the top while squeezing from the bottom. The *istwa* in this chapter are told by women being consumed like a *peze souse.*[2]

The *griyo* describe the pernicious effects of structural violence, what Paul Farmer et al. defined as "a series of large-scale forces—ranging from gender inequality to racism to poverty—which structure unequal access to goods and services."[3] This structural violence is felt in their daily lives, for example, from small farmers' inability to feed their families due to U.S.- and World Bank-imposed free market policies that have destroyed their subsistence production, to the large landowners' control of irrigation systems. It is felt in the lack of medical care for their infants because the government budget includes almost no social spending.

As prevalent in the *istwa* are women's deployment of their internal resources to leverage small advantages in the daily battles against structural violence. When they cannot increase their power, still they try to keep the margins of power from shifting further to the individuals, political institutions, and economic systems that oppress them. It sometimes takes all their energy just to hold on to what they have, materially and spiritually.

In so doing, the women expand the definitions of political action and resistance. They demonstrate what American religious scholar Howard Thurman called "the creative capability of personality to grow in the midst of no-growth circumstances; to find faith in the midst of fear, healing in the midst of suffering, love in the midst of hate, hope in the midst of despair, life in the midst of death, and community in the midst of chaos."[4]

The women's negotiations with dominant power usually go unseen. The boundaries of those negotiations are often small and may be viewed as personal. The women do not necessarily articulate the theories behind their actions, or the connection to larger social movements. Yet the deliberateness of their acts indicates clear refusal to cede ideological or personal space to their oppressors.

Detecting the prevalence of dissent among Haitian women necessitates radically changing one's perceptions of what resistance is and where to look for it. It requires asking, What are the forces that these women overcome each day to sustain themselves and their families? What negotiation is involved in their maintaining their humanity? And what sort of "personal" or "private" actions may, with a widened gaze, be revealed to be as political as a union strike?

Not all women are protesting or even fighting defeat. Some may have given up, for the time being or permanently. Still, what might look to be a completely beaten-down victim might be something quite different, as Roselie Jean-Juste, survivor of domestic abuse, illustrates. Her hand crippled by a beating from her husband, her face and carriage showing the strain of life on the run from him, at first glance Roselie seems broken. On the contrary. When she came to our meeting to give her narrative, Roselie had just left a human rights advocate from whom she was seeking help. She also was engaged in complex self-protection strategies, including sleeping at a different house each night. And she was vehement about having her full story, including her husband's name, told in this book so as to publicize the man's brutality and pressure him to stop.

MAINTAINING LIFE

> *There is a Haitian saying. . . .* Nou lèd, Nou la. *We are ugly, but we are here. For most of us, what is worth celebrating is the fact that we are here, that we against all the odds exist. To the women who might greet each other with this saying when they meet along the countryside, the*

very essence of life lies in survival. It is always worth reminding our sisters that we have lived yet another day to answer the roll call of an often painful and very difficult life.

—Edwidge Danticat

Given Haiti's extreme circumstances, mere survival can be an implicit protest against attempted extermination. Often only sheer will, coupled with tremendous creativity and resourcefulness, allows the maintenance of body and spirit.

Maria Miradieu's resistance is in her renewed efforts to defy starvation in her children and to assert her human value each day. Every morning this woman rises at four o'clock to prepare a meager pot of rice for her four children before heading for the crowded, noisy market to garner a few *santim*, pennies, from selling mangoes. Her protest includes fighting off physical exhaustion aggravated by the weakness of hunger. As she has no money for the bus, it requires mustering the strength to walk miles to the market, enduring fast and careless cars, the stench of open sewers, and dust and filth. On the job, she publicly ridicules anyone trying to barter down her already-low price so that she can maintain her dignity and preserve the tiny margin of profit she desperately needs.

In Haiti, more than one in ten children do not make it to the age of five. Of those who do, the average life expectancy is just over fifty-three years.[5] But these figures recount only a small part of the story; the full wretchedness of the poverty cannot be conveyed in tidy numbers. So how is it that Haitian women continue to cope and persist?

The *istwa* in this chapter reveal many strategies. Ingenuity, for example, is a form of resistance when survival means creating something out of nothing. Yolande Mevs recalls returning home empty-handed from a long day of wandering the streets, seeking food for her worm-bellied kids:

> I told them, "Little ones, today I ran my head into walls everywhere. . . . Everything that could have saved me, didn't." I took a pot I had, I put a little salt in the pot. I made salt water. Only my first child didn't drink it. All the other children drank the salt water and then they went to sleep.

In Haiti, this type of effort is called *sou fòs kouray,* on the strength of your courage.

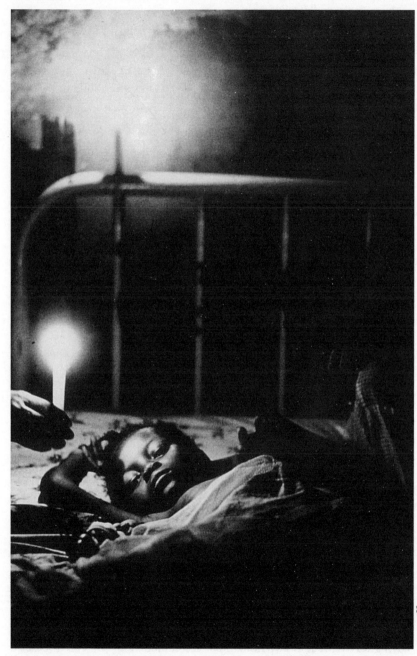

© Maggie Steber

RESISTANCE IN SURVIVAL   { 27 }

Vita Telcy describes her efforts to meet her strategic needs and interests this way:

> Rich people eat three times a day, me I can't. When I harvest five cans of corn, today my family can eat half a pound. Tomorrow if there's a cup, I'll cook it. I maximize those five cans like so: one can to send the children to school, one can to send a sick child to the hospital, one can for all the family to eat. With what's left over, I find seeds to plant to make sure I can grow next year. This is how I see resistance with an economic face.

What happens at the level of domestic partnership, also, is central to women's resistance strategies. In one of many examples, as in Celine Edgar's story in the introduction, women speak of consenting to relationships in the hope that a man will provide additional economic support for the household.

DEFYING DEGRADATION

I learned to be vigilant in the nourishment of my spirit, to be tough, to courageously protect that spirit from forces that would break it.
—bell hooks

A market woman bends down and raises the pink plastic bucket of tomatoes and onions to her head. All the while she sings.

"Your heart is happy this morning, *Madanm*," I say.

She surveys me. "It's not happy, no."

"But I see you're singing."

"I'm making an effort. I'm trying to *kanpe djanm*, stand strong."

Using the resources available to her, this woman's song is one of countless acts of defiance that Haitian women wage each day to sustain pride, dignity, and hope.

The story of Lovly Josaphat is another example of holding strong. Lovly is raising six children alone, after a first husband was murdered by a death squad, and a second fled after raping her oldest child. Lovly lives in Cité Soleil, the poorest and most densely populated 2.5 square kilometers in this hemisphere, where the family slogs through sewage to reach its stifling one-room home. Lovly's survival requires overlooking or accommodating problems as best she can, this in turn demanding resilience and psychological fortitude. For example, after detailing the pervasive violence found in Cité Soleil, Lovly says, "But I like my neighborhood. It's quiet there." This attitude does not signify acceptance—she denounces the conditions elsewhere in her *istwa*; it is her attempt to change the effect of the problem when she cannot change the source.

HOPE

This hope of the poor is an elusive, underestimated, yet determinant stratum of resistance. The "secret weapon" . . . is insurgent hope that, like a phoenix, rises from the ashes of charred villages, pulses in hands that have been shackled and hearts that have been broken.
—Renny Golden

Her rangy body is too large for the milk crate on which she is sitting. Yolande Mevs scratches her left calf with her right foot. A survivor of coup violence from the slum of Martissant, she says, "We know that we can't live without hope." That hope is heard often in the phrase *fòk sa chanje*, this must change. It is inconceivable that life will forever remain this desperate.

What keeps hope alive in Haiti? From a Western cause-and-effect analysis, it should have fled the country long ago. And yet, as Haitians often remind each other in rough moments, they cling to their stubborn belief in change because they don't have the luxury of despair. Nun and agronomist Kesta Occident says:

We Haitians give ourselves reasons to live, reasons to believe that one day our lives will change, even if not for ourselves, then for the generations after us. If they kill a woman with misery and hunger, she'll die with the hope that her kids will live better.

A common Creole proverb is *Kote gen lespwa, gen lavi*. Where there is hope there is life. Hope for *yon alemyè*, a better go of it, *yon pi bon demen*, a better tomorrow. When asked how they maintain their hope in the face of such suffering, poor Haitians readily offer up their reason: *Nou pa gen lechwa*. We don't have a choice. In fact, they do have a choice. Despair, crack cocaine, grain alcohol, and suicide are also available to them. While some Haitians do go down these roads, many more get by in dire times through the crucial resource of positive expectation.

Squatting over a blackened pot and poking at the burning charcoal under it, Lovly Josaphat says,

When I was a child . . . life was easier. I would buy sugarcane, eat it, and my stomach was full. Now life is hard from time to time. . . . But I know that I'll live again the same way I did when I was a child. I never get discouraged.

RELIGIOUS FAITH

Yolande Mevs exhales loudly and picks the edges of her wide polyester skirt off the ant-ridden ground. "The Eternal has shown me how to resist. . . . God gives me strength and courage." Often despite tremendous misery, the Haitian women here have managed to sustain themselves through spiritual faith.

The relationship between religion and resistance is integral to these *istwa* and to Haitian history and culture. As for vodou, Haiti's predominant religion, that it still exists is itself an act of rebellion. In colonial days, French slave-owners tried unsuccessfully to stamp it out. Especially during an "antisuperstition" campaign of the 1940s and in a post-Duvalier wave of attacks, *vodouizan,* vodou practitioners, were repressed and even murdered. But these efforts have failed to curtail either the faith or the practice. Instead, vodou not only has thrived but also has served as an important vehicle to instigate other forms of protest. For instance, the story of the slave revolution began with a ceremony in the dark woods at Bois Caïman. In another example, the *lwa* Erzulie Danthor has been invoked by *vodouizan* throughout Haiti's history to rid the country of abusive leaders. After the 1991 coup, for instance, pictures of Erzulie appeared on battered wooden doorways throughout the country to hasten the downfall of the regime.

Vodou also provides everyday strength to the poor, the fervent belief in a set of supernatural forces reinforcing their assemblage of resources. In the perspective of *manbo,* priestess, Florencia Pierre, "If those country people didn't serve *lwa,* who walk with them, help them, encourage them, they would have all died already."

Like vodou, the Christian faith provides a crucial form of succor. The encouragement gained from an added power in their corner—an omnipotent one, at that—is expressed in many of the *istwa*. Moreover, the Catholic *tilegliz* movement shapes religious convictions into a foundation for political solidarity and struggle. Too, Christianity—especially the *tilegliz*—offers institutions, networks, and resources that have been mobilized repeatedly for collective protest.

SOLIDARITY

North Americans usually understand solidarity as political support for people engaged in justice movements. Haitians, like other Latin Americans, expand the definition to include neighbors' sharing burdens and supporting each other's personal struggles. An oft-invoked Creole adage is *Mizè yon fanm se mizè tout fanm*. The misery of one woman is the misery of all women. Repeatedly, poor women speak in the *istwa* of solidarity with other women as one of their main reserves of fortitude. As Lovly Josaphat says,

> If you are sensitive to me, I am sensitive to you. If I see a man abusing a woman, I might go to him and say, "No! Don't beat her!" If he beats her, I get angry.

Poor Haitians employ solidarity as a means to survive economically, as well as psychologically. Although hunger and want drive some to hoarding their meager resources, more typically, pooling money, resources, and labor serves as the only buffer against losing a home on rent day, or losing a crop from lack of labor at harvest time. *Tilegliz* activist Marie Sonia Dely explains, "If one person boils a breadfruit, it is for us all. We'll eat today. Another day, if God wills, another person will have a breadfruit. That's how many people are spared from dying of hunger." Yolande Mevs offers another example: "If I go to someone's house . . . if she has a can of rice, she won't hide it. She has to give me some, so I can go feed my children."

Haitian women have formalized the philosophy and practice of support into thousands of organized groups. These solidarity networks are composed on the basis of geography—a village or a neighborhood—or of sector, such as factory workers or *tilegliz* members. The forms of mutual support range from simple encouragement to counseling for rape survivors, rotating child care, and revolving loan funds.

CONSCIENTIZATION AND EMPOWERMENT

Conscientization programs are a central agenda of many sectors, including grassroots women's groups. Much like the consciousness-raising movement of Western feminism, Haiti's tradition of conscientization has helped women change the way they view their own worth and power. The tradition has contributed to women's militancy in demanding personal and social validation. For example, while it might seem to some that Venante Duplan's gritty experiences would have limited her expectations, she defies this with a common attitude:

> Don't think that a man has priority over you. You must keep in mind that you have as much value as any Haitian, as any woman. Even if you're not a professional, even if you're not an intellectual . . . We all have our place in society, and we all have our role to fill.

Too, exchanging personal experiences and analyzing social rights and responsibilities have built upon Haitians' historically strong political awareness. Conscientization and a woman's sense of empowerment are critical variables between a spirit of resistance and one of resignation or defeat. They are also key reasons why the ruling class and political regimes, which have conquered political and economic power, cannot seize control of the ideological terrain.

The significance of critical consciousness, including the concept of empowerment, needs to be mitigated in the Haitian context. Alone, it does not lead to control over one's own material and social situation. The impact of oppression extends far beyond muting people's voices or degrading their sense of self. Still, conscientization is a necessary first step in mobilizing women to take that control.

SPEAKING TRUTH TO POWER

"What I have witnessed, I have no tongue to tell," said Michaelle Jean-Louis during the coup, passing a withered hand over her eyes and sucking air through her teeth. But now that women have attained the political space to grieve and speak freely, they are finding ways to voice the horrors they endured. The healing has begun.

Under decades of dictatorship, and especially during the three years of the coup regime (1991–1994), for a Haitian woman to publicly acknowledge her own or a family member's abuse was to risk more violent repercussions. In the tautological logic of the military, to be a victim of state violence, or to be related to a victim, meant that she was necessarily guilty of a crime. Even worse, protesting an attack or an assassination was taken by the regime as a direct affront. So people mourned the death of loved ones in secret or reported their personal suffering to only a trusted few.

Chenet Jean-Baptiste, the soft-spoken director of the Catholic Church–sponsored Justice and Peace, reports, "During the coup there was little we could do besides collect testimony from victims. This didn't do much to change the situation, but it was very important to the victims." Today, this form of testifying is another type of resistance critical to these narratives and to contemporary Haiti. "A wound only festers if left all covered up. . . . It heals only properly if it ventilates in the open, with plenty of light and fresh air to cure it," says the father of a "disappeared" in Argentina.[6] As Haiti has struggled to come to grips with years of genocide, documenting the brutality has been vital. It honors the mothers, partners, siblings, and friends whose lives were lost to military violence. It also helps people reclaim their integrity and worth.

After representative democracy was restored in 1994, human rights organizations and radio stations were besieged by survivors wanting to tell their stories. An independent National Commission for Truth and Justice convened and began documenting thousands of cases of rape, torture, attack, and murder perpetrated by the coup regime. The commission's report of these atrocities, entitled *Si m pa rele, If I Don't Cry Out*, is almost twelve hundred pages long.

Another part of the survivors' healing, attaining justice for the crimes, still eludes them. Despite the importance of a few high-visibility prosecutions by the Haitian government, most notably the November 2000 conviction of senior coup officials and others for a 1994 massacre, the fight against impunity proceeds at an agonizingly slow pace. Pressure from many quarters of civil society to prosecute and make reparations for thousands of individual cases is backed by reams of documentation. Additional pressure from Haitian and international human rights groups is focused on the urgent need for reform of the judicial and police systems. Still, the demands for justice for the nation of survivors have languished.

The *griyo* tell of the catharsis of finally speaking out, often wiping away tears on their skirts. For numerous women, this is the first time they have openly stated their truths. Mesinette Louis angrily stomps a bare heel on the earth. "The thieves raped my daughter but the girl is always ashamed for me to speak about it. Yet because I am speaking into a cassette, I must say that!"

Discussing post-coup Chile, American activist writer Margaret Randall wrote, "No easy way to describe or decipher the process by which a people can be broken, but silencing memory is certainly a big part of it."[7] Conversely, proclaiming the names and lives of murdered loved ones helps to commemorate and ensure memory. This is why Marlene Larose, whose baby shared her womb with a bullet, demanded that I include in this book the names of coup victims Marie Paul Jeune and Carline Champagne. Marlene said, "You *have* to put their names in so people won't forget these strong women, these great militants."

Another example of the significance of memorializing: After her daughter died of trauma from watching *zenglendo* rape her mother, Lenyse Oscar stared blankly with the eyes of one barely holding on, and said in a voice dulled by grief:

> I can't speak without calling her name. If you hear me call her name each time I speak, that's because she's in my heart. She never takes a step outside of it, she never leaves. That's why each time I speak, I call the name of Wilmide Oscar.

The South African Freedom Charter states, "Our struggle is also a struggle of memory against forgetting."[8] Retaining memory of the terror also becomes a component of resistance and vigilance. Human rights activist Marie Josée St. Firmin says, "We remember and keep alive the desire that the horrible things which happened earlier in our history never recur."

≋YOLANDE MEVS≋
My Head Burning with the Burden

Well, what gives me the strength to live, I can say that it is God. Absolutely! I have seven children, they don't have any father. So I'm struggling with the children by myself. I can't give them food. I can't put them in school. There's no way to sleep. The godmother of one of my children gave me one corner of a little wooden house for me to squish into with these seven kids. Lord, I've become sick with misery.

It would be too hard on me if it weren't for the will of God. I take God as my husband. Whenever God decides, he sends some support. I hold on to the bond of God with his soldiers of goodwill.

To this day, there are people who, when they see me in the streets, say, "Man, Yolande, in spite of everything, it seems you'll never get old. You poor thing, God gives you strength, huh?" Yes, when I'm falling, God gives me the strength to stand up. And I have to say, after all I've been through, I should have died already. I have a strong heart to tolerate all this.

The day was June 10, 1994, close to midnight. I lived in Carrefour Feuilles when this incident happened to me: Five men appeared at my house. Armed. Masks on their faces. They beat me on the head and then they broke both my arms. Three raped me. Two men took all my things and put them in a car. I can't take them to court because I don't know who they are.

Rape, it's like experiencing death. I don't know if all women die; for me it was death, sister.

They kick us around in Haiti worse than dogs. If we went to the radio about these incidents, the police would chase after us. They would beat us with sticks, give us tear gas. But even if you get your bullet, you're strong. You're strong in the name of the good God. So, I ask for a little justice. We women must stand up, so we can get justice in the country of Haiti.

I've plunged myself into a women's organization here. This women's organization has helped me, because I had finished dying when that *zenglendo* incident happened to me. God gave me a little satisfaction, you understand. What makes us have strength is the workers at the organization. When I told one of the women in the group about the rape, water couldn't stay in her eyes. An American journalist came to see us and she cried for the state we were in: finished. She cried for our penitence.

We have a strength, we have a hope. If it hadn't been for the women in the organization, I'd still be struggling to survive that experience. That's why I say that after God, it's the women, they are the ones who give me strength now, because I know we can't live without hope.

I've also been able to resist because I'm strong with people. Thanks to God, I get along well with everyone. If I go to someone's house, that person knows who Yolande is. If she has a can of rice, she won't hide it. She has to give me some, so I can go feed my children. Like my godsister's child, I get along well with her. On days when I wake up and have nothing to give the children to eat, I say to that girl, "Give me a can of rice. When I have money, I'll pay for it." After I've gotten it, I say, "Eternal One, I've bought this on your credit, you know. You need to give me money so I can go pay for that rice." Well, when I get money, I pay her back so that when the children are hungry next time, I can go find her again. What do you think, sister? God shows us another way for us to keep our children alive.

I will stay with my children. If God wills tomorrow, maybe when I have to lean on a cane, my children will carry the cane for me. Wouldn't you say? I have to struggle with them because my mother struggled with me. And today, here's my mother in the house with me, eighty-five years old. My mother depends on me; my children depend on me. And there are times when I wake up and I don't have one gourde to give my mother or my children.

I put myself into the street, my head burning with the burden. I get out there to struggle and see how I can make ends meet. That's what life is. That's how a woman's life is now in Port-au-Prince. Like that, yes, *cheri*.

I remember one time during the embargo of 1993 and 1994, there was a huge rain. I remember it as if it were today. I wandered and wandered the streets. I couldn't find any food to bring home to my children. It was eight o'clock at night. I went into my house, all the children climbed on the bed and lay down. I told them, "Little ones, today I ran my head into walls everywhere. All the holes were blocked for me. Everything that could have saved me, didn't." I took a pot I had and put a little salt in the pot. I made salt water. Only my first child didn't drink it. All the other children drank the salt water and then they went to sleep.

Well, because I never cease fasting and praying, the Eternal has shown me how to resist with the children. I am always at the Church of the Immaculate Prayer. I always go to church, and fast and pray. God gives me strength and courage. Even when I have nothing, I hold on.

⋐ALINA "TIBEBE" CAJUSTE⋑
A Baby Left on the Doorstep in a Rotten Basket

My name is Alina Cajuste, alias Tibebe. I will never drop the name Tibebe. It is a slave name.

Only now do I feel that I'm starting to live. I never had a childhood, I never had a grown-up who cared for me, took me in. Only when I was grown did anyone treat me as a human being. Now people say to me, "You must get better, you must learn to laugh." And I say, "Well, I never had that opportunity since I was born." That's how my life has been.

This is a sad sad story to the world. As a child I was given away to a woman to live as a *restavèk,* a child slave. A woman who used to come sell in the market in Leogane told my mother to give me to her. My mother had no support, so she had to give me to this woman. I don't know how old I was. My mother was totally illiterate; she didn't give me my age.

When you work as a *restavèk* at someone's house, you're a slave. What did this woman make me do? I had to get up before three or four o'clock in the morning to make the food, sweep the floor, and wash the car, so that when the family woke up everything would be ready. Then I had to wash dishes, fetch water, and go sell merchandise for her in the countryside. When I came back from the marketplace, I would carry two drums of water on my head, so heavy, to wash up for her. Then I'd go buy things to make dinner. And I couldn't even eat the same food as her. If she ate rice, I only got cornmeal. I didn't even wear the same sandals or dresses as her child. My dresses were made out of the scraps of cloth that were left over from what was sold in the marketplace. I couldn't even sleep in a bed.

She treated me terribly. She used to torture me and beat me and break my head open. I was climbing Calvary, my own mountain of suffering. I would ask her if I didn't have a mother or father. She would answer, "You want to know? Here!" and she would take a stick and beat me.

That was how I got treated when I was a *restavèk.* That's how children who are given away to other people's homes live. Like I said, you're a slave. Now there are a few places that look at *restavèk* as human beings. But before, you were in major slavery.

One time things got really serious for me and I underwent a lot of torture. This woman sold cloth, and she went to the marketplace with a permit which gave her the right to sell. One day when I went to Leogane to sell for her, she forgot to give me the permit. And what happened? The police came. The police arrested me with all the merchandise. They thought I was going to escape with her goods.

They locked me up and wouldn't release me. I spent three days in prison and the woman didn't come get me. After three days she came to the area to ask if anyone had seen me. They told her, "Oh, Tibebe's in prison." My mistress would have left me there forever. A neighbor who was selling in the market said, "Why don't you go help her?" The mistress said, "She stole my merchandise." The other woman said, "Tibebe's no thief. She's just a child."

A long time ago when you were in prison, they did nothing for you. Other prisoners had to share their food with you. So, by the time I got out, I was in terrible shape. The woman who kept me never even asked me how I was She didn't even take me to get washed. She just sent me right back to work. She said, "Go and fill two drums of water," so I just kept right on working. She never even considered me a human being.

When they released me, the neighbor said to her, "You took someone's child to make her suffer misery like that? She helps you, she brings in money to give you. Why do you do that? You didn't give her food, you didn't ask her if she had eaten today. You should have taken up her case first, just shown the permit and gotten her released, then bathed her and cleaned her up. Only then should you have gone after the merchandise."

My mistress answered, "And what about all the money I had tied up in that merchandise? What are you saying to me?"

The neighbor said, "Oh, that poor little thing." She told the others, "All right, I'm going to find her mother." And she went, truly true. She found my mother, whom I never knew from the time I was little.

Then the neighbor came back and told me, "Why don't you run away? Before you go out to sell, collect your things and put them on the porch and escape." And I did it. I really did escape. When I ran away, that was my second Calvary to climb.

When I got to Gressier, an officer stopped me as I was walking along the road. He asked me, "What town are you going to?" I said, "I'm going to the place called Darbonne. That's where they tell me my mother is."

Then the officer saw the cuts and bruises on me. I had a big cut on my foot, and he said, "Did they beat you? Someone who beats a person like that . . . What did you do? Did you steal?" I said, "I'm no thief. I've never stolen anyone's money."

He said okay, and a group of police took me to see my mother. They insulted her. They said, "*Madanm*, you have a little girl, you don't know who she'll be tomorrow. Why did you give her away?" My mother said that she used to do the wash in one man's home. The man raped her. And then I was born.

I asked my mother how she had had me, why she had had me. Then I asked who and what my father was, how he had made me. That was when my mother explained to me how I was conceived, how I was born. While she was washing and ironing at the home where she lived, the son of the household grabbed her and threw her down on the ground. He held her down and ripped her body apart. My mother was bathed in blood and that's when she conceived me.

While she was lying on the ground, the master of the house came and said, "What are you doing lying there? You seem very relaxed." He said, "You're supposed to be doing washing. What do you think you're doing? Staying in a guest house?" He forced her to get up. She had clothes to wash and iron, and supper to cook.

Soon she started feeling so sick she couldn't work. But when they saw that my mother was slowing down in her work, they said, "Girl, you can't stay here and continue like this!"

My mother explained her situation to a neighbor who went and told the lady of the household, "That girl is pregnant," and told her what had happened. The woman said, "I don't know what you're talking about. It's impossible that one of my children would sleep with some servant." "But your son raped her! You must take the child." The woman answered, "Oh, you think that my son would want that type of person? That's not possible."

When they saw that my mother's stomach got big, and that she couldn't hold her body very well, they said they couldn't keep her in the house. The man who raped her said she was too low to bear his child. My mother was a *restavèk*; she didn't have the right to give her child the father's name or even to acknowledge that it was his baby.

So she went and lived in the street. I was born right in the middle of the street at an intersection. I came out black. I was so black I really couldn't have access to my father. A market woman who was passing by cut my umbilical cord with a Gillete. Another woman came to bring my mother a towel. They made that woman my godmother. Anyway, I don't know that person. I don't even know her name. I just heard this.

From the moment I was born, it's been humiliation. When I was baptized in the middle of the street, they just gave me a little paper but it got lost. My birth was never even registered.

I told my mother, "Ah, so my whole life, it's been spent in the street." She said, "Well now, that's because of your father."

When I was just a baby on her shoulder, my mother went back home. That's when she gave me away to the woman who abused and tortured me. Actually, after my mother gave me away, she'd forgotten me.

I said, "Well then, Mama, why don't you show me to my father? Maybe my father's family will take me." So my mother showed me to someone from my father's family. When the relative saw me, she cried. She said, "Lord, you look so much like my family, you must be my relative. We'll take you." Then she cried and said, "I heard someone say that my brother had grabbed a girl who was working in his house and that she had had a baby girl who was never recognized. We'll take you. But we have to go back to your mistress's house." She said, "Take me to the woman you lived with." I said, "I don't need to show you that woman. When my father had me, he didn't recognize me as his child. After all I've suffered, *now* you say you're interested in knowing the people I lived with?" She said, "No, we must meet the person before we hold onto you, so she doesn't get us into trouble and say we stole you." I said, "Okay, we'll go back to the house and show that woman that I'm worth something."

Truly true, we went back to my mistress's house. She said, "Oh, Tibebe has relatives?" My aunt said, "Yes, she has family. It was my brother who fathered her but I never knew her. Now that I see her, I'm very happy. I'll take her." So she adopted me. But she didn't *really* adopt me. I was still an orphan. The family of the person who raped my mother didn't really accept me as part of the family, but my life was a little better than it had been at the woman's house.

The woman I had worked for had just called me Tibebe. That was the only name I knew. So now I asked my aunt—she said yes, you may call me your aunt because you are a person the same as me—"But what's my real name? Where's my birth certificate?" My aunt answered, "You don't have a birth certificate."

But she said, "I remember when they threw your mother out, your father got engaged to another girl. So then your father got married, and that child was born about the same time as you." The person who raped my mother was Cajuste. That sister of mine was Alina Cajuste. She had died. So now my aunt took the birth certificate and gave it to me. I must tell you I was never really born and registered. Alina Cajuste is not really my name. It's the name of a dead person that I have. My aunt said, "Now you are Alina Cajuste."

I asked, "*Am* I a human being? Then why did you let me undergo so much misery? Live with a person who tortured me?" My aunt cried as if someone had died. Me, too, I felt water flowing from my eyes. She said, "Listen, my brother said you weren't his. The mother was just a servant at his home who used to wash and iron clothes." I said, "Oh well, *se lavi*. That's life. It seems that my life is to be spent this way. It seems I'll never exist in this society."

I said, "What can you do to get me into school?" She said, "You're already grown. School won't take you. We should show you how to sign your name." I said, "Sign my name? That's all?" She said, "Yes, that's all we can do for you. And I'll give you one little room to live in. I can't do anything else for you."

Then my father became poor. All his business and his money were lost. He got very sick and I was the one who had to take care of him. When he was dying, he called for me, calling me Tibebe because that's the name I always went by—while I always called him *msye*, sir, to his face. He said "Tibebe, I am your father." I said, "*Now* you tell me." He said, "Everyone has regrets." And he spoke to me of his errors. I said, "I'll help you. Whatever I have, I must help you with that. Don't worry, you don't need to acknowledge me as your child." Then I was happy. Up 'til then, he hadn't even admitted he knew me. I'd been an orphan. I had been a person who had been rejected and now I was able to help him.

All of his family was living abroad. None of them helped with his funeral. I had to make all the arrangements and pay for it all myself. I kept saying to myself, "Look at this child that he never needed, and now I'm doing this funeral." I repeated this the whole time. When I was at the burial, I told my father, "You never took care of me. If you had taken care of me when I was a child, now I would do more for you. But it's a *restavèk* doing your burial now."

Then his sisters got mad. They said, "This is a child who was given away to someone to be a servant. Why does that child have our brother's last name?" They didn't recognize me. To this day, only that one aunt recognizes me. If she's going by in a car, she'll stop to speak with me even if she won't welcome me at her home.

Once she drove by and I said to the woman selling in the market next to me, "That's my father's sister, you know." "You're kidding!" the woman said. "If she's your relative, how come she drives a fancy car and you're living in the streets?" I told her that's because I'm an indigent, and because I was cast out as a servant's child, like a baby in the bulrushes. A few other members of my family recognize me—I don't mean really recognize me as a person, no, just acknowledge that I'm alive.

If you're a child born of rape, everyone, even your mother, considers you worthless. That's how my life has been up to the present; my life is burdened this way. I feel like a baby who was left on a doorstep in a rotten basket.

Once I got down so low, I was crying in the middle of the street. A woman asked me, "Why are you crying like that?" I said, "I can't see any future except to kill myself."

She said, "I'll take you to an organization." I said, "I'm not going into any organization to get beaten up and killed." In those days the military was killing people who were organizing. She said, "No, it'll be good for you. This will help you so you won't kill yourself."

And truly true, I went to a meeting. I sat down, holding my handkerchief in my hands. I was thinking about my life. But then all the women introduced themselves to me. I told them I was called Tibebe, the slave name I've always held onto. They asked, "Why do you want to kill yourself? You don't have the right to kill yourself." They tried to sing with me but I said, "I don't know how to sing." They asked me if I knew how to read. I said no. So they did a little literacy school with me. They said, "Here's how you mark to write your name." Then they asked me how old I was. I'm an illiterate so I never knew my age. They said, "Go get your birth certificate to show us." Then I went and got my birth certificate. There was a woman there named Rica who read it for me. She said, "You were born in 1952." I said, "Ah, tell me again." She said, "You were born on April 7, 1952." I said, "Okay, thank you."

The women's group helped me and my knowledge. They showed me that what the woman had done to me in the *restavèk* system was violence and torture. It was the women who made me understand that you don't beat children. I came to see that when someone says something humiliating to me, that person is humiliating herself, not me.

That's when I started to become like a child. I started playing with the women. They said, "What makes you so playful?" I said, "*Medanm*, women, I've never played in my whole life. I stayed in a woman's home as a *restavèk*." Then they said, "But what about the games you played with other children when you were a child?" I said, "I never played as a child." Now whenever I go to meetings, the women always play with me. Now I know what it feels like for a child to play.

I've come to live my childhood, the one I never had. Only when I was grown-up did anyone treat me as a human being. Now I can smile and laugh, before I couldn't.

The women looked at me as a human being, the same as themselves. That's where I was first given encouragement. I saw that I was living. They made me feel like I exist in society. I became a person.

⋘ LOVLY JOSAPHAT ⋙
I Always Live That Hope

In Cité Soleil, I've suffered a lot. When it rains, the part of the Cité I live in floods and the water comes in the house. There's always water on the ground, green smelly water, and there are no paths. The mosquitoes bite us. My four-year-old has bronchitis, malaria, and even typhoid now. The doctor told me to put him in the hospital but I don't have money, so I leave him at home. The doctor said to give him boiled water, not to give him food with grease, and not to let him walk in the water. But the water's everywhere; he can't set foot outside the house without walking in it. The doctor said if I don't take care of him, I'll lose him.

They've made me undergo a lot of misery in the Cité. I have six children; not one goes to school because of money. I can't send them to school. The children cry each time they see someone else going to school. Titid said he was going to build some schools in the Cité. I would have sent my children there for free, but it never happened.

The morning after Titid left the country, my husband went off to work. When he was returning, FRAPH killed him. They shot him near the sugar factory. They killed my husband because he said that Titid had to return to the country no matter what. FRAPH wouldn't even let me go look. When I went outside to pick up his corpse, they said to me no, they would shoot. There were FRAPH everywhere, shooting in the Cité. When I went outside to look for the corpse, they broke my head open here and here.

They wouldn't let me pick up his body. They dumped it in Titanyen.[9] They dumped his body in Titanyen and left me with six children on my hands. We couldn't even live in our house. FRAPH came and destroyed the house. This little two-room house I had, they threw me out. I had to sleep in the streets with six children.

I suffered a lot for the president. FRAPH used to accuse me of being political. When I was taking care of my asylum application at the International Organization of Migration to leave the country with my children, FRAPH came looking for me to kill me. They said I was into politics, that I was for Titid, that they would kill me. I went into hiding in an area they call La Pleine. When I came back one day to get the children from a friend's house, FRAPH found me and beat me. They beat me on my feet, and my behind, which swelled up like so. They almost broke one of my feet, they beat me so much.

Then my fifteen-year-old girl was coming home from school one day. My second husband held her down and raped her. I had married this man so we could leave the country together. We got political asylum together. It was he who raped my child. He told the child that if she told me, he'd shoot her. At first, the child didn't tell me. Afterwards, though, I saw she was crying. I asked her what was wrong and she explained it to me. Lucky for my daughter, she hadn't yet developed so she couldn't get pregnant.

She was a little kid, she was ignorant. He wasted the life of that child. But they didn't do anything to the man. To this very moment he is a maroon, in hiding. They never found him, though they say he's in Leogane. Everyone says to me, "If it were me, I'd have killed him." I say, "I didn't put him on this earth. God can judge him."

Whenever someone talks to her, they harass her, they say, "Oh, your stepfather raped you." They insult her. She starts crying and comes to tell me. She says, "Please, Mama, send me to the country, send me out of town so I can hide somewhere." When she tells me that, I cry.

© Maggie Steber

To this day, all these things give me an ulcer. After what happened to my husband and me, I shouldn't be living in the Cité at all. But I didn't have any place else to go with the children, I had to stay here. People pass by and say, "*Woy,* wow, this is a place for animals to live." If I found somewhere else, I'd live there. But I say, "Oh, well, we have nothing. There is where we have to live." I just shake my head and say, "One day without fail, God will deliver us."

Me, I cry. The cause is my six children. My last child I had with the man who raped my girl. Five with the other man who died. Tomorrow morning I might get up and the children are coming and going and I don't have any money to give them food. I said that when Titid came back to Haiti maybe I would be better off, but it seems like I've gotten worse. Now, a little can of rice sells for six gourdes (U.S.$.40).[10] Oil sells for two and a half gourdes (U.S.$.17). Seven and a half gourdes (U.S.$.50) for a little can of peas. I can't afford to buy any of it.

My friend Vevette might give me a little scratch of food. She sees I have nothing, so if her husband is working in town and gives her a little money, she gives me a big plate for me and the children. I just give the children our two spoons and let them eat. Sometimes there's not enough for me. But sometimes the kids give me some of theirs. They say, "Mama, you didn't get any. Here, take mine." A friend may give me money for food one day, and then the next day no one in my family will eat.

I'm suffering. I pay $120 (U.S.$40) for six months' rent. I'm not working anymore. I used to do commerce, sell second-hand clothes. Now I don't have any money to invest in the clothes so I can go out into the streets to sell. I sit around all day. I'm not doing anything. I don't have anything, either. I have one mattress, and I sleep with three children on it. Three others sleep on the ground. I put the mattress up on six blocks so when the water comes in, the children don't get wet and they can sleep.

My ten-year-old says to me, "Mama, don't have any more children, no. When I'm big I'll work so I can take care of you." He says, "If you have any more children I'll be mad at you, because the country is too expensive and you don't have any money. The six you have is enough."

Sometimes I sit and cry and think of life. At times I wake up in the night and can't fall back to sleep. I get up, I sit and think. The children say to me, "Mama, why are you sitting there?" Then they get up and sit with me, too. They say, "Stop worrying, Mama. You'll get skinny." I say, "Ah, let me worry." I worry about the life of my children. I see they're getting bigger and I can't do anything for them. They need to go to school; they need to learn a trade. When my first husband was alive, the children could go to school. Now he's not here anymore.

Me, I'm a woman; I can't do anything. And I won't find a man to live with me and help me because there are too many children.

My daughter is fifteen; she needs a skill that she can do tomorrow in case I die, so she can take care of the others. She doesn't have one. I don't have money to buy dresses just for her; I buy one and we both wear it. Sometimes she sees her friends who look nice, dressed in pretty clothes, and she says, "If my mother had money, she'd buy them for me, too." My child who's ten says to my other kids, "Your mother has nothing and your father is dead. Don't you dare ask my mother for anything." They might need shoes or a shirt, but I can't get it for them. If I were working, if I were doing commerce, I would take care of all of them.

I want where we live to change. I want the high cost of living to end. I want my children to go to school, I want other people's children to go to school. Most of us where we live in Little Haiti[11] are suffering. But we must have *tèt ansanm*, unity. If we did, there wouldn't be such price-gouging; the cost of living wouldn't be so high. If everyone acted in solidarity with each other, what someone now sells for ten dollars, she might lower to nine dollars. If everyone were to change, the country would become normal. Otherwise, we'll always suffer.

Cité Soleil has no *tèt ansanm*. All the people do is fight. There's a big party of civilian bandits in Cité Soleil who have arms in their hands. These gangs might take your child away and rape her. It's no good. In the part of Little Haiti where I live, you might just be sitting in front of your house and someone could throw a stone and break your head open. You might never even know who threw it. We women, they might attack us even though we haven't done anything to them.

Just the other day, a bandit shot a child to death in the Cité. I just appeared at my doorway, and bandits with guns were running in front of my house, hiding, shooting at the policemen's heads. I said to one man, "Why are you doing that? You might shoot and take out anyone, someone who wasn't even involved." He told me, "I can kill you just like the kid." When he said that, a neighbor said, "Don't talk with him, Lovly. Don't talk. Don't talk."

But in Cité Soleil there are good people, too. Like my neighbor Vevette, who brings the food for me and the children. She's like a mother for me. She says she likes me because I'm not rude and I appreciate everybody.

I do like everyone. The misery of one woman is the misery of all women. If you are sensitive to me, I am sensitive to you. If I see a man abusing a woman, I might go to him and say, "No! Don't beat her." If he beats her, I get angry. I don't like that at all. If I see two women fighting, I always enter into the middle. I say, "Don't you dare fight. Don't you dare fight." Before I sleep I say, "God, for everyone who has done good to me, I ask for nothing bad to ever happen to them."

Some people are discouraged. They see that the president came back and that he didn't do anything for us. Life is still expensive but, like old people say, *Piti piti zwazo fè nich li.* Bit by bit a bird builds her nest. The country was crushed under the three years of the coup, but now bit by bit it will be fixed. Every time someone does a little work, it will get better.

When I was a child, I had hope. I saw that life was good. If I had a gourde in my hand, I could buy something with it. Life was easier. I would buy sugarcane, eat it, and my stomach was full. My stomach was fine. Now, from time to time, life is hard. But I know that I'll live again the same way I did when I was a child. I never get discouraged. Me, I always say that I have hope. I have children; one day, even if I die, the president will do something for my children. I always live that hope.

A Woman Named Roselie Who Fought Back

I have experienced a lot of pain in my life because of a man I was in love with. His name is Jean Richelère Lizaire. He married me at seventeen, and now I have twenty-six years on my plate. I had four children with him.

When we'd been married for about a month, the maid of honor from our wedding came to spend a few days at my house. During the night, I turned the light on and found her together with my husband. He got off the bed and began to beat me. I screamed for help. In Haiti when you hear someone scream for help, you must investigate. My mother came and found me. He was beating me hard, many times, in the face.

I tried to live with him but we were always arguing. I tried to ignore every time he did something to hurt me. Sometimes I did things to hurt him. But in 1995 he became involved in a *rasin*, roots, music group. I didn't like the kind of friends he was making; they didn't respect themselves. He started smoking cigarettes and drinking rum. I could smell the liquor seeping from him.

Once in 1996, I came back late from church because there was a jam-up in the road on the way home. He started complaining. I told him it wasn't my fault there'd been a traffic jam. He hit me and I told him, "I know what's wrong with you. You're preventing me from praying!" He dragged me into the bedroom and punched me right near the mouth. He punched me in the ribs and I fell to the floor unconscious. He'd hit me in a very serious spot. I still can't sit over a bucket of clothes to wash, and when I bend down, I feel a sharp stabbing pain near the rib. It hurts me so much.

I had three kids in school. I didn't have the money for tuition or uniforms. The entrance fee was $75 Haitian (U.S.$25) for the three, and then there was an additional fee of $9 (U.S.$3) each month. I took what little money I had and went to the city. I worked with the money and multiplied it to $200. My husband asked me to lend him $100 so I gave it to him. When the start of the school year arrived and I needed to purchase the uniforms, I asked him for the money. He told me he'd used it to buy food for the household, but that was a lie. I always bought the food from my own little resources. Fifteen days went by and the children couldn't attend school. I asked him again for the $100. I managed to pay the tuition but still he didn't give me the money for the uniforms. I had to send them without uniforms. But I kept asking him for the money. He

Roselie Jean-Juste

said if I wouldn't stop asking, he would leave the house. True to his word, he didn't come home to sleep.

I went to see my uncle, who is also my third child's godfather. He loaned me the money, and I bought the uniforms. When my husband came to the house and saw them, he asked me where I got the money. I told him. When he heard this, he said my uncle was my lover. Of course I told him no. My child's godfather *can't* be my lover! I told him he was a savage, brutal man and to look at the way he was acting.

When I said that, he hit me several times in the face. When he was through hitting me, he told me he'd kill me because he was married to me and he could do whatever he wanted with me.

I kept suffering with the children. Sometimes when he was beating me, the children would cry, "Daddy, Daddy, don't do that!" He told me he was going to break me so I'd stop being so wise.

One night he came home after I'd gone to sleep. He slapped me hard and that startled me awake. I sat on the bed and said, "Richelère, I don't have any quarrel with you. Why are you hitting me? You've been with me since I was sixteen years old. I married you. I have four children with you. You don't have to do this stuff to me. I've never cheated on you. I'm a poor woman who's struggled all my life. I don't run around behind your back, but you mistreat me anyway."

He told me if he ever caught me cheating on him, he'd kill me and send the corpse to my parents. I said even if I had reached a state with him where I'd have to sleep under a bridge with the children, I'd never take another man. Regardless of whatever tribulations I might be undergoing, I could never cheat on my husband. He answered by hitting me and slapping me again. He constantly hit me in the face, head, and ribs. He said he'd beat me so much that he'd make me walk with a hunchback and that he'd break my nose to make me ugly. I told him that rather than making me a hunchback, he should just leave me and let me live. He said, "If I leave you undamaged maybe you'll find another man. I have to damage you to prevent that."

I said, "You can just forget that. I can't allow this. I can't let you damage me. I'll leave your house and your children." He answered, "I'll never take care of children for any woman. The woman is supposed to take care of the children by herself."

Another time I went to St. Joseph Street to buy a needle and thread. Little did I know my husband was following me. I left there on foot, while he took a bus and got home ahead of me. When I got home, he bolted from the room and pulled me up by the neck. He asked me what I was doing on St. Joseph Street. I told him I went to buy a needle and thread. He pulled me up by the neck again and asked me how come he got home before me. He said I saw him and deliberately lost him. I told him I never saw him. Finally he said, "Too much fooling around. You're messing with me." Then he grabbed me by the neck and started beating me. He hit me on the back of my hand with a stick and broke a finger. Since that time I haven't been able to sleep at night.

After that, he left the house and didn't return for twenty-eight days. Meanwhile I carried on with business as usual, selling merchandise in town. He returned to divide up the things we owned. He took things that were mine, and things he had bought for me. I told him he could just take them.

I continued living there with my children, but he had no thought about their existence. He had no idea if they drank, slept, or how their tuition was paid. On the days that I can provide, they eat. On days I can't, they suffer. That's the way it is.

The last thing he said to me was that in order to kill me he would join up with the *zenglendo*. I don't want him to kill me. I know he's looking for me. I won't let him find me!

I haven't been able to sleep at all. For eight days my eyes haven't closed day or night. I'm afraid he'll come kill me.

I still don't know when it's going to end. I've decided that he's abused me too much. I could never live with him again because he's caused me too much suffering. I didn't leave before because when a woman is married, she must respect the law. If you're married and you sleep outside of the home, the husband can kill you. If you go to court, the law will ask you where you were sleeping. So I respected myself and tried to cope. But now I've given up. Even if he accuses me of something, I can't sleep in the house so he can kill me and leave my four children motherless. If I leave him, he'll kill me. If I call him to court, he'll kill me. If I divorce him, he'll kill me. But I won't stay with him.

I went to court to file a complaint so I could leave my husband's house. I don't want to be accused of anything later. When I got to the courthouse, I spoke with some women who told me to go to General Hospital and get x-rays of the broken finger. The hospital will give me medical documentation of his abuse. My hand trembles whenever I try to do anything with my finger; I can't do anything with it.

I like to go to church and he never could stop me even though that always bothered him. Prayer has helped me. Sometimes I run into a priest or a nun who talks to me and encourages me. I have a lot of courage that I get from God. That's God's grace. Alone I couldn't go on.

I hope that tomorrow God spares my life. I know God won't ever give my husband the power to kill me. I pray a great deal, and I always meet people who encourage me. I talk with them, and it gives me strength.

In addition, I have a strong backbone. Not eating doesn't cause me problems. My only problem is I don't have money to feed my kids. I'd rather not eat than see my children go hungry. He dropped them on me to raise alone. Not only does he make me suffer, he makes the children suffer. I don't want them to suffer! I've resorted to borrowing, doing almost anything to take care of them.

Children are intelligent. Whatever they see their mother and father doing is what they'll repeat and do tomorrow. There's a Haitian proverb that says children are like little fish and they'll follow the big fish. I don't want my children to follow my footsteps. I want them to grow up differently so they don't repeat my mistakes.

I shouldn't have had four children by the time I was twenty-six. I should have learned a skill so I could have been a useful mother and have a better tomorrow. Unfortunately that wasn't what I grew up to find. Those opportunities weren't in my environment. Now I'm trying to help my children reach different opportunities, so they don't retrace my path.

I don't understand Haiti. Day after day work is being done to stop violence against women. Women are fighting back, but still, they just don't have any respect. Men abuse them anyway they please. Men beat women, kick them, pull their hair, shake them by their heads. I have a nonstop headache from the way my husband beat me. I feel my brain move whenever I bend down. I can't take it. And there are other women in the same situation as me. Their husbands knock them to the ground, walk all over them, and break their bones.

That's why I'm doing all I can. I'll always fight. I'll divorce him no matter what to remove him from my spirit. Even if he kills me, at least I'll have left an example for my friends. They'll talk about a woman named Roselie who struggled and fought back.

I Don't Have the Call, I Don't Have the Response

When Aristide left Haiti, the *zenglendo* overtook the area. They shot everything they saw. The *zenglendo* came into my house, they beat me, they slapped me. Four of them raped me, martyred me, vanquished me, sliced through me. Lucky for me my children weren't there, my mother wasn't there, it was only me and my little baby in the house. They beat the baby, they tied her mouth. Lucky for me my child didn't die. But to this day she doesn't speak.

Since the priest [Aristide] came back, we've gotten a little relief. But still, they're dumping bodies on the ground. I sleep with one eye open, one eye closed.

My life has reached a terrible condition. The *zenglendo* took everything from my hands, every little bit I had. It's not like I had jewels, but at least we could eat. Now I am living by borrowing from the loan shark. I don't know what to do to pay back the money. Now I'm living in a hallway with my six children and grandmother. I've become degraded. I ask for aid, I ask for help.

After the rape, I suffered so much shame. The people where I was living abandoned me. I've been humiliated in my own neighborhood, Carrefour Feuilles. They criticized me for what happened. I have no more value as a human being. I don't have the call, I don't have the response. They look at me like I was something I'm not. People make fun of me. "This is a *zenglendo*'s mistress. Huh, you think you're important." First the thugs destroy you, then the neighbors humiliate you. Even your children aren't respected.

Thanks to God, what gives me a little breath now, what allows me to stand up to speak, is that someone from a women's group came around. She helped raise us back up. She told us, "Being raped doesn't mean that a woman is finished. Even when you think that a *zenglendo* has shamed you, it's not true. Don't believe you're degraded. Don't think that when the evil men finished doing what they did to you that you should let yourself go and drink poison. You must always hold strong, pray, and put yourself with other strong women so you can create a sort of solidarity. Find people to help you raise your heads up again, so you don't let yourself be humiliated."

She told us, "You must give yourself strength as a woman. Don't think that a man has priority over you. You must keep in mind that you have as much value as any Haitian, as any woman. Even if you're not a professional, even if you're not an intellectual, don't debase yourselves. Don't say that others are more than you. We all have our place in society, and we all have our own role to fill."

Well, when I met up with people from the women's organization, I felt myself comforted, and I felt that I had strength. It is the hour, it is the time for me and all of us to have a change. I believe that little by little in the future, I can come back to the level I was.

All strong women, we take a stand. What we want is what must happen. We can't let other people decide for us, we must decide for ourselves.

School

I am here today to tell you about my life from my childhood on. It's been a mass of problems.

When I was nine years old, a woman saw me one day while I was at the marketplace with my mother. She said, "Oh *Madanm*, let me take your daughter to come live with me." So my mother sent me to live at this woman's house. And she conducted herself well and was good to me. Then a priest saw me. He liked me, too, and took me to his house. They were treating me well, but they never put me in school. I was really unhappy with that, so I went back to my mother's.

I had always liked school a lot, so when I went back to my mother's, she put me back in school. I worked hard. They chose me to play all sorts of roles in the theater pieces.

For the closing ceremony, there was going to be a play and a party on Sunday. We all practiced parts. But on Saturday I got a fever. The fever I had, it was because I didn't have any shoes. I had some plastic sandals that I used to wear to school, but I wanted to have shoes to wear in the theater piece. I didn't want the children to make fun of me so I felt I couldn't go to the play. Well, I lay down with fever.

The following Monday, I went to get my report card. The principal said, "So, you didn't show up on Sunday and now you think you can just come and get your report card? No way!" I thought about how hard I'd worked; I would have been first in my class. But they failed me. It wasn't right for them to ruin that whole year because I hadn't performed my role in the play.

In September, my aunt came to take me to go to Port-au-Prince. More problems! I didn't know Port-au-Prince yet. Back then, a long time ago, in the countryside, you always heard that everyone in Port-au-Prince was happy. I was excited to go. But my aunt never put me in school there. What she did was make me stay home and take care of her youngest child. They just kept me there to wash the girl in the afternoons, make food for her, take her to her godmother's house to get her hair combed, wash clothes, and do the house work.

All my aunt's children went to school except me. Each time I saw her children going to school, I cried, I cried. I had gone to her house with all my books, my notebook, my uniform. Even though my aunt saw that, she would never even let me attend afternoon classes. But I couldn't find anyone who'd give my mother a message for me so I could go back home.

This was the biggest nightmare of my life. I could have gone far in school, because I know I am very, very, very intelligent. And every time I stop and remember these things, I always want to cry.

Now, well, in that house, my aunt's husband would aggress me in my sleep. This husband of my aunt, he took advantage of me. I always called for my aunt, told her I wanted to go home, that there was something eating at my heart.

The man hated me. Why? Because each time he wanted to have sex with me, I didn't want to. So each time he saw me, he beat me. There was a time when I was washing the child and she didn't want to be washed. She started crying for her father. The man didn't even ask me what was wrong with the kid, he just attacked me with a whip. He beat me and put marks all over me.

Another time I was in the house—I was always in the house—and my aunt said, "Bathe the child." After I finished bathing the child, she took off her shoes and started playing in the dirt. My aunt told me to wipe her dirty feet with a wet cloth. I asked another of the kids, "Can you wipe her feet while I'm making up the bed, so I can put her to bed?" The man came and beat me. He beat me and I fell and shouted for help. I said, "If you're going to beat me unnecessarily, send me back to my mother." I said that if they didn't, I would run in front of a car and make it crush me. And I ended up back home.

When I got home, I went to the home economics center where I learned sewing and embroidery and that kind of thing. Life was never good again. But whether life was good or not, I survived. I took responsibility; I did a little selling. I was getting by.

Then I had yet another problem: The principal of the school I had gone to liked me from the time I'd been a child. Well, after I got back, when I saw that he still liked me, things happened. He offered me a job, so I started to work. And one time I needed to pick up my paycheck. The school was closed so I went to his house. This time he put his hands on me. I had never responded to his advances before. But this time I lost my virginity and got pregnant. That's how at twenty-one years old, I had a child with him. He continued on with me for awhile, but after two years he didn't take care of the child anymore. I suffered so much misery for that child.

Because of the way I'd been raised, I'd always said that my children would be raised well. Ah, the problem of children, the problem of children. My parents didn't have the means to give me a good life. They thought that if they gave their child to be a *restavèk* in some home, that person could help her advance.

Now more people understand that even if life is getting harder for them, they have to make more effort. They must raise that child well because tomorrow the child will be the staff of their old age. That's why I left my one-year-old daughter with my mother and went to Port-au-Prince to work. After I started doing marketing, buying and selling a few things in the street market, I sent for the child. I sent her to school.

Well, my life has not been sweet for me at all. I am going to be fifty and my whole life has been misery. But good or not good, my child and I lived. I struggled. I suffered to earn her tuition with my little marketing business. I did it. I put her all the way through school. And today she's a preschool teacher.

2 RESISTANCE AS EXPRESSION

It is through the creation of art and culture that the spirit is fed and kept alive and our common humanity is expressed and exposed.
—Suzanne Pharr

I have to speak. The word has to get out. If I didn't have a microphone to speak with or people to listen to me, I'd stand in front of a chicken and talk. I'll die with the words on my lips.
—Lelenne Gilles

Haitian painting is rich in brilliant colors, whimsical scenes, and joyous tones. This richness is particularly manifest in the abundant paintings of jungle scenes. With their majestic trees clothed in thick foliage, tigers, lions, and giraffes, these images might have come straight out of Brazil or Kenya. The scenes raise a conundrum: almost no Haitian has seen rain forests or jungle animals. Haiti is the most deforested country in the Western Hemisphere; most of its mountains are brown and denuded. And except for a few rare specimens, Haitian wildlife has been reduced to rats, bugs, and birds.

"How do they manage to paint such beauty," I have heard foreigners ask, "when their lives are so filled with despair?"

The answer may lie in the inversion of the question. Perhaps Haitians paint such vivid, ebullient art precisely *because* so many domains of their lives are filled with despair. Haiti is poor, yes, but it is also filled with richness. Searching out that richness where it exists, and inventing it where it does not, are ways to maintain hope and resilience. For those seeking a brighter landscape, expression can offer relief, sustenance, and a path toward change.

The *istwa* in this chapter look at three variants of resistance: expression as a challenge to personal subjugation, popular culture as the validation and empowerment of a people, and expression as social protest.

Haiti is fissured into two disparate societies. The first one is exclusively black, Creole-speaking, rural, and poor. Its members are usually *vodouizan* (although often Catholic at the same time) and closely tied to their African heritage. The second society includes mulattoes (there being virtually no white Haitians) along with blacks who speak French along with Creole, maintain an urban connection, and are Francophile. They largely shun vodou and what are derogatorily termed "Congo" traditions. Though comprising only roughly 15 percent of the population, this sector controls almost all the wealth and institutional power in the country.

Until very recently, the second group has also controlled official cultural domains. In the period of slavery, the dominant classes and government forbade public demonstration of African customs, including music, celebrations, religion, and languages. This social control has extended to more recent days, with the prohibition of Creole from school, church, and legal institutions, and the persecution of *vodouizan*.

Popular culture has remained forever vibrant in quotidian and covert domains. But through a form of apartheid maintained by the powerful, the majority has been traditionally denied formal social, political, and legal access. As market woman Lenyse Oscar says, "In Haiti, if you're not an intellectual, if you're poor, if you're a kerchief-head, no one takes care of you. They despise and mistreat you." And while this apartheid has oppressed all the Haitian poor, women have been doubly burdened—both as members of a disempowered group and as oppressed members within that group.

In recent years, new forms of foreign penetration—notably by the United States—have further endangered traditional popular culture. Along with undermining the local economy, the invasion of foreign goods into local markets has meant that peasant women are increasingly wearing cast-off American T-shirts with their commercial slogans, instead of the locally made, conventionally styled dresses. Many have grown ashamed of their formerly omnipresent head scarf. Whereas in homes throughout Haiti one used to see leaf medicine—potions of dark liquid and herbs stored in old bottles and sealed with cloth stoppers—one now sees U.S. pharmaceuticals, often long-since expired, tucked under the eaves of thatch roofs. Increasingly, the snack of choice from street vendors is imported popcorn instead of the roasted peanuts and coconut candies that were prepared for generations by Haitian women from local products. Words like *cool* now pepper Creole speech, and American music permeates the radio waves. Even crime patterns have been influenced, with assaults styled after those of Brooklyn gangs.

EMPOWERING POPULAR CULTURE

Expression is about power. The expression of the dominant drowns out that of the dominated: men drown out women; the landowner drowns out the peasant; the boss drowns out the worker; the foreign superpower drowns out the Third World country. As journalist Lelenne Gilles puts it, leaning forward on her wobbly chair, "Those who can't speak are those who can't eat."

Control over the production and demonstration of expression, over the margins between silence and speech, and over the content of the public record, have long been hotly contested in Haiti. After Jean-Claude Duvalier fell from power in 1986, the silenced citizenry ratcheted up the campaign to bring their voices to public spheres. Personal, social, and political expression that had been confined to private or underground domains erupted into public, open sites.

The advances have imbued marginalized sectors of civil society with a new pride, sense of self-worth, and commitment to their own self-determination. Gracita Osias, a literacy worker, says, "There's been no cultural value placed on the [peasants] and there's been so much richness and capacity lost . . . But little by little peasants are beginning to establish their value [and] bring up their morale."

In the 1980s, progressive journalists and advocates developed a new form and function of radio—*the* media for a population that overwhelmingly cannot afford television and cannot read newspapers. Radio stations have served as open microphones in which the democracy movement and the poor can speak their minds. A free-speech format has allowed citizens from the grassroots to present local and national issues from their own perspective, for the first time. Lelenne Gilles describes the work of these stations as "going to all corners of the country to collect speech from the mouths of those who didn't have the right to speak for themselves."

Moreover, the spreading use of Creole on radio, beginning in the 1970s, gave millions of people who did not know French access to news—also for the first time. In moments of political upheaval, each rare transistor radio became a convergence point for a small crowd eager for news.

Popular radio was not attained easily: Throughout the late 1980s and early 1990s, the military repeatedly shot at these stations and destroyed their transmitters. When possible, station owners and staff immediately repaired their equipment and returned on the air. Young journalists attained folk hero status as they were arrested or forced underground. Under the coup, activists broadcast from secret locations with mobile transmitters. One group even established a Creole program from a Dominican station, relaying stories over the border. Barred from broadcasting news, peasant station aired songs with developments encoded in the lyrics. What has happened in Haiti confirms James Scott's assertion that "printing presses and copying machines may be seized, radio transmitters may be located, even typewriters and tape recorders may be taken, but short of killing its bearer, the human voice is irrepressible."[1]

Another major recent advancement has been the supplanting of French with Creole in many social and political arenas. Though known only to a few, French had always been Haiti's official language. Until the 1980s, it was the only language employed by the media, the state, the Catholic Church, and other official spheres. Children were beaten in school for speaking their mother tongue. Most citizens could not understand their primary school classes, their own legal trials, or the bill of sale for their produce. Beyond the material implications, the psychological impact was devastating. Peasant organizer Vita Telcy explains, "When the big educated folks come among you and say two or three words in French, they squelch all you have said and you come to understand that you're nothing." Nurse and labor organizer Yanique Guiteau Dandin says, "When they told us not to speak Creole in school, it was like saying to the people: do not speak."

Creole, the language that evolved from African tongues and French colonialists, contains the imagery and soul of the culture. As a result of popular mobilization, Creole gained its place in the 1987 constitution as a second official language. Linguists and Creole advocates developed an orthography, and citizens began teaching themselves and others to read and write the language. People are forcing the language's integration into formal domains formerly controlled by the elite, such as in the legal system. All of this is slowly changing the balance of power between the poor and the ruling classes.

Market woman Alina "Tibebe" Cajuste's life and *istwa* narrate past developments, as well as how far this movement still has to go. "Huh!" she said.

> At the parents' meeting . . . everyone looks at me funny behind my
> back. Why? Because I don't express myself in French. But I say,

"That's just how I speak. . . . But it's my right. . . . I'm living in a Creole country. I must speak the way I speak."

Another domain in which popular expression becomes a tool of empowerment is vodou. The vast majority of the people[2] practice the religion and rites the slaves brought from Africa, one based on a belief of one God, a life-giving force, and of *lwa*. Repressed for centuries, still vodou flourished, its faithful finding ways to practice underground. For instance, *lwa* were depicted as Catholic saints so that their images could be displayed openly without retribution. Peasants' ability to maintain their African worship has been an emboldening, counter-hegemonic feat. Popular educator Claudette Werleigh says, "Vodou is the religion that has been able to travel and to survive not only slavery but colonialism, and then the neo-colonialism that we've had after independence." The empowering elements of vodou extend to gender; women have as much centrality and authority as men within the practice.

Since the mid-1980s, *vodouizan* have made great advances in their claims to religious freedom. Vodou's place in society is "rising up from under the table," as *manbo* Florencia Pierre says. *Vodouizan* no longer risk death because of their faith.

In fact, vodou's public image has become respectable, even trendy, among some in the dominant classes. Americans and Europeans now travel to Haiti and pay a fee to become vodou initiates. About this new phenomenon, Florencia says, "They used to say that people who . . . go to vodou ceremonies were people who . . . were unenlightened children, ignorant, unsociable. . . . But now they want to catch a free ride on its back."

But the poor still have not won the culture war. Their negotiations remain blocked in many areas. For one thing, foreign cultural domination is growing exponentially. And universal literacy remains a pipe dream.

In the mid-1980s, a nervous Catholic hierarchy, encouraged by the military junta, aborted a nascent national literacy project. To this day, the government has not implemented any viable literacy program, while private initiatives have done little to abate the level of illiteracy.

The critical import of literacy is expressed by two underfed and underemployed women as they sit on undersized chairs in the sky-blue kindergarten that serves as their literacy classroom. Rubbing a chapped elbow, Maryse Joachin says, "Before I knew how to read I was nothing." Julie Nicholas states,

We're not into those little **X**'s anymore! We're done with those little **X**'s! Now we can sign our names. We don't have to be ashamed anymore.

CULTURAL EXPRESSION AS RESISTANCE

Beyond personal and social expression, the post-1986 opening has put popular culture at the service of gender and class empowerment. Standing amidst corn in her small hillside garden, Mafi Elma says, "If I am made to feel I am nothing in society, if I am told I'm inferior, I won't find strength within myself to stand up to defend my rights. On the other hand, getting support from my own culture, I can resist in the struggle to get my rights."

Since the mid-1980s, such public sites as churches, schools, universities, and the media have become headquarters for bold political speech. *Rara* celebrations, masqueraded, musical parades of vodou societies, serve as massive demonstrations of popular will. There, symbolic costumes, ribald songs, and bawdy street drama act out political opinion. Mardi Gras can serve the same purpose. In the 1998 carnival parade, for instance, a national women's group *Kay Fanm*, Women's House, had its own float, a truck decorated with a naked and defiant woman. As it lurched through the tightly packed, drunken crowds, women atop the truck threw tracts and sang feminist chants. Bright murals evoking imagery from the national heritage and vodou convey earthy political commentary on walls everywhere. Clandestinely scrawled graffiti brings primary-color messages to street corners. Cartoons, guerrilla theater, and songs deliver often ironic social statements.

The erosion of gender constraints has not kept pace with that of cultural constraints. Haitian women's mouths are still gagged relative to men's, in both public and private spheres, as their socioeconomic and time constraints are much greater. Too, speaking is not the same as being heard. But the degree to which poor black despised women are now able to speak out is a victory. And women are gaining power from that exercise.

The empowerment takes at least two forms, the first involving women's personal voice. Speaking of her brilliant-colored canvases with images of skulls rendered in violent brush strokes, Martine Fourcand says, "Painting was a way to try to limit the effects of the destroyers on my individual life. My painting allowed me to live in the extreme constraints we were suffering under." Today, personal expression allows women to assert themselves and expand their identity, humanity, and self-determination.

Second, expression is one more weapon in women's battle for economic, political, and gender justice, as Alina "Tibebe" Cajuste attests through her poetry. In a small stifling room packed with women from her grassroots organization, Tibebe critiques U.S. domination:

> Don't corner me!
> You sent for me,
> You made me come.
> Don't corner me!
> You are the sky
> filled with stars,
> Why are you cornering me?
> You've harvested my garden
> to send it overseas.
> Don't corner me!

I'll Die with the Words on My Lips

Since I'm a journalist, I choose to be a voice for those who can't speak. I want to make the big ears listen.

Those who can't speak are those who can't eat. They can't live, they can't drink, they can't breathe. They don't have the right to anything because they're not considered people in our country. These are the people I feel it's necessary to stand with, work with, be their spokesperson, give them a microphone, help them speak out so they don't suffocate with what's inside them.

I started this fight in the '80s when I was in school. Some students thought that, as privileged people, they didn't have any responsibility for the have-nots. But the have-nots and the weak always get my attention. In school I was always questioning why people couldn't fight back when their kids were sent back home because they couldn't pay. I always stood up and asked the question at the bursar's office: Don't those kids have a right to education, too? All my teachers told me they were waiting for me to become a journalist.

My awareness increased when there were huge movements of mobilization to crush Jean-Claude Duvalier's regime during the 1980s. We saw the necessity of helping out through the microphone. At that time, you know, there were no radio stations working with the poor. Also, there were only two television stations: a private one and a state-owned one, and the state one knew exactly what the private one was doing. There was an urgency for people to spread information through any means possible, whether by tracts or radio or newspaper. So after my studies, when Radio Cacique called me in '85, I went without thinking twice. It was different than other radio stations, Radio Cacique; it was a station of struggle. I gave a hand to this radio station, which was both young and full of youth. I knew my place was with them, because there was a task to be done. Through this radio we waged a battle for the poor, for the factory workers in Cité Soleil and in all the shantytowns. We went to all corners of the country to collect speech from the mouths of those who didn't have the right to speak for themselves. Of course, the radio station was later destroyed, but the work is still being done.

We won a brief victory on February 7, 1986, when Duvalier fled Haiti. I think you know there was this wonderful outburst. Everyone could talk. Everyone could express himself.

Lelenne Gilles

Nevertheless, after February 7, there was an effort to rob us of the little peace we'd won. I had to hide because they were after me and a lot of other reporters. Political tension was rising. Soldiers arrested a journalist from the radio station and tried to force him to reveal my address. He didn't reveal it. They beat him and threw him on the street. Finally they let him go. That same day, two armed men in civilian clothes showed up in front of my house. They approached a child and asked him, "Where is Lelenne's house?" The kid answered, "I don't know that person." They didn't find me that day. Later they even searched my house.

I went underground, to somewhere I always go. Two days later they showed up at this place and made an all-out search. I was forced to leave Haiti quickly. I spent about three months outside the country. Eight days after Ertha Trouillot was inaugurated as president in 1990 I came back to the country. I swore to myself that I would die here. No, I won't go into exile again for anyone.

Right after the 1991 coup against Aristide, I went into hiding again. I spent six months totally underground. I didn't go out at all. My complexion changed completely, I became very pale.

They tried to gag our mouths but they couldn't. I wasn't the only one hiding—there were a whole bunch of us. The phone was the only means of communication between journalists. Each journalist had the phone number for one other reporter. I talked to you, you talked to the other ones. We couldn't work under our real names. Everyone had a pseudonym, everyone had a number, everyone had a code so we could gather information and disseminate it. We were scared the phone company would tap our phones. But we had to do it, we wanted to do it. It was from there that the news spread, that people outside the country became aware of what was going on. A big international movement of solidarity was developing to expose the crimes being committed in Haiti.

There were almost no radio stations left functioning at that time, because the army had destroyed most of them. Three months after the coup, only Radio Nationale was functioning, and it was the mouthpiece of the coup leaders. However, there were Haitian radio stations in the diaspora. When they needed information, they called journalists in Haiti. I used to give the news to Miami, to New York, and sometimes to Canada, the Netherlands, and Martinique.

I didn't have a mike in my hands but I had a telephone. They would call me. I would lie under my bed and broadcast news by the phone. I spent an hour or two giving news and explaining what was happening in the country. Now, you're probably wondering how I got the information. I couldn't go out in the streets to get it. I used people from my home who could go out. They would come and tell me, "Here's what's happening." I had other friends and reporters who would verify and exchange the information.

I used to get anonymous and threatening phone calls, but I said that I would die while speaking, I had to speak. I would die with the words on my lips.

Finally I decided I just had to go out. But I was put under a lot of pressure. For instance—I'll never forget this—I was walking down Capois Street. I'd just bought a chicken for my mother to cook for dinner. There was a car filled with people parked right in the middle of the street, and I heard someone shouting, "Oh my God! There's Lelenne Lavalas! Lelenne Lavalas! There's an Aristidiste!" Everyone knew Lelenne who worked at Radio Cacique. They ran after me. I ran inside the store where they'd sold me the chicken so fast that I almost went straight into the freezer.

Then in 1992 I got arrested at the cathedral. There was a mass while grass-roots organizations were preparing a political mobilization. There were a lot of reporters present, a lot of people. Even before the event started, a group of armed civilians appeared. They arrested me and accused me of receiving money from Aristide in Washington and distributing it around to the people in the streets. They pointed their guns at me and forced me into a car. They struck me and jabbed me with their revolvers while they drove me to jail. All the people in the jail were people who had spoken to me. They had even arrested a street vendor I'd been speaking with. I'd just been standing in front of her because I was buying a candle for the mass from her. They arrested her and asked her to tell them what I was talking about. I spent a day there, but I was freed because the media had already spread the news. Thanks to this solidarity I got free. In any other case I would have been killed, just like so many others.

The right to speak, you see, has always been a process, a battle. In the '80s, the soldiers and Macoutes would just break into the radio stations to arrest reporters, kill reporters, disappear reporters. But the journalists didn't give up. I wasn't intimidated by the fact that a lot of reporters had been victimized, or their houses were burned down and their families attacked. It didn't really bother me, a young girl just out of school. On the contrary, I was driven like an electric current to continue what our predecessors had to stop doing because the dictatorship had interrupted it. Even today, we've only won a part of that battle and we're still struggling to consolidate the victory.

I've dedicated my life to working with the press. If I didn't have a radio to speak in, I'd stand under a tree to speak out. If I didn't have a microphone to speak into, I'd stand in the middle of the street. The people would pass by and

I'd tell them, "Ladies and gentlemen, here's what's going on. In this rural area they just fired fifty workers for their union activities." If I didn't have a microphone to speak with or people to listen to me, I would stand in front of a chicken and talk. I'll die with the words on my lips.

That's what I tell you. I have to speak. The word has to get out. This is the way I can contribute, what I can do, what I can give. I must tell you that life isn't easy, but I made a choice. I must speak. Everyone has secrets, but I know every secret has something it can teach others. So, me, I put everything out.

It's a struggle, a determination, a conviction. I've dedicated my life to that. I have a boy, Sonio, and an adopted girl, Liline. I'm living for them but also for the majority who don't have their full rights. It's not a question of just doing a job. I'll continue regardless of all the obstacles that arise along the way. If I don't, people will end up not having the space to breathe. In spite of all those difficulties in life, I've decided to continue this fight. That's how it is.

☜MARCELINE YRELIEN ☞
Singing a Woman's Misery

All the humiliation and exploitation I suffered as a peasant woman living in the countryside, that's what made me become an artist. A woman's misery made me a *sanba*, bard, a person who writes songs and teaches people the songs. You have a choral group behind you, and you who know how to sing, you call out, and the chorus answers you.

I, the woman making these songs, am not a woman who really knows how to read and write. The state doesn't concern itself with helping the poor that way. But I can write my name and a few lines.

In 1980 I fell into the struggle based on the misery I was living. I knew that I couldn't stay by myself my whole life, that there were other women like me who were suffering the same misery. I joined the *Tèt Kole Ti Peyizan Ayisyen* movement, the Heads Together Small Haitian Peasants movement.

They arrested both women and men in *Tèt Kole* because we were talking about our situation and how we could get out of it. At times I've had to go underground, sleep in the bush. I've had to run four or five kilometers to go hide in the forests so the officers couldn't come destroy me. Other women comrades who were working with us collected our children, fed them while we were suffering—being beaten, arrested, and humiliated in prison. Women acted in solidarity and held demonstrations to get each other released. It works the same way in other areas, too: all the women embracing each other.

All that made me become an artist so I could talk about the lives of all Haitian women who are struggling to get out from under this bad system of exploitation. That's why I make songs: to speak about life from what I know of my own situation.

You might hear about some big crisis that's happened, when poor Haitian men or women—because you never find a rich person that's been killed, no—have died under bullets. And you know there's no justice that will bring the killers to trial. I made songs about July 23, 1987, the day the local landowners and Tontons Macoutes massacred 139 peasants of our organization. I made songs about the coup d'etat of September 30, 1991, when people showed so much resistance. I make songs so we can keep track of history, so people will hear and remember. The songs are also meant to show what we can become tomorrow.

I sit down and make a beautiful song that tells the story, that gives the history of something that happened. I notice especially that none of the things that women have done in Haiti appear in history. All the battles that women have led, from our independence in 1804 on, never appear. I make songs about great strong women who raised women's rights off the ground. I make them so all women can know just how long we've been struggling to get out from under our oppression, so the women's struggle for rights and equality can continue on, go farther.

We published the songs on a cassette in the name of the movement. Women from all over the country can learn these songs, study and master them, and understand the lyrics which talk about their own lives.

There are other big *sanba*, men and women who don't know how to read, who also make these songs today. It's when we look and see that we don't have any justice in the country that we make songs. We make them so that all the things that happen to the poor and the women can be told.

> Don't forget, poor women, don't forget
> Don't forget, working women, don't forget
> March 8 is Women's Day,
> Don't forget.
>
> Men stomp on women's rights
> So we can be their maids.
>
> They plunder women's rights
> Forgetting that women made them.
>
> They may kill us with bullets,
> But we'll remember Women's Day.
>
> We remember in Chicago
> They killed 129 women.
>
> March 8, 1905, women took the streets
> Reclaiming their rights.
>
> March 8, 1908, Chicago's women
> workers seized a cloth factory.

March 8, 1910, a strong woman called
for a big women's gathering.

We have Défilé Lafolle
She collected Dessalines' body.

We have Anacaona, a strong woman
She refused to accept the Spanish.

Don't forget, poor women, don't forget
Don't forget, working women, don't forget
March 8 is Women's Day,
Don't forget.

Getting the Poetry[3]

I'd never had poetry in my life. The only poem I had ever heard was a nursery rhyme called "Baby" that my children recited for me. I just thought of my poems myself. I did them without ever having heard any poetry and without anyone helping me.

I am a person who doesn't know how to read, who doesn't know how to write. But I'm intelligent, my spirit works. It's a river that flows to the sea.

The first poem I composed was on a Mother's Day. People were celebrating, everyone was giving their mothers gifts. And I just sat there, because my mother was far away. I said, "Okay, I'll create a poem about Mother's Day." I made "The Rape of Haiti."

> Haiti is a beautiful woman,
> but what a woman with no luck!
> This woman wraps her head in a red kerchief
> wears a blue dress
> and old sandals
> yet all the men like her.
>
> But really, this woman has no luck!
> All the men who like her are raping her
> They'll never bow their heads
> What a woman with no luck, this Haiti.
>
> Haiti had a young man who loved her
> who courted her properly.
> Everyone was happy
> that he would marry Haiti.
> But that man'll be forced to rape Haiti.
> What a terror.
>
> What a woman with no luck, this Haiti.
> This man will court her again.
> Haiti is happy that this man will marry her.

But his feet are tied.
He doesn't know if he should run or sit.
Both his feet are tied.

I'm the child of rape, that's how I made "The Rape of Haiti." It's thinking about my life that makes me do poetry.

It was my present for Mother's Day. When I did that poem for the women of my group, they stood up, they applauded. Some hugged me. They were happy! They asked me how I did it. They said, "You know how to write?" I said, "No, I don't know how to write. I think all the time and I'm always experiencing misery. I just copy the misery."

What really encouraged me with poetry was a child named Nicole who used to buy things from me in the marketplace. She was the only person among the rich who treated people well.

One day Nicole said to me, "You don't have anything to sell? Not even a little spoon?" I said, "Ah, I don't have anything to sell. But would you like me to give you a poem?" She said, "Oh? Is that right, market woman, you can give me some poetry?" That's what she called me, market woman. I said, "I'll give you poetry."

She invited me into her home. Now, I'm a market woman. I just stand outside households; I don't go in. But she invited me to her birthday party, and she made me sit in the room. There were some people from New York who were all dressed up. I don't live in a world of nice clothes. I had on torn sandals, my feet were dirty. I felt so humiliated.

A woman asked me, "What are you doing here at this party?" I said, "This girl is my friend." She said, "What do you mean, your friend? You're just a market woman!" Nicole said, "This friend is going to recite a poem. I want her to recite it before everyone. She has so much intelligence, even if it's undeveloped." That woman and some others said, "Ah, we're not staying at this party." Nicole said, "Okay, if you want to go, go. But this is my friend."

When she said that, she gave me hope. She said, "All right then, do the poetry for me." I stood up and said "The Rape of Haiti." Then everyone who had said, "Why'd you bring that woman in here?" came to hug me. They congratulated me. Then they went and got a dress for me to put on. I said "I won't put that on, thank you very much. I will stay as I am." I didn't want to be humiliated even more.

I told one man, "You will not torment my spirit. It means nothing to me that you told me not to sit next to you. I needed to do poetry for Nicole, who recognizes me as her friend, and I came to recite poetry as my gift."

Nicole said, "Your poetry is so beautiful. And you're not ashamed. Other people would be praying, they'd be so scared." I said, "That's where my pride comes in. I can do this because of how I've been humiliated. Since I was born my life has been my humiliation."

Humiliation is when you go somewhere and you don't speak French and they make you sit in a corner. Humiliation is when you don't know how to read and you don't have nice clothes. And now I feel pride because I have the words, the spirit, the knowledge. I can say a word that makes someone happy or that someone higher than me will hear. My whole life doesn't have to pass in humiliation. I can give poetry that will make people who had looked down on me see me as something.

Still, people don't take it seriously since I don't know how to read. I can't make a profit off my poetry. When a savant makes poetry, people say, "Oh, listen to this beautiful poetry." The savant would know how to write it down and make a book. And then he could make some money off of it. When someone illiterate makes poetry, it's like a joke. People say, "*Woy*, how weird! Where did that person find that language?" When you're illiterate, you think all the same thoughts as a writer, you just don't know how to write your thoughts down.

At the parents' meetings, I go and ask the principal, "How is my child doing in her work?" Everyone looks at me funny behind my back. Why? Because I don't express myself in French. But I say, "That's just how I speak. I'm an illiterate. But it's my right to speak this way, I'm living in a Creole country. I must speak the way I speak."

Alas, when you don't know how to read, it's like a disease. My children suffer humiliation in school because I'm illiterate. They even threw Carel out of school because of it. What happened was that after I had taken her to school, the other students said, "What are you doing in this school? Your mother doesn't dress nicely." They said, "If it were me, I'd never admit that that's my mother. I'd make her drop me off in the streets so no one could see her." Carel said, "No, that's my mother. I'm not ashamed. She's the one who bore me. She put me in school. She's the one who feeds me. I wouldn't be able to eat otherwise. She's the one who must come get me." She got mad at them and got into a fight. So, they threw her out of school.

My children copied down the poem, "The Rape of Haiti," and took it to school. The other kids asked, "Where did you get that great poem?" My kids said, "Our mother composed it! She recited it and we copied it down." They said, "Oh yeah? Your mother can say these big things?" My children said, "Yes, that's why we're proud of our mother. Our mother speaks beautiful language."

So the other kids said, "Write it down so we can have a copy, too." My children said, "No way! You're always insulting our mother because she's illiterate."

Now that they know I'm a poet, when my daughter Roselore's friends come to the house, they always come seeking out poetry from my hand. They say, "Roselore's mama, how did you do that?" I said, "I thought. I just thought."

Analfabèt pa bèt. The illiterate are not ignorant. When you're illiterate you think a lot.

They ask, "What pushed you to send your child to school?" I answer, "Children, you ask a big question. You see, I've suffered humiliation all my life but I have knowledge. Still, I know how much knowledge has been lost because I'm not a savant. I put my children in school so they could have a little hope and do better than I have." Here's a poem I made about that.

Look at the misery of an illiterate woman
deceived by the state schools.

How much money are you asking me
to enroll my child in a state school
which belongs to the people?
One hundred dollars?
I don't have one hundred dollars to give you.

I'm a seller of sour oranges
who doesn't want her child to sign with a cross
as I do at the Big House.
Why don't you give me a chance
and let my child into the school?

I'll give you all I own
so you can give my little one some
knowledge so that she won't
sign a cross at the Big House.

Her mother used to practice her crosses
beneath a mango tree.
I won't give my child a chance to bear a cross
beneath the mango tree.

Give her a small chance, make her live
so that she can read
so that she won't make mistakes
in front of Professor Low-Score.

Listen to me, please.
Give me a chance.

The revolution in state schools
never happened.
Still, the mother who cannot read
will make sure her child can.

Roselore's teacher tried to throw her out because I couldn't pay what I owed the school. The children said, "Teacher, give Roselore a chance. Let Roselore stay in school. Don't send her back home. Her mother will come pay." But Roselore started to cry. She said, "My mother doesn't have any money." The teacher said, "The students spoke with me. I won't send you home, Roselore. Your mother seems to be very wise. When she comes to the parents' meeting, she's always asking if you give me any problems. I'll keep you in school. From time to time, when your mother has some money, she can come pay."

These poems, I don't know how I make them. Poetry just comes to my head when my heart is in distress. Here's one that I call "Rainbow." When I recite this poem, people always cry.

Rainbow, rainbow.
Why, rainbow?
You leave the big fields of the landlord alone, rainbow.
But only a little garden for us poor, a little river,
A trickle of water have I, rainbow.
You are sucking us dry.
But give me a chance, rainbow.
My back is strained
Filling your pockets to cross the sea, rainbow.
But rainbow, my back is strained,
Give this poor indigent a little chance, rainbow.

That's how I have come to think—always in terms of poetry. That's what makes my brain work, what makes me live, too. My whole life doesn't have to pass in humiliation. I can give poetry that can make people who once looked down on me now see me as something. I can live as a human being should live in a country.

Under the dictatorship, there wasn't a lot that people could do when their eyes began opening, when they were angry. Then, you could just go around the edges of a problem.

It was during school that my will to change the country took off. I felt there must be a battle. So I started working in the movement for Creole. The issue of Creole was really taboo at that time. In school we weren't allowed to speak Creole; we were forced to speak only French. When they told us not to speak Creole in school, it was like saying to the people: do not speak. French was only spoken by a small elite. And the whole school system perpetuated the power of that elite.

We built students' organizations to really launch the fight. It was an act of resistance to say you weren't going to speak French in school. Struggling inside school to incorporate Creole was resistance against the whole social structure.

The next step in that battle was to see if at least Creole could become an official language so the country could really have a new face. The whole population was marginalized by the requirement to speak French, since most speak only Creole and don't go to school.

This was in the period when Radio Haïti was broadcasting in Creole, when the battle for *Haïtiennité*, Haitianicity, was taking off. *Haïtiennité* was a search for identity within a system dedicated to controlling how we could express ourselves.

Beyond the identity question, reporting news in Creole was a big deal because it helped the population start getting, as we say, conscientized. Having news in Creole on Radio Haïti for the first time helped people understand what was happening in Haiti, and in other countries like Nicaragua and the Philippines where similar struggles were underway. Today that might not say a lot, but it was an enormous battle back then.

The struggle to speak Creole was an important step in our lives. Most of my generation of activists started off between 1970 and 1980 with that as their first involvement. That's where we started this struggle to allow, little by little, an unblocking so that the people could resist the dictatorship.

My mother and my father are peasants. Well, what can I say? I'm a peasant, too. It's in my blood. No matter where I live, even if it's Port-au-Prince, I always make a little garden. My garden plot is truly a mark of the peasantry. I plant beans, I plant corn, plantains. No flowers.

Oh, you find so many strong people among peasants. But they're a category of people that's always been ignored. There's been no cultural value placed on them, and there's been so much richness and capacity lost. Now there's a Ministry of Culture and all that, but as regards *popular* culture: people aren't really digging to research this treasure. This country is losing everything it has—it doesn't even have a national agricultural plan—but it still has that one strong element of culture.

The country's culture means all our habits, our customs, our language, our way of seeing life, our music. The reserve of culture, where it's strongest, is found in the middle of the peasants. The peasants are full of the capacity to resist and to continue expressing their culture.

The greatest root of all Haitian culture is vodou. It's true there are many people who criticize vodou. It's true vodou has good and bad aspects. But it remains the fundamental element of the culture.

The gifts peasants have to express themselves—a people who don't know how to read or write—are so strong. These people can sit and compose music that other people, who've gone to school to study it, could never do. I know a person who makes songs . . . Truly, his music and the variants he puts in it are extraordinary. There's so much capacity in peasant music that's being lost—just one of many things.

But little by little peasants are beginning to establish their value, bring up their morale, express themselves. We need to lift up the peasants, each one, by supporting them and giving them the strength they need to continue.

I went to school with my older brothers in the countryside. But there came a great drought that brought a lot of hunger, a lot of misery. My parents couldn't pay for school anymore. But it was something that always obsessed me. Well, when the drought improved, I returned to school. I was lucky enough to make it all the way through teacher's training school, so I got more elevated training than a lot of peasants.

I could have used this training to raise myself up to another social class, but I went to work in the countryside, where I came from, in the peasant milieu. I worked with youth who never had the chance to go to school. Well, the youth didn't just learn to read and write, they also worked in crafts and popular theater. They learned to use drums, dance, sing, and drama to express themselves through the elements of their own culture. Those youth truly feel they've become human beings, because they can stand tall even in front of students with means.

I also work in a peasant organization, especially with women. The hard lot of women in the country has always struck me. We found the women's organizations always had to get a man to come and take notes because the women couldn't read and write. So I made it a priority to give them a higher level of training. Plus I always work in their gardens with them.

In the program, we teach peasants math, a little history, a little geography. They become familiar with maps of Haiti and the world then. When they listen to international news on the radio, and hear of some country that has relations with Haiti, they can say, "Ah-hah!" They know more or less where that country is. After that they learn the fundamentals of how to write a letter. We make the students do a composition. They go out into the villages, and then write what they see. You get the person to observe, write her ideas, express herself.

Recently we did a seminar at the literacy center where an old woman, sixty years old, participated. She couldn't really read, but wow, could she write! You truly felt you were in the presence of a poet. Me, though I've gone to school, I'm not a poet. But that woman . . . It was sheer poetry.

Written information is coming at the people all the time; it's really invaded their lives. They're not in a completely oral system anymore so they need to know how to use the skills.

Knowing how to read and write is a great power. In Haiti, especially among peasants, this power is doubled. In the countryside, a person who knows how to read is a king. He's the one who writes letters for everyone, who drafts up land titles, who fills out the birth certificates. If a boy needs to write a girl a letter to become engaged, he's the one who does it. And the person who asks him to write the letter has to pay. The one who knows how to write is living off the others, is dominating the whole community. If there's a job in the community, he gets it. Writing up land titles for other people gives him the power to steal land. For example, if on paper he's supposed to put two acres, he can put four. If he's the one personally buying the land, he can put down any amount of land he wants.

Okay, this is a short story of my family history. I tell you this story to show you the importance of knowing how to read and write. I had a relative who knew how to read. Since he's dead I can cite his name—there's no problem there if you put it in—it was Chaleron. He used to make false land titles. When people brought him documents, he used to add acres to the proper amount. He shacked up with my father's mother. Chaleron gave my grandmother a gift of eight acres of land. I believe he only paid for two acres. But since he was the one that made up the papers, he put eight acres. The other inheritors eventually discovered this. My grandmother only had one child so this got my father involved in a big land problem. My grandmother was old by that time, so they took my father to court instead. My father didn't want to share the land with the other inheritors. The trial lasted fourteen years. That put us in a heap of misery, a heap of problems. We lost the land, you see. Plus, my father had had a lot of means and he could have sent all his children to school, but he spent all his money in the court. The other inheritors demolished our house and after that we went to live somewhere else. We've been nomads ever since.

So in the literacy work we do with peasants, I always insist on the power of knowing how to read and write. For democracy, this is the whole struggle. The people can't leave all that power to the elite anymore. They must have that power, too. But not to be able to change from the poor class to a higher economic and social standing. It's in this interest that I put all of myself into literacy work.

There was a period when people couldn't even do literacy. Under Duvalier, if the state learned you were teaching people to read and write, they could arrest you. Same thing during the coup. They said if you were teaching people to read, then the people might speak out, and that might be communist speech. We have the illiteracy rate we have because the state wanted it that way. If only 15 percent of the people are literate, you can see how power is concentrated in the hands of a small elite.

The elite that know how to read and write, that have this intellectual knowledge, they traumatize the peasants, scare the peasants. As soon as the peasants know that they have the right to learn, to gain understanding, to speak, they won't have to bow down before the rich anymore.

FLORENCIA PIERRE
The Cultural Soul

This is Florencia Pierre. I am a woman of Haiti. I am a dancer and an actress in theater and films. I broadcast on the radio, right? Plus I am the mother of two children. Well, I should say that I am the mother of all the children of Haiti because I love children very, very, very much.

I began dancing when I was nine years old. It was something I started by myself in Leogane. As you know, in Leogane there are *rara*. And I went into the *rara* to start dancing. Frankly, I never knew one of those dances before. It was a gift from God and the *lwa*. Dance was what allowed me to hold on. Then I started to accept it deeply, to take it seriously. At the age of sixteen, I went to Port-au-Prince to advance myself at Viviane Gauthier's school. That was when I started learning the folkloric dances, why you dance them, what they are called, what clothes you should wear, and so on. That's how I came to pierce the four corners of Haiti and even go to foreign countries, to spread this thing.

To be honest, I must truly enter into vodou in order to understand how Haitian folkloric dance works. If I'm doing a choreography, I have to know the character of that *lwa*; I have to know how he or she manifests him or herself, what sort of clothes he or she wears, so I can present it exactly as I should. For example, foreigners, they don't know who Erzulie Freda is. They can read about her in a book, but they would have to attend a ceremony to see who she really is. I can show a person who Erzulie Freda is through choreography, who Saint James Major is by choreography.

Culture plays a big, important role in Haiti. And the central soul of culture is inside vodou.

Vodou gives us a lot of strength, it supports us so that we can combat all bad things. If those country people didn't serve *lwa*, who walk with them, help them, encourage them, they would all have died already. Also, it's the *manbo* and *oungan*, vodou priests and priestesses, who serve the spirits who are the ones who prepare remedies for children when they're dying of diarrhea, because there aren't doctors who will go up into the mountains and do anything for the kids.

Some forget how *vodouizan* play a big, big, big role in society. People forget that it was a vodou ceremony at Bois Caïman where we first developed the plan to take our independence. Vodou lets us fight people who want to infiltrate and deter us.

Florencia Pierre

Also, there's no discrimination in vodou. A person who is barefoot, a person who is well-dressed—they receive you the same way.

In fact, in vodou women have the same rights as men, too. The same way a man can be an *oungan* and has the right to lead a ceremony, a woman can be a *manbo* and lead a ceremony, too. If anyone has more rights than the other, it's the woman because she's responsible for the temple, she's the one who takes care of it. When a woman leaves the temple and goes back into society, she loses a lot of that power and those privileges. For example, when some women leave their homes, their husbands tell them, "You have no right to go out. You can't do this, you can't do that." No: in vodou a woman has the same rights as a man. There's nothing the man can say to her; they're serving the same *lwa*. That's why women who come out of vodou are strong, they know what they're defending, and they won't let a man do whatever he wants to them.

Now, some bourgeois people say that they're part of the religion, too. They're not so interested anymore in saying nasty things against vodou. They used to say that people who do Haitian folkloric dance and people who go to vodou ceremonies were people who—excuse the expression—were unenlightened children, ignorant, unsociable people. But now there are bourgeois who just hear some good vodou singing on the radio, with good drums playing behind it, they say, "Hmm! This thing, if it takes off, it will really take off. Let's jump into that." They're exploiting the *rasin*, roots, movement so they can get ahead. They see that it's a movement with a lot of people behind it, giving it strength, so they want to catch a free ride on its back. Everybody wants to do the roots thing, to act like they're part of the scene. But truly, these people are not from *Ginen*, our African ancestry, they don't truly have the spirit of our homeland. Not one day in their lives did they say, "Here's a bottle of rum. Let's give it to Ginen."

A long time ago, I must tell you, when someone danced, they said she was a prostitute, she was impoverished, she was a bad thing. Well, now there are many people who are going to dance schools. Why? Because of the roots folk culture movement. Because they want to learn to dance the way the folk dancers can dance. In order to do that, they have to go to dance schools. Now poor people can't even dance at the schools because they can't pay for it, because the bourgeoisie have totally descended and taken the schools over.

The people who are the true roots are the peasants who rise each morning with a glass of water in their hands. They face the four walls and call out to the *lwa*, "Here we are under your protection. After God in the heavens, you command us. We here and our children are on your bond: you will give us food today, you will give us drink today. After God, it is you who raises us up." These people are the root of *Afrik Ginen*, our homeland Africa. From the time they were children, they were born into this culture, they were raised in it, they grew in it, they slept in it, they ate in it. That's what they know.

I talked about how vodou has been rising up from under the table. Dance has, too. I'm one of the people who've struggled hard so that Haitian folkloric dance can enter full force into society and not lose its identity. This is why many, many people in the society know Florencia Pierre.

Dance is what put my feet inside society. To be accepted into society is no small game; you have to have parents who are big shots. When you're a poor person from an undesirable class, you must make a lot of effort to struggle and rise up. It's this dance that allows me to send my two children to school. It allows me to pay rent on my house. It's what allows me to help my little family.

I'm giving dance courses for many people in society who would never have known who Florencia Pierre was. But through the dance and the theater, many people know me. And I help a lot of other people feel like they are part of society, too.

I have no mother; my mother died. I can tell you that dance is my mother, dance is my best friend, dance is my husband. This dance is a language. It's a means, a tool, to allow you to speak, to recount your suffering, to recount your pain, your joy, to recount the happiness of your heart. It is dance that does everything, everything, everything, and is everything for me.

When I am dancing, I feel like I'm living. I do it with love.

MARTINE FOURCAND
Expanding the Space of Expression

During the period between dictatorships, 1986 until 1991, there was a resurrection of free speech. One could finally say things that should have been said for the past two centuries. But when the coup d'etat occurred, the perpetrators shut down all speech. It was three years of terror and hell for the population.

The coup d'etat, to me, was an occasion when the powers of the hemisphere regained control over the country. The first matter of importance was to abolish speech by violence. The second most important thing was to make the repression last until self-censorship took over and the practice of questioning power was halted. At the heart of this censorship and self-censorship you came to see the unfolding of the dominant ideology—not just of the hemisphere, but rather of the planet.

The problems were so severe during that period of repression. Even though many of us were working in active resistance to the coup d'etat and the occupation, the powerlessness we felt each day was virtually annihilating. Anyone could be shut up in a house and in the middle of the night hear the cries of someone being killed less than fifty meters away, and not be able to do anything. That situation of extreme powerlessness is conducive to destroying people. Yet even under these conditions my artwork allowed me to maintain my political commitment.

During the last two years of the coup d'etat, painting was what allowed me to hold on. Painting was a way to try to limit the effects of the destroyers on my individual life, on my capacity to reflect, on my capacity to react. My painting allowed me to live in the extreme constraints we were suffering under. It let me preserve and expand the space of expression.

Martine Fourcand

3 RESISTANCE FOR POLITICAL AND ECONOMIC CHANGE

Life is a struggle. You fall but you must get up.

—Tikann Lerius

Power concedes nothing without a demand. It never did, and it never will.

—Frederick Douglass

Turning her head away from the circle of women under the tree, Dania Gerome spits expertly through a crack in her front teeth. "You ask me if I am political. How can I not be? Everything is political. If I am hungry and she"— she gestures an arm to me, the *blan*, foreigner—"has lunch to eat, but I can't eat any of it, that is political."

Americans who have worked throughout the world often express amazement at the level of political acumen they have encountered, unparalleled either at home or abroad, among the general population in Haiti. A strong tradition of popular education and conscientization has offset the dearth of international contact, media exposure, and formal education. Once, way back in the bush, miles from any primary road or electric line, I encountered a woman who was bathing in a river. She paused in soaping her body to make sure that I was aware of that morning's developments vis-à-vis U.S. policy toward the refugees imprisoned in Guantánamo. I have met many Haitians, who, whether squatting under a precarious palm-frond lean-to selling fried dough or breast-feeding a baby beside an open sewer, could reel off an analysis of the nuances of the World Bank's development plans for Haiti. Many more could report exactly what steps the grassroots movement is taking to challenge the plans.

As political consciousness develops, and implicit or hidden acts of protest grow in strength and quantity, over time they may take on explicit political intention and move into open, collective dissent. James Scott wrote, "Under the appropriate conditions, the accumulation of petty acts can, rather like snowflakes on a steep mountainside, set off an avalanche."[1]

Millions of small statements of resistance have fueled Haiti's two-hundred-plus-year history of dissent. In turn, a deep knowledge and pride of that militant and revolutionary history have imbued in the average citizen a political awareness that energizes the tradition of daily, individual protest.

Working collectively, people can move forward from defending the space to live to proactively defending their class interests.[2] While the forms of resistance discussed in the two previous chapters indicate that the Haitian population has refused to let the elite and the state capture the ideological terrain, such resistance alone cannot effectively challenge power or bring about structural change. This chapter explores overt, group protest by women within the national liberation struggle.

HISTORY OF WOMEN IN THE POPULAR MOVEMENT

Haitian women spanning all classes have participated in collective opposition since before the revolution that won the slaves their freedom, and Haiti its independence, in 1804. Of the preliberation period, sociologist Carolle Charles wrote, "Resistance took many forms, including suicide, poisoning, participation in *marronage*, and rebellions. Black slave women killed their children and performed abortions as a way to set the terms for control of their sexuality and reproduction."[3] In 1792, Cecile Fatiman, a *manbo*, helped lead the Bois Caïman ceremony that officially started the war of independence. A handful of women, such as Marie Jeanne, Sanite Belair, and Marie Claire Heureuse, were noted for their involvement in that war.

Records of women taking to the streets for political and economic justice date back to 1930, when they demanded an end to the U.S. occupation. Since that time, women have been active in virtually every citizen campaign.

But until very recently, women's participation has been almost exclusively behind the scenes. Their roles and contributions typically have remained in the shadows of male activists. As several sons repeatedly urge her to finish speaking into the tape recorder so that she can take them home to supper (which interruptions she ignores), health care promoter Selitane Joseph says:

Women died fighting but you won't hear their names. They'll talk about Charlot Jacquelin [a male activist and martyr] and other male heroes, but never the women. They broke off branches and leaves to cover up those facts.

All but a very few women who have been publicly noted for their political activities have been the wives of leaders. And during the recent coup years, human rights and media reporting generally characterized military attacks on women as retribution against their male relatives, effacing the women's own militancy that made them targets.

Poor women note that their marginalization within the popular movement in many aspects parallels their marginalization in society. Rosemie Belvius, a well-known organizer in the Artibonite region, says that in grassroots political groups, "Women's power never comes to the fore." For most women, a rigidly gender-proscribed division of labor places limitations on their capacity to engage in organized social movements. Being responsible for virtually all household and child-rearing labor, while also engaging in income-generating activities outside of the home, many women simply do not have the time for activism.

Too, husbands and male partners often oppose women's political or social participation. Tikann Lerius, a member of a peasant women's collective, grows impassioned as she explains, "We notice there are many men organizers who go around and get people to join their organization. At the same time they keep their women sitting at home, making babies, getting old." Many men object to "their" women working with other men, and tell their wives they had best not neglect their "women's work." However, as several of the *griyo* note, some husbands strongly encourage their activist wives.

When grassroots groups exploded throughout Haiti in the mid-1980s, many did not allow women members. Claudette Phéné, her sweet smile belying her fierceness, tells of showing up at meetings to be told, "Women don't you come stand here! Men only!" Claudette once arrived at a community meeting only to have the men shout out, "Close down the meeting!"

Long-time activist Yanique Guiteau Dandin recalls the sexual harassment women activists underwent in the 1980s: "Something every woman [in the movement] experienced during those days was [being] seen by the men as a sex object. . . . There was always a message that, well, you had to fool around with them a little."

Gazing above the tin rooftops, Yanique reflects:

The women were in the midst of a bunch of men who had ideas for change but were nonetheless very antidemocratic in their behavior towards women in the movement. Before women had their own autonomous groups, the men couldn't really understand how the women could resist the same way as them.

For these reasons, in the mid-1980s many began organizing independently. They initiated women's sections of their peasant and worker collectives and their Christian base communities. They also founded autonomous women's organizations that allowed them full voice and effective participation. Often this was done very delicately. Barely audible above the choir practice going on next door, church activist Marie Sonia Dely explains,

> You know, in Haiti the men are so macho. They don't want their women to leave the house. If you asked women to meet each Sunday, they would tell you right out, "I can't, no. My husband won't let me come each Sunday." If the man saw that each week his wife was going out, he might say, "I never find you at home," you understand, or "I can't accept that." So we do it in a way that the husband won't get upset. You can't try to take them away *whoop!*—like that. It's little by little, little by little, then further down the road you can take them totally.

Though things are changing, women's voices and initiatives within the popular movement continue to be severely restricted. In mixed-gender groups, women are often excluded de facto from participation and leadership. In the noontime shade of a narrow porch, Dori Elma explains, "In [my organization] there are three groups: men, women, and mixed. But we notice that men are still the head of everything." As for women organizing independently, adult educator Claudette Werleigh recounts men throwing rocks at buildings where all-women meetings were located. And Yolette Etienne says that now that "women in development" is the hot issue for international aid organizations, men are reporting fictional women-run community activities so that they can get the funds designated for women.

Still, as the *griyo* describe, women are beginning to insert themselves qualitatively and quantitatively into the popular movement, where they are forcing greater political access and economic empowerment for themselves *and* their male compatriots. "This work is huge," Marie Sonia Dely says, "but we have the will."

STRATEGIES OF RESISTANCE

Among the priorities of the popular movement have been organizing the poor to amass their strength through unions, collectives, and coalitions. In the Haitian context, organizing has a revolutionary connotation, given that one of François Duvalier's most effective means of maintaining power was to sow division. Under his and his son's reign, almost every *bouk,* small cluster of huts around a central dirt courtyard, contained at least one Tonton Macoute who deeply penetrated and cleaved family and community.

Solidarity is its own terrain of resistance. In chapter 2, women tell how solidarity can translate into economic survival, as the sharing of battered pots of rice back and forth increases the number of households that can eat. Marceline Yrelien, from the drought-ridden, battle-scarred northwest corner of Haiti, describes a form of mutual support that was critical under repressive regimes: As activist women moved in and out of prison, they took turns feeding each other's children and holding demonstrations for each other's release. Josette Pérard explains a further level of solidarity: "The women know they must stick together to defend themselves and realize change, the women's rights they are after: the right to life, the right to health, the right to schools, all the rights they yearn for everyday." Labor leader Yannick Etienne expresses it this way: "You can't eat gumbo with one finger."

When covert resistance is needed so that they can live to fight another day, women have used subterfuge and subtle craft, what they call *teknik.* Yanique Guiteau Dandin explains that under the dictatorship, radical women joined a Duvalierist women's organization because it was the only structure that offered them security as they went into shantytowns to mobilize opposition. Louise Monfils worked under the searing sun in the fields with farmers, talking low as she bent to the ground to weed, because that was the only place she could organize without arousing the suspicion of security forces.

Many of the protest tactics exploit the narrow social spaces reserved for women: domestic domains and the marketplace. *Bat tenèb,* to beat back the darkness, has been a common tool of protest during times of repression. Women create ear-splitting dins as they bang together utensils and pots. According to Claudette Werleigh, women have used their time together at the village pumps, collecting water, to exchange news. Other women have reported how they do laundry side-by-side—beating clothes in rivers with sticks and laying them on rocks to dry—for the same reason, to strategize in periods of repression. During the coup, Alerte Belance took advantage of the public space of the market, another women's domain and one of the few places where citizens could gather at that time, to whisper news of political developments. In those days, too, women used the marketplace to pass clandestine messages back and forth on notes scribbled on the ragged orange gourde bills they exchanged for goods.

Since that time, throughout the nation, all-women and mixed-gender groups crowd into courtyards, where they shade their eyes against the sun and figure out strategies to augment their political power. Chanting, dancing women and men march through towns to make their demands known. They mount torrential protest campaigns, shutting down towns and regions through angry strikes; the smell of burning rubber likely indicates another road blockade. Rare is the public event that does not become political, given over to heated exchanges on current events. Citizens use celebrations, blank white walls, and mealtime conversation to rally support for their political programs.

Many individuals have given their lives to opening the space for a new state and economy. The purpose of the centuries-long state-sponsored violence has been precisely to suppress those individuals' efforts. Claudette Phéné explains why the violence has been futile; she shakes a work-worn finger as she recalls telling a colonel:

> Death today is death, death tomorrow is still death. I'll still be here.
> If you shoot me, I'll leave behind children who'll leave behind even
> more children.

Feminist activist Olga Benoit explained this in her own way just after the coup had been reversed. She told me what her women's collective had been able to accomplish during the prior three years through clandestine meetings and underground organizing. She proudly showed off posters celebrating women and tracts denouncing the regime, all of which had been widely circulated with secretive ingenuity. Then she threw her arms out wide and smiled hugely. "But the most extraordinary victory of the past three years is that—look—we're still here!"

Resistance for Political Change

With the end of the three-decade Duvalier dictatorship, the population began not just pushing at the margins of power but actually negotiating alternatives. Chief among the aspirations, and uniting all others, has been a commitment to participatory democracy. Unlike liberal or representative democracy, where people express their will only through occasional elections, participatory democracy allows all members of civil society to have a voice and a role in their communities and nation. As important as being active participants in their political system is that citizens also be the system's beneficiaries.

In her *istwa*, former Aristide minister Myrto Célestin Saurel says the first agenda item of the popular movement after Baby Doc was overthrown was to "prevent the dictatorship . . . from re-emerging in a different form." The *dechoukaj*, uprooting, sought to dissolve the old systems of repression of the Tontons Macoutes, section chiefs (rural sheriffs), and armed forces. Chasing Macoutes from a village, burning the homes of infamous torturers, getting corrupt figures fired from government posts—all that was part of the agenda to *bay tè a blanch*, clear and level the field.

Demands for government reform, in which women have been active, have helped attain the popular ratification of a new constitution, regular election of constitutional government, and greater civil protection. With public education, popular protest, and strategic campaigns, the movement continues its work for more progressive laws and transparent, responsive government.

In one of the largest mobilizations in recent history, women are participating in campaigns for the arrest and prosecution of the perpetrators of coup-era political crimes. Backed by human rights groups and a few legal advocates, women also are working for lighter legal burdens of proof in rape cases. In addition, the justice campaign calls for reparations for coup-era victims and an end to impunity for criminals. The tactics include petitions, demonstrations, press work, mock trials, and legal advocacy. The survivor of torture and extensive mutilation, Alerte Belance declares in furious, rapid speech:

Justice, exactly, that's what we need. . . . So there will be no more Alertes in this situation, never ever ever.

Resistance for Socioeconomic Change

An exhaust-blackened banner swinging over a busy street in Port-au-Prince reads: *Si pa gen lapè nan tèt, pa ka gen lapè nan vant.* There can be no peace in the head if there is no peace in the stomach. The women state throughout their *istwa* that social and political rights have limited meaning when their children have not eaten since yesterday morning. Claudette Werleigh expresses it another way: "We can't have political empowerment without economic empowerment. For isn't it the power of capital which prevails?"[4]

People in the movement for economic justice are attempting to leverage a transition—to use the popular phrase Aristide coined—*pou nou sòti nan lamizè pou n rive nan povrete ak diyite,* "from misery to poverty with dignity." To do so, they must impact what anthropologist Catherine Maternowska described as "the underlying grid of poverty, . . . the way that structural forces transgress people's most basic human rights."[5] These structural forces have led to a macroeconomic policy that prioritizes profits for the wealthy and satisfac-

tion of international donors' conditions. Citizens are demanding that primacy be given, instead, to their own empowerment. Specific demands include higher levels of employment and lower prices for basic goods. They include government policies that valorize domestic agricultural products through higher import tariffs and reform of land tenure systems, both of which critically impact the people's ability to grow food and survive. Women are battling for legal reforms to protect the economic well-being of children and single mothers. As the primary laborers in multinational corporations, they are also on the front lines in demanding fair wages, better working conditions, and the right to form unions to advocate for these demands without reprisals.

Women in thousands of organizations across the country also demand that the state provide social services and develop a social infrastructure. They are calling for government to adopt a basic-needs strategy, including access to food, potable water, health care, education, literacy, employment, credit, and rural development. Kesta Occident describes how popular mobilization is forcing the government, in small measure, to respond: "For instance, there was always a tendency for the poor peasants who needed roads to have to construct their own. Now they are learning that they can stand up and tell the government they need the road, and get the government to make it."

Resistance for International Change

The targets of the battles extend beyond the borders of Haiti. They also address power structures within the international community and the global economy, which are mirrored in domestic structures. Foreign hegemony over Haiti has been denounced by a mass movement spanning classes and social sectors, going back to the introduction of the Spanish colonists. At that time the warriors were Indians who, until they were enslaved and exterminated, fought the Spanish invasion. The Africans who were later brought in to replace the Indians as laborers then overthrew the French colonists. When the United States invaded and occupied Haiti in 1915, Haitians mounted a guerrilla war. Then, from the 1950s to the 1980s, they fought U.S. political and economic support of the Duvalier regime. And in the 1990s, they protested implicit or explicit U.S. support for the coup regime, which included CIA employment of two of the three leaders of the coup as well as key leaders of FRAPH.[6]

Today the popular movement is demanding stronger national sovereignty so that Haiti will no longer be subordinated to more powerful states, lending agencies, and international trade and finance institutions. The movement is protesting the foreign-imposed economic policy of structural adjustment, or what Haitians have labeled *plan lanmò*, the death plan. The "medicine" imposed by the United States Agency for International Development and international financial institutions is characterized by the government of Haiti as "basic reforms aimed at combating structural imbalances."[7] More accurately, the plan prescribed for Haiti determines systems of resource flows that serve wealthy Haitians and foreign investors, while further impoverishing and disempowering the poor. The main components of the structural adjustment program are: reduction of state spending, shrinkage of government through massive layoffs, privatization of state-owned enterprises, financial liberalization, export-led production, and elimination of import tariffs and restrictions.[8]

The popular movement is organizing against structural adjustment. Advocates and justice organizations contend that the structural adjustment plan entrusts the provision of people's basic needs and national infrastructure to unconcerned private hands, undermines Haiti's sovereignty, further diminishes the already abysmal percentage of state expenditures committed to the poor, and causes government policy to be guided by the interests of investors and international financial agencies. Activists are mobilizing against free market policies, forced upon them by the U.S. government, the World Bank, the International Monetary Fund, and the Inter-American Development Bank, which are destroying local production and food security.

Another component of the program involves the sweatshop labor of large numbers of peasants who, no longer able to sustain themselves, have been forced into Port-au-Prince. There they fight for jobs in factories, many of them owned by foreign corporations, which pay anywhere from U.S.$.70 to U.S.$1.50 per eight-hour workday for the manufacture of push-up bras, electronic widgets, and other goods bound for foreign department stores.

Through unions, peasant associations, and their autonomous groups, women are fighting back. They claim a special interest, carrying as they do a disproportionate increase in economic burden.[9] So, too, do their children, who have the weakest voice of any citizens to fight for their needs, and whose small bodies are most vulnerable to hunger and illness.

Protests in recent years have taken such forms as a sit-in in front of the National Palace, complete with a row of empty cooking pots. For several years a street theater troupe, its members dressed in large papier-mâché heads of grotesque, three-horned demons labeled "IMF," have paraded through carnival. Workers from soon-to-be-privatized state-owned enterprises have staged general strikes. Peasants from across Haiti have traveled in the beds of old trucks to dingy back-alley organizing centers in Port-au-Prince for education sessions on the exploitation of Haiti's "comparative advantage" of poverty. Activists have gone to Washington, D.C., to lobby the U.S. Congress and World Bank and to educate American supporters. Organizers have voyaged as far as Senegal and Brazil, and hosted partners from El Salvador and Cuba, to exchange strategy ideas on fighting the free-market policies of neoliberalism.

In the convent where the sisters speak in hushed voices and move quietly through clean corridors, Kesta Occident spends brief periods away from the battle zones of villages in southwest Haiti. There, stirring a cup of strong black coffee thick with sugar—the national beverage—the agronomist-nun says, "There's an alternative movement that is not only national, but that unites the poor. The pariahs of humanity are fighting against the same empire that produces more exclusion, that produces more hunger, that produces more poor on the face of the earth."

My Blood and My Breath

They killed me that night in Titanyen. Of course they did. Who could have survived what the wicked did to me? I died and I was revived. God resuscitated me for a well-defined reason, so I could speak for all the other victims who didn't make it. It is through the grace of God that my tongue wasn't lost in the bushes, which is what allows me to speak and explain to you what Haiti is going through.

A lot of people like Alerte Belance went to the killing fields of Titanyen but none ever came back alive. Many mothers have lost their children there, children they struggled to give so much care to. They'll never see those children again, because they went to the bushes of Titanyen.

I am an activist. It was during the time that Titid declared his candidacy that I dipped my body into activism. I organized people to vote. All the poor men and women of Haiti looked up and saw that Titid was leading a campaign for the presidency. Myself, Alerte Belance, I saw that God sent Moses to us Haitians to lead us across the Red Sea. Titid, I call him Moses. All Haitians of conscience who wanted the country to have a change after thirty-some years of dictatorship stood up when we saw that Titid was mounting a campaign for the presidency.

I was mobilizing all my friends in my neighborhood so that together we could send Titid to victory in the elections, so we could finally have a president who could hear the cry of the poor and the people. I told the people at the market that they should vote for him, and they agreed.

When the president was elected, many mothers of children, fathers of children, all went out and cleaned the streets. I was the one in my neighborhood committee who had people out cleaning the streets. I was the one who always took up collections of money to buy a truckload of water to clean the streets. It was our will, not for money, that made us do this to change the face of Haiti. Those streets were clean!

I organized my friends and the people in the marketplace into a team. Whenever I could find a newspaper, I ran to buy it so I could run and show them the news. I was the one who, when I heard news on the radio, ran to tell it to the team.

The president came to power. They let him spend just eight months in power, then they gave him a coup d'etat. The soldiers with no conscience took money from the biggest ones, the bourgeoisie. They made Titid lose the presidency. The Haitian people spent three years in exile. Three years of misery, three years of bone-crushing horror. Massacre! It was three years of massacre against the mothers of children.

There were a lot of activists in the market. People there were really organized. FRAPH always used to come through the marketplace and trample it, because they said that this group is a *lavalas* group. We always ran and hid when they were ravaging the market.

They ravaged everyone who had been Titid's supporter. Killing, they were killing many people who had cleaned the streets and done other neighborhood activities during the eight months Titid was in power. They put more pressure on me because of the role I played in organizing. Each time they saw me they taunted me by calling me "Godmother of the Militants." It was meant as a threat. That's why I had to leave the area altogether, why I left the marketplace and went into hiding. That's why I spent two years as a maroon.

At the last minute when Titid and the other big chiefs signed an accord at Governors Island in New York to say that the president was to return on October 30, 1993, they began carrying out the lion's share of the massacres. The big thugs with their gangs of bastards went out to break us all, to stop the return from happening.

Still, we believed the foreigners; when they signed the Governors Island Accord and said that the president would return, we believed it. So I came out of hiding. That's how the bastards got me, when they were attacking so many mothers and fathers of children to keep our president from coming home. That's why they came to kill me at Titanyen. They came for me on October 15, several days after I'd returned from hiding.

The vicious ones chopped me up during the night; I spent a night in the weeds bleeding.

This story really is a piece of history for Haiti, even with the level of crime that occurs there. They sliced me into pieces with machete strokes. They cut out my tongue and my mouth: my gums, plates, teeth, and jaw on my right side. They cut my face open, my temple and cheek totally open. They cut my eye open. They cut my ear open. They cut my body, my whole shoulder and neck and back slashed with machete blows. They cut off my right arm. They slashed my left arm totally and cut off the ends of all the fingers of my left hand. Also, they slashed my whole head up with machete blows.

Yes, they killed me. The death squad was so convinced I had died that they dragged me further away to dump me. When I was in the bushes, what passed through my spirit and my head were my three children. I am their mother, I am their father. What was I imagining in my head? It was: How will the children ever know where I died? How will my family ever know where to find me, because there's a big distance between where I lived and where they dumped me, in this place called Titanyen.

When I saw the work they did on me, I called, "God, let the people finish me off and be done with me." As soon as I spoke that in my mind, I knew nothing else. I was taken by sleep.

I woke up when I heard a big horse walking around in the bushes. I said, "*Woy*, Jesus, if this horse walks on me, he'll finish me off, and I can't get up to move my body away." While I was thinking this, sleep took me again. I didn't know anything else.

I was killed when the men kidnapped me, took me out to the bushes, pulled their machetes on me like that. But it was God's will for me to come back from the dead to speak for all the other victims of Titanyen who didn't live. Truly, God wanted me to live for all people who want change, for all women who are struggling for women, for women's sacrifice, for women's betrayal, for all those who stood up to revolt and say the nation of women is suffering too much misery. God spared me.

I woke up again the next morning and found myself stuck on top of a briar patch where the *zenglendo* threw me. My whole body was full of prickers. I didn't feel them, though, because my whole body was dead. I'm not positive where I was because I couldn't see—my eyes were stuck together with blood—but I think I was up in the air, perched on the side of a hill, just over a hole. I felt myself shaking, my whole body was trembling. I unstuck my eyes and then I saw that I wasn't too far from the road. But I couldn't see up or down, I couldn't move to the left or the right. Anywhere I turned, I would fall into the hole. I said, "God! Help me!"

With my left hand I took hold of my right arm, which had been severed and was just hanging on by a little flap of skin, and I started rolling and falling. God made me not fall into the hole. My whole body was cut, my eye was cut, I couldn't see where I was going. By pushing myself by my feet off tree trunks, I dragged myself out of the bushes and lay my body by the side of the road. This was God's dream, this was his idea. When I lay beside the road, I raised up the stump of my arm, which was still hanging, so passers-by could see I was alive.

Someone was coming along the road; he backed his car up to look at me. With my tongue cut out, I said, "Collect me, my brother, take me to the hospital." The man said no, he couldn't pick me up because if he did, the police would say he was the one who did this to me. I said, "No, I won't let anyone say you did this to me. You just take me to the hospital and then leave. They won't know you." He said no, he couldn't.

But God was pulling for me again. That man went to the police post and gave a statement, and came back with the justice of the peace and the police. They collected me. That was God's work, because God spoke to the hearts of those men, made them consider the state I was in, so that they would agree to collect me from the ground. They took me to the General Hospital in a car with sirens that carried me like a cadaver.

As soon as I got on National Route Number 1 heading back to Port-au-Prince from Titanyen, there were people running behind the car. Because I was a woman and because of the state I was in, like a piece of ground meat, and because I was very well known from when I was out in the marketplace selling, when I got to the General Hospital a chief had to force people with his stick to leave the hospital, so many people had charged in there.

I recognized all the people who were there because, thanks to God, I never lost consciousness. The whole time I was in the operating room, while they were sewing my tongue, while they were sewing up around my temple, sewing up my face, I felt the needle. I had a ring on my left-hand finger; the vicious ones had tried to take it, but they couldn't. The doctor knocked himself out to get it off; I felt that, too. The doctor called my sisters to give them my ring. I was conscious the whole time, even though they gave me anesthesia. Myself, I see this as the work of God. It couldn't be the work of man for me to have maintained consciousness, to be able to recognize everyone after having just spent a night in the woods spilling so much blood. I told God, "Thank you," in all those instances.

Some journalists heard about my story and came to see me in the hospital. They took pictures of my mangled body and put my story on the radio. The army found out I was still alive and sent people to the hospital so they could finish me off there. But my doctors told the men I'd already died, and they snuck me out of the hospital into hiding so I could heal in safety.

In hiding, I spent two months on oxygen because my nose was cut in half, my tongue was cut in half. I couldn't breathe, I couldn't swallow. But I maintained consciousness. I had a vision, I saw that I had died. I had died and I was revived.

It is only not me, Alerte, whom the death squads killed at Titanyen. They killed mother after mother of children. They killed doctor after doctor, student after student. Mothers of children lost their children without any reason.

There was no one to cry for help to, to call the criminals by their names: Thief. Assassin.

I may be a victim of the coup d'etat, but I am a militant victim. Three months after I came back from the dead at Titanyen, I was on my two feet. I was crying out for help so that people of conscience could hear my cry, as a mother with three children, as a young woman thirty-two years old, so that they could help me get Haiti out of the situation it's in today. I traveled around the United States trying to beat up on the misery of Haiti and the Haitian people. I spoke about women whom the cruel death and terror gangs were raping, little children they were raping, babies in the cradle. I went on television and the radio; I talked to U.S. congressmen, journalists, human rights activists. I spoke at demonstrations, press conferences, churches, congressional hearings. I filed a lawsuit against FRAPH with the Center for Constitutional Rights in New York. My case became part of a complaint to the Organization of American States about the coup regime.

Many people who see me say that if they'd become a victim like me, they'd never have been able to speak about it, to travel to tell what happened. They wouldn't have been able to take tours around the world like I do to say, "Here. Here is what I suffered."

To tell it well: My family wants me to leave off this business of politics. I've a lot of friends who don't want me to be involved in human rights work, to speak about Haitian issues at all, at all. But I have to. In my mutilated state, my neck nearly cut in two, my tongue cut in two, my right arm cut in two, my left hand cut in two, God resuscitated me for a reason. He put his force in me so I could struggle for women to have not only life, but rights and freedom of speech. Left to my own devices, alone, with just my own courage and feelings, I wouldn't have been able to return to speaking about politics again to inform those who didn't know. I always feel myself animated with a huge amount of strength and courage so that those who don't know what's happening in Haiti can know. Every time I want to quit, strength returns inside of me again so that I, Alerte Belance, can speak to women of the entire world so they'll open their eyes to what's happening. God gave me the strength and the resistance, the opportunity and the courage to bring this case to you so that you'll stand up and join in the call for help. We must stop women from being tortured, from being dragged through misery.

I remember lying in the hospital bed and trying to imagine how I was going to live in the situation I'm in now. I don't have two arms. My left arm sticks to my body but serves no purpose for me, because I have the ends of four fingers only and my hand doesn't close. I can't do anything with it. My right arm, I lost it.

In Haiti I was a market woman. I had to cook food to sell in the market so I could care for my three children. But now I can't take care of myself. I can't even bathe myself, someone has to help me. I'm pregnant, but I don't know how I'll take care of the baby. I won't be able to change his Pampers or fix his milk. But God always puts a person of conscience before me to help me survive with my children. It's thanks to good neighbors that we survive.

The devil has raped the confidence of the people. I can't live in Haiti now; I would always have to be in hiding. But if I heard that justice were established in Haiti, that there might be justice for me. . . . Oh, how I would love to return to my country to live, especially since my physical situation is so disfavored in society and I can't do anything for myself. I would reunite with my family who would help me with the remaining days that God gives me to live.

⋙ YANNICK ETIENNE ⋙
A Grain of Sand

From the time I was very young, I've been involved in social issues—right up until today. The question of change, or working with other people to make a difference, has always interested me.

When I was sixteen, I went to study in the United States and got involved in social movements there. Most of my experience dates back from the 1970s, beginning in high school in 1971.

The social issues that were being debated really hit me in the head. It was during this period that identity politics were coming to the fore. I was becoming aware that I was black, that my cultural identity was black. At that time, college students were fighting for black studies and affirmative action. I participated so there would be more black professors and more programs for black minority students. The movement within the black community, like the Black Panther Party, was very strong. I joined a black student newspaper organization. Politically, though, my focus was international. I was part of the oppressed people and determined to fight against that oppression.

I started to develop an anti-imperialist conscience and connected with a lot of different struggles in the United States. I participated in a lot of demonstrations, especially so the United States would stop bombing Vietnam. I was in the International Club, I founded the Haitian Student Organization. Whether it was with my Jewish friends, or with South Africans, or for equality and social justice in the United States, or the liberation of the Haitian people from their oppressors, I was always there. All this heat you had in the 70s! Later things slowed down, but I maintained the spirit of struggle.

Well, I always stayed in touch with what was going on in Haiti. The dictatorship got stronger and all those people fled Haiti. I'm the daughter of someone who left the country because of political repression. I fought so Haitian refugees, the "boat people," would be accepted. I was always bringing support to the refugees or working on literacy with them.

After I started graduate studies, I decided: I have a country, too. I have to go back. So after living more than fifteen years in the United States, I decided to take my participation back to Haiti. That's where my responsibility lay. I left my family, everything, and returned in 1985.

Now in '85 and '86, there was this movement to bring down the dictator. And of course, I was knee-deep into it, in poor neighborhoods, in the burgeoning democratic movement, in all those things to make Jean-Claude leave, so that there would be a different government, another society. Because I believed in total social transformation. I was more interested in being in front of the barricades so the people's words could be heard. When I say the people, I'm talking about the popular masses. I mean workers, peasants, the poor, the unemployed.

I stayed in the poor neighborhoods, and that's where grassroots organizations were really developing. In the neighborhood I was working in, I taught people how to read and write and established a health center for women and children. We started talking about salary problems, working conditions, sexual harassment—all these questions. And it's from there, while talking to the women—most of whom were factory workers—that I realized the exploitation in the factories. Since I had a more radical orientation, I thought confrontation was easier in the factory environment since you were clear about who the enemy was. It was the boss. You could target him more easily, you could confront him directly.

So, I went directly into that milieu. You have to work from within to see how things are inside. Yes, yes, I got a job in a factory; I did cleaning and I was also mobilizing people inside. Of course, with the spirit I had, they fired me.

There are roughly forty-five foreign assembly shops in Haiti. Most of them are Haitian-owned subcontractors. Most of these plants make clothing or electronic pieces. There are about twenty thousand workers in these factories.

The conditions for workers in the sweatshops are, oh, they're terrible. They work under such repressive surveillance. The workers don't get enough to eat, and they're working really fast under high pressure because they're working on piece rate since factories don't pay the minimum wage. The supervisors and bosses shout at the workers and abuse them. They tell them, "What you do, that's what you get!" That means they'll get in income only what they can sew, whether it's minimum wage or not. Minimum wage is thirty-six gourdes. But what they do, they set the quota so high that people can't make enough money to take care of themselves. The women don't get breaks; they have to push, push, push so they can meet the quotas. The workers might have to sew two-hundred dozen pieces in a day: two-hundred dozen sleeves, shoulders, et cetera. If they don't meet the quotas, they never make even that small bit of money. They might earn only fifteen gourdes per day. Or they might even get fired.

The workers might be very thirsty and can only find hot, filthy water from an unwashed barrel to drink. It's usually stifling and hot in the sweatshops. The bathrooms are backed up with sewage and stink horribly. To clean them to a usable condition, you'd need a lot of water. But they don't have water. When people need to go to the bathroom, they have to wait until there's a break to run into the street and do what they need to.

Even though I got fired from the factory, I'm still in the workers' midst. We talk wherever we can meet. I go to their houses, or I meet them on their way home and talk with them on the road.

I talk to them about their problems and from there we ask, "If there are all these problems, don't we need to get together? Don't we need to organize?" Then we start delving into different issues—work issues, the problems they face in the home, trying to educate their kids. We build trust, and then that person brings another person who brings another person. And that's how you get a group, and you arrange for a meeting. You say, "Here's our problem, and here's our program. Are we going to post up flyers or distribute them inside without the boss knowing we did it? Are we going to denounce all the problems?"

They decide what they want to say to the boss and in what form, since they can't say it directly. They get excited but also frightened because they don't know what the reaction will be.

One of the things we're trying to do is translate the laws into Creole and make them more accessible to the workers, so they can understand their rights and how they're being violated. So they can know, too, how to battle. I do training workshops on rights. I pass along news that's relevant to them.

This is very important, because I'm only a grain of sand who has certain advantages that society hasn't given the workers. I have a responsibility to help them continue the battle. Because the workers are the future. They're the hope.

We're currently involved in a campaign against Disney Corporation for its violations of workers' rights here. People in the United States, Canada, Europe are starting to become aware that buying an article of clothing involves people making profits off the backs of exploited workers. But it's a tricky battle. It's hard to risk losing the jobs if the international companies close. On the other hand, you can't accept the exploitation. That's why we really need the international solidarity.

It's very hard to organize in Haiti. You know Haiti is a slippery slope: one day you might have a space and the next day that space is closed.

During the coup, especially, there were terrible moments. You never knew if you would be alive tomorrow. You never knew who might see you while you were in the streets buying candy or an avocado, point a finger at you, and say,

"Ah! This person is an organizer." Then you could hear a bullet and find your-self on the ground. All this fear!

You have to realize, too, the harshness of the women's lives; sometimes they simply don't have the time to get involved. They come from work, they have to fetch water, they have to go borrow some money somewhere, they have to do the marketing, they have to cook, they have to do the laundry, they have to keep an eye on the children to see if they're doing well in their studies, they have to pay someone to help the kids with their schoolwork since most of the mothers don't know how to read. There are responsibilities. All these problems slow down the process.

Sometimes husbands, brothers, entire families get scared, they tell the woman not to get involved in these things. Then we have the Protestants in Haiti who believe that everything comes from the sky. You might get a worker who's involved with a church and she might say, "You shouldn't get involved in this, it's dangerous." Well, I have another orientation. Jesus fought against false prophets. He came with radical ideas for his time. He didn't sit with his arms crossed, he was a pioneer, he took initiatives. He saw all the injustice and he op-posed it. I tell the workers that's how I see things. If you're a true Christian you shouldn't be afraid. But I'm talking not to their religious sense but to their con-science. It's their choice if they want to follow the minister and their husbands.

It's hard to organize, too, because sometimes people accept the labor condi-tions since, bad as they are, at least they have a little stability of income. They can't refuse that job because they have to take care of the child, the house, themselves. But you find a lot of people who resist because sometimes they just get exhausted by the conditions and have to speak out.

For instance, against the sexual advances the managers make on the women for them to get or keep their jobs. Most often, women accept: they don't feel they have a choice because they're too desperate. But some women just stand right up and say they oppose this.

From the minute workers place their first complaint, the boss starts pressur-ing them. Oh! He tells them that if that's how they see things, he'll fire every-one. If they don't like it, they can leave. They're all dead-end jobs, but you know how little work there is in Haiti and people need them so badly. That's what's most infuriating. The workers suffer all this, and then they don't even get paid enough to take a sick kid to the doctor.

And if they suspect that a worker is interested in joining a union—just sus-pect, you hear?—they can fire her. They'll watch to see if she's talking with other workers in front of the factory, and then she's in trouble. Management says, "Hmm! She's a hot-head, someone who will cause us problems." You see? And then she'll lose her job. And as for workers getting their legal rights to bonus, severance pay, and vacation, forget it! That rarely happens. The other problem is that the bosses have total impunity, they can do whatever they want. And the state doesn't do anything. Laws just exist on paper.

That's what affects me most: when a worker, especially a female worker, loses her job in the process of defending her rights. This is what's hardest for me, because the boss can fire her for whatever reason. And when you're on this person's side, you're struggling, motivating, giving support, and then *blop!* they fire her. . . . Ah, it's hard, it's very hard. It's something that kills your morale. It's tough to go to her home and see four or five kids who haven't eaten since early morning, or for three days. When you're unemployed, you have to take one day at a time. You can give up at any time.

And then we have to start organizing all over again, each time they get fired.

The women are the central pillar. They're the ones taking care of their kids. They're the ones sacrificing themselves for their children, you see? They have a strong spirit of sacrifice. I tell you, they drain their blood so their children can have a better tomorrow. They don't want their children to find themselves in the same situation they've been in.

At my age, with the confrontation I do, I never know when my hour might be up. This is why it's critical to pass along the information that I have in my head, to help others continue on. It's in this spirit that my little grain of sand might help others advance. Because the battle will be very long and hard. The country is small but the problems are vast.

That's my story. That's how I got here. I'm starting to have gray hair, and this is the way it's going to go for the rest of my life. I don't see any other alternative as long as things don't change, as long as this state that we have doesn't change, as long as the women, the children in the shantytowns, the unemployed, the workers, don't get out of their situation. This is what gives me the energy and strength I need to continue this struggle. And I hope it's a radical change, revolutionary. I don't see any other way. No other way.

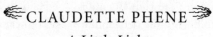

When that basket is on your head from the first light of morning, you go search for life wherever you can find it. There are times you get wet in the rain or big ants bite you, just so you can look for assistance to give your children. You go look, husband on one side, woman on the other, for some support. That's not to say you find it. Tomorrow, if God wills, you might find fifteen gourdes (U.S.$1) working for the big landowner for the whole day. Then he says to you, you little poor peasant women: "I can't pay you today, no. Come back tomorrow." When you do, he'll say you didn't work well and he'll pay you at twelve and a half gourdes (U.S.$.83). Tomorrow, if God wills, you go buy half a sack of sour oranges, you put them into piles of four for one gourde. If you make five gourdes in profit, you can't buy a lot with that. You buy a can of ground corn, five cents of grease, and tell the kids to get some wood, come boil some water.

Peasants from the countryside who are asking for life don't come to beg; no, it's just that you can't survive. There are times you sleep with only water in your stomach, you take a little salt and put it under your tongue because of hunger, you sleep. Hunger in the stomach is not sweet.

You, a little peasant, you have your pride, but sometimes you have to hold your pride and hope you don't choke on what you have to do. You leave the children in a bad way and you go do a job so you can pay back interest on your loan to the rich man. Tomorrow, if God wills, you the little indigent, instead of being able to make some food for yourself, your kids, and your husband, you give your money to this rich man. The old people say, *abse sou abse*. Abscess on top of abscess. If the peasants could work, had a good little business in their hands, they wouldn't need to borrow at those cruddy rates. But now the rich man stays rich; you, you'll always stay poor. Once when I borrowed two hundred dollars to pay back four hundred dollars, the big bourgeois who owned the two hundred dollars called me to court me so I would repay him. I offered him a deadline for repayment, but he said no, he wouldn't accept. Even though he'd already eaten! He had no conscience. Now I have to go do work for his wife. I don't want to do it, no, but I'm obliged to.

We women in the Artibonite Valley, we know misery better than the next woman. We endure it. Every day I have my mother telling me, "Good Lord!

Look at this country, this sad Haitian nation." We Haitians have resources and capacity we could fulfill, but the rich landlord takes our capacity. We could put our heads up high, you bet, but they force our heads down. We can stir things up, but under the system of the landowner, we can't fix things properly.

All this devastates us Haitian women. We can't raise our children the way we want to. Today you can give your child a little ground corn, tomorrow you can't. The child is crying in your lap, but what are you going to give her? She isn't a little baby anymore, but you're obliged to give her your breast. You can't find money to send your kid to school. Instead you tighten your belt, you lie down and sleep, you worry about tomorrow.

We have suffered too much. Suffer, we suffer. They say, *Mizè yon fanm se mizè tout fanm.* The misery of one woman is the misery of all women. But it is *not.* There are women who, when they pass you in their cars, would rather give you dust than anything else. Then you see the bourgeois with their strollers. They press a button, and *clap!* it opens. They press a button and *clap!* it folds down. Yourself, a little poor person, you don't even have a mat on the floor for your baby to lie on.

We're tired of carrying baskets. We're tired of having the middle of our heads worn away. You see here? The basket has worn off all my hair. I weave extensions into my hair so no one can see I'm just a peasant woman. Why? Because we would like, when people look at us, not to say we're peasants with dirty feet. We have what it takes to live, it's just that the biggest always suffocate the smaller ones.

We women, we have resources! We can do things! We get up early in the morning, we don't get discouraged. Us in the Artibonite Valley, there is nothing we don't do. If we find land, we'll work it, we'll make a few cents. Whatever it takes to give our children some education, we'll do it. We make half a gourde turn into five gourdes. We buy a mosquito coil, we sell it for sixty cents, there we make twenty cents profit. We buy a small box of matches, we walk down the street calling, "Matches, matches, matches!" In a minute, we've made five gourdes. We women have capacity!

We women are always present in the struggle, too, always there. We sing a song that goes like this:

> Women, women!
> We are tired of suffering misery, O!
> If you see us uniting
> A solution we'll find.

When you get into an organization, you change completely. What makes you change? I come to see you, know you, share ideas. That allows a change in both of us.

I belong to an organization called the Women's Commission of the Development Movement of Small Farms in L'Estère. I'm the coordinator. I'm also a farmer, so we set up another association called the Small Farm Women's Group. We do a little reforestation; we weed the area and do a lot of gardening, planting flowers. We also plant trees so our roads can be beautiful. There was also a group of five young men in Gonaïves who called themselves Group Five. I said to them, "Guys, this is something I like a lot, participating in groups. You five, how would you like it if I came into your group to make six?" The men said, "Oh, we have no problem, Claudette. If you want to make six, you can come make six." We hung on, trying to get our strength where we want it to be. Our area couldn't evolve without organization.

I started working with poor women for them to understand, in life, you can't just let go of your head any which way. I'm here for that. If they don't understand, and if I have more light than they do, I inform them. I do a little theater with them. I show them how to sew, how to make little blouses. In our organization, that's our objective: the woman who can't, and you who can, you get together. We're always sharing what we know so that tomorrow, if God wills, we can advance further, we won't turn to the left or go back. We never get discouraged. We're always walking.

You don't do this for money, you do it for free. That's what they call *gratis ticheri*, free for you little sweetie.

Because of problems getting assistance, each Saturday when we have a meeting, we put a gourde in the fund. When we get up to fifty gourdes (U.S.$3.33), we give it to a peasant. She can buy a small basket of mangoes with it. When she sells them, she gives us back a gourde to put in the cash box so it's never empty. And when they need to borrow, we don't give loans for the normal 100 percent interest. We lend people ten gourdes, they pay back ten gourdes. If there's one of us with a problem, if there's one of us who's sick, we give her some aid, too.

There are those in the group who can't send their children to school. So we made a small literacy center for the kids. We teach them in Creole. Sometimes when we look at what we have in our cash box, we can send a child to school in the mornings.

The grown-ups were thirsty for a little school in the afternoon, too. There are those that say the biggest abuse was that they didn't learn to read. Well, now, we have a literacy center of twenty women; the women are always there.

There are times you see how men humiliate women and shut them out of organizations. Sometimes when a man sees a woman coming, he says, "Close down the meeting! Women can't attend." But I always go into a meeting even if it's not intended for me. I know the advantage of unity. I went to a meeting about land reform that the government put on and the men said, "Hey, this isn't a women's meeting! Women don't you come stand here. Men only!" I said, "Myself, I am a man, I am a woman. Whenever I see people putting their heads together, I must be there." They were obliged to accept me and let me stay. When I showed them a woman's capacity, that a woman should participate in everything, the men came up to me and gave me their hands. Afterward they sent me a letter asking me to participate in the next meeting. Actually, now I'm the secretary of the group. Now if they go a day without seeing me, they have to come looking for me.

God gave me a good husband. He never has any problems with my work because he's a secretary in a committee, too. We always give each other support so we stand proud.

When the army was in power, if they heard you were involved in organizing, if you were a leader for Aristide and the people, if you weren't a member for the bone-crushing system, you could get in a lot of trouble. But when I heard Titid was coming back on October 30, 1993, I came out from underground. I dressed up in the national flag, my Aristide T-shirt, my head wrapped in a banner reading "*Vive lavalas.*" I took to the streets for Titid, selling candy, shouting "*Lavalas* candies, *lavalas* candies!" Everyone came running, everyone wanted to buy *lavalas* candies.

The Macoutes had warned us that if Titid hadn't come back by October 31st, they would kill all the people in his party. Titid didn't come home so *whoosh!* we knew the Macoutes would come make trouble. When they came, they asked for me, Joel Gabrius, and Charles Suffrard because we were organizers. None of us were sleeping at our own houses but they found Charles' little brother and beat him instead. They said, "Okay, tell your brother who came to beat you. Tell Charles Suffrard he's lucky we didn't find him. We beat you to a pulp for Charles to see." When I came home, my mother said, "All right, Claudette, go to Port-au-Prince." I said, "Mama, I'm not going to Port-au-Prince. I'm going to stay here in L'Estère."

That day we saw an officer's car coming. My mother said, "Get your body out of here! The chief has come to get you." I ran, my son on one side of me, my husband on the other. I became a rat in the forest. I went to hide in a place in the mountains, a place they call Sillon Mountain.

When I finally came home, I asked my mother, "What did that chief want?" She said, "I don't know what they came to do. They got out of the car, came into the yard and shot. They said they came to look for Joel Gabrius and Claudette Phéné." My mother said, "I told you, child, not to get involved with an organization so you wouldn't die!" I said, "All right, Mama, if some peasant doesn't have a little light, and we have light, we must give it to him. We started the battle, we must finish the battle." She said, "Well then, you're no longer a child of mine." I said, "Mama, you'll never get rid of me. There will be a time we clap bravo on the heads of the Macoutes. When I clap they won't stand." My mother said, "You believe that?" I said, "Yes, Mama, I believe that!"

And there was a time I ran into Corporal Dol. Dol had promised to shoot me. I was coming from St. Marc on a truck and there he was at an intersection. Dol told me, "Get out of the truck, Claudette." I said, "I won't get down. You need me, you come up here and get me." I told him, "Death today is death, death tomorrow is still death. I'll still be here. If you shoot me, I'll leave behind children who'll leave behind even more children." Three or four people in the car said, "Driver, go!"

My mother made me go hide in Gonaïves. I said to the women in my group, "I leave you behind, but don't ever let go, always have meetings, hold on. Our custom is to always continue on. Continue!"

Even if God doesn't send something right away, we hope that in what we're doing, we'll find benefits so we little peasants can stand. When the women talk about their tribulations, we tell them not to get impatient. We're always here to develop our community and fight for change. We don't let people lie to us, tell us they'll come give us plantains but instead give us rocks. We never take that from people. We remain strong here in our own community.

On our main road we planted fruit trees and flowers. When you come into our area and you feel the wind blowing on you, you'll know that here we are, we women who planted these little trees. We're always here and we're joined together.

Jumping over the Fire

"Globalization" is one of the latest fashionable words. Globalization could be something interesting: all people together benefiting from each other's experiences, sharing the riches of the blessed earth. Knowledge circulating from one group to another. That would be a beautiful thing if that were the meaning of globalization.

But the way the big countries define it and apply it, globalization is more in the interests of those producing than all the people who are forced to buy. That is to say, you who used to grow your own plantains, who didn't need to buy plantains, are told, "You don't have to grow plantains because we make enough for you to buy them from us when you need them." But where do you get the money to buy these plantains from overseas?

We're given a spot in the market that causes the poor to become even poorer and the strong to become even stronger. They decide which activities ought to be our principal ones and which plans we should follow that will supposedly bring us to the road of development. For example, it's clear that in the plans the richer countries have for Haiti, agriculture has no value. They say to us, "Look, you're so close to Miami, you don't have to plant rice. We'll sell you rice." This makes obvious sense for them, but no sense for the people of Haiti.

So this is globalization: The big countries produce most of the things you need, and you who are smaller have to depend on them. You don't have a voice to say, "Here's what I want."

Globalization is based on assumptions about communication, neoliberal politics, open markets. It assumes that everyone has access to the market. But Haitian women have lost so much from globalization and the new markets that capitalism has brought. The production through which women used to be able to maintain their livelihood and culture is being destroyed.

Now everything is for sale. The woman used to receive you with hospitality, give you coffee, share all that she had in her home. I could go get a plate of food at a neighbor's house, a child could get a coconut at her godmother's, two mangoes at her aunt's. But these acts of solidarity are disappearing with the growth of poverty. Now when you arrive somewhere, either the woman offers to sell you a cup of coffee or she has no coffee at all. The tradition of mutual giving that allowed us to help each other and survive—this is all being lost.

Yolette Etienne

And not only is the whole society for sale: there are more people who are selling than buying. Searching for life here is like pouring into a hole without a bottom. Women must get by on the strength of their courage alone.

When we talk about globalization, we have to focus on women because they're the hardest hit by its destructive aspects. It's a two-edged knife, very sharp. The money invested for the development and the promotion of women is not really intended to help them. Women are *à la mode* in the development terrain today. Mm-hmm, but let's ask the heads of these projects and organizations: How many women are in the decision-making roles? What place do women have in them? They're just being used to serve the Machiavellian plan.

The paths are traced out for women to sell used goods from abroad—junk, clothing, food—everything that is not made in Haiti, let alone in the women's own regions. All the women, who are the pillars of the rural zones, they abandon their production because they have no means to do it. They're fighting over the bones.

The stated aim of the development agency where I work is to help the poorest struggle to attack the causes of poverty. Our option is to work with women. If you're speaking of globalization and development, you can't leave half the country out. No matter where I go in the country, there are two things that the women express: They need to feel that they're in control of their own lives, and they need to break their patterns of isolation. But they don't even know how to read and they feel they can't take their lives in hand. It's like having their eyes closed. If there's one thing they want, it's to be adults, be able to make decisions, do what they want with their money. That's my role, to help make that a reality.

Another thing that undermines their autonomy is credit that makes no sense. Women are offered a little credit or aid but then abandon their own production because they have no means to sell their products. That's the trap in credit: The more a woman depends on it—which can never be profitable because the options don't allow her self-sufficient production—the greater the chance that she'll never become her own master.

Isolation is another big problem for women. In much of Haiti there are few opportunities for women to meet at all. When a woman lives in one area, she might die there without ever having left it her whole life. Even a horse or a donkey that would take them a couple of villages over is a luxury. It's true that Haiti is a very small country, but the distances are great due to the travel conditions and the money involved in transportation. At most a woman goes to a little marketplace and returns home, and she never knows that five or ten kilometers away there's another woman living the same reality.

Also, a woman enchains herself because she knows it's up to her to find food for the household and take care of the children. She'll jump over the fire to guarantee survival. Then her husband and family give her constraints. She's the last person that anyone would see as having the right to go out. Men prevent women from having access to even a little drop of information or contact. But still, these women take on their backs the weight of society, of tradition, and of men.

What I want to believe is that globalization will create more communication, and women will understand they are not alone. It's clear, in a society dominated by men, that men don't want this to happen. Men will do everything possible to prevent information from reaching the women where it could be a tool of their liberation. If women could get together, they could change all this. Haitian women could communicate with other poor women in Haiti and in other poor countries, as well as with those in developed countries who believe that women are human beings and must live as whole people.

For us, development, including globalization and integration, must mean that you accomplish for yourself and accomplish for the country, so that all of us can live together for the collective good. Development must accept our specificity in our country, in each of us, in our people. It's clear that all the strategies that have come from outside, and not from the soul of our people, will never work.

True development is something more complicated than just meeting basic needs, although those are fundamental. It's something much more integral, linked to our own identity. We have a right to be Haitians with all that that entails. True development means that there's space for our own cultural elements: how we feel, how we eat, how we express our happiness, how we express our pain, how we want to work. This doesn't mean that we won't integrate at a global level, but that we maintain what's unique to us and use it in a way that serves us.

There are a lot of possibilities for how we enter the globalization debate, how we integrate into the global society, the planetary village. For instance, the technology and communication means now being developed can allow little countries to take a step forward. With more information, peasants could acquire the knowledge they need to better their lives, and in a rapid manner. Now, the only person they know in the market chain is the speculator who takes the product directly from their hands. As producers they don't know what the global market price is. With better information they could know the price for the coffee they produce at home and how much profit they could make from it in the market. They need information to negotiate squarely and with their eyes wide open, to say, "No, here's the condition in which I'll sell what I have to sell," you see? In this way, the poor could profit the same as the rich.

Another interesting possibility of globalization is the solidarity that could develop through improved methods of communication. In a global sense, when we have information about other people on the earth, we realize that we're not isolated. The peasant who is in the most remote hill of Haiti, and people suffering in other places, can teach each other how to improve their lives.

What do I think of the question of resistance? We can't mount a strike-for-strike resistance or a muscular resistance. We can't be in competition with big countries in the global system. What we do, we stand with all our pride. And from where we stand, very slowly, we advance and we confront what's being imposed on us. Even if it's too big for us and we can't act on a global level, we get together with others to put up a struggle so that we remain players, so that we maintain a space from which we can confront the logic that's being forced on us.

In the organizational work I do, each time we enter into an activity or program, we ask ourselves, "Will this activity tie the people more detrimentally to the path of shame, or will it give them a hand in their own development?" The question is how can you assist both the peasants' groups and the women's groups to strengthen their economic power not only to improve their status, but to give them force to unite and apply pressure on the problems?

There's a cultural element in resistance, too. The strength of the Haitian identity permits it to veer around the big countries, you see? Each time they think they have us safely locked up, we slip away and escape, and the big powers have no idea through which exit. So it's extremely difficult for them to perpetrate their schema. It might seem that there's never a strong *direct* resistance, but in fact people are getting around the plans. It's very difficult for a Haitian peasant to assimilate and integrate into his or her life and soul things that are imposed from outside. That's one of the elements in the failure of all these plans.

For example, now our government is saying agriculture isn't a priority. They say we must plant flowers and other cash crops for export, and we'll get rice and other important food crops we need from other places. But Haiti is based on planting food, understand? The peasant is resisting because he can take on coffee. Those hills with their coffee trees are now owned by the peasants who can say, "Here's the area in which I want to work, here's what I've found to give me results." Then the government is caught between two fires; it's forced to choose between a plan from its own people and a plan from outside.

Even if the majority of the Haitian people don't know how to read, this doesn't mean they don't know their own path. Despite the fact that there's no land, despite the fact that the hills are bare, seventy out of one hundred people in the country of Haiti are peasants. And those peasants' essential demand is to find a way to work so they can realize what they need in this life.

You should see the enthusiasm that people are entering into this struggle with! They're resisting the destruction of local markets. There's a phenomenon in Haiti now where second-hand clothes from abroad are flooding the market and poor people are buying them. But some women's groups are developing cottage industries for sewing clothes. Proud people aren't buying second-hand imported clothes because there are good, inexpensive clothes produced right here in Haiti.

Another example of resistance is how we're using credit. In my work, we're now helping the women understand what type of credit they should accept and for what purpose. You have women's groups only taking a type of credit that reinforces their autonomy and that nourishes national production.

Another way we can fight the powerful countries' macroeconomic plans is by sharing strength with other poor countries. In the past, a peasant might have heard more talk of Miami than she would of Jamaica. But that's all different now. There are some exchanges happening with Cuba, for instance. Developing regional solidarity creates closer relationships in the Caribbean so people realize they're not alone in the struggle. The more we work together, the more there's a chance we can break the shackles of the plans imposed on us all from the powerful countries.

These alternatives are like a machine that is just getting up and running. It's a little step at a time. People are developing another economic logic. And they're learning to go forward on their own.

We're in a world that's transforming, you see. We can effectively enter globalization through a model of our own choosing. We'll use the same term, but we give it another content and value to let us chart our own paths for ourselves and our children.

We *must* enter into globalization and integration, but for the profit of ordinary people. This is my work and my role: to make these aspirations a reality.

Women in particular have a large role to play in constructing a development model that profits the family, the country, the whole blessed earth. I continue to struggle and stay tied with every Haitian woman who believes this country can be saved and that it must be we who save it. That's where I believe hope is and why I believe women can build our own true strategy of development. Through our resistance and our alternative strategies we can ensure that Haiti enters into globalization in a way where little people as well as big people, women as well as men, have their place.

The bamboo symbolizes the Haitian people to a T, eh? We are a little people. The bamboo is not a great big tree with a magnificent appearance. But when the strong winds come, well, even a great tree can be uprooted. The bamboo is really weak, but when the winds come, it bends but doesn't break. Bamboo takes whatever adversity comes along, but afterwards it straightens itself back up. That's what resistance is for us Haitians: We might get bent by globalization, but we're able to straighten up and stand.

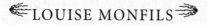

LOUISE MONFILS
The Samaritan

If I need to meet Jesus, I meet him in my brothers and sisters, I meet him in the work I am doing, in helping them live as human beings.

In my everyday life, what does living the gospel mean? Not praying, singing, clapping, making a lot of noise. That's not it. It means that those around you can know that a brother or sister has come into their midst. It's answering the cry for help by someone at night. Imagine someone on a Sunday morning saying to a sick person all alone and in need, "Oh, today I can't help you, I have to go to church." That's not where it's at. No, you've got to use this morning to help that person, do things for him, give that person courage, help him live.

You're taking a better communion that way. It's not opening your mouth and taking the host, answering, "Amen" to "The Body of Christ," while being mean and a nuisance to your neighbors. Or sending your own kids to school while you keep the little girl you are also raising at home to cook food, clean up the dishes, and wash the clothes of your own child. That little girl could become something tomorrow, but if you turn her into a beast of burden in your home, don't let her learn to read and write, then you can't say you are living the gospel. Pay attention to what I'm saying: you have to help her any way you can. Then when Jesus comes back, he can say: "I was sick and you cared for me; I was in jail and you set me free." Only when your concrete, daily acts match your preaching can your work be considered a work of the gospel.

If you know someone who needs some legal advice, and you, you understand the law, you should accompany that person to court and help her know how to defend her rights. That's what the Gospel of St. Luke says: "Today the spirit of God descended on me and sent me to give the good news to the poor. Those in prison shall be freed, the blind shall see." You should sit down with her and tell her, "According to what the law says, here is where your rights start; here's where they end." That's living the gospel, that's helping people. Are you hearing me, sister?

Do I need to kneel in front of somebody to confess my sins? No, I need to work together with my friends, my family, my brothers and sisters so that we can fight together for change. It's going for a taste of water and letting the river carry you away.

So I went with the tide of the *tilegliz*, the church of the poor. I left Port-au-Prince and went to the mountains. I started forming groups, without a penny. I didn't have any money, and I wasn't paid for my work. My friends and I climbed up and down the mountains, through the briars, to bring the gospel and help people work together. I was responsible for a *tilegliz* in a rural zone. Each Sunday I celebrated mass for the group. It didn't matter that I was a woman, because the spirit of God was in me to send the good news of the poor. I was helping people be in solidarity with each other. There was a Samaritan who fell under the hands of an assassin . . . We asked each other, "Who is my neighbor?" as the good Samaritan asked. Everyone on the earth is your neighbor, because you are a human being.

We were collecting information from the peasants so we could use it to help them understand their situation better. You synthesize what they've told you with what you saw yourself, and analyze it to understand the situation better. You extend the consequences to the whole country since all the peasants have the same problem. Then the peasants can use that information to analyze important questions, like: How can they protect their land? From there we would organize peasant groups.

Sometimes I traveled to other areas of the countryside to meet with other groups. When I came back, I'd share what I'd learned with people in my own area. It went like that, back and forth. I met with other groups, shared with them, then went out and created more groups. I helped create about ten or twenty peasant groups.

You need to step into other people's skin. I would enter the field where the peasants were working and say, "Hey! How's it going?" I would start chatting with them and lend a hand with the work. When it was time to eat, they'd invite me to join them. Even if I weren't hungry, I'd say, "Sure, let's go eat." I would eat with them and drink some water. And then we'd talk. This work takes a long time.

We studied the chapter in the Acts of the Apostles where the disciples put their goods together. And the people realized that they needed to work together.

They built a collective silo to store seeds and grains. Each area had its silo. But the Tontons Macoutes burned those silos in 1987, with the peasants' food reserves. Have you heard of what happened here in November 1987? Well, the elections were destroyed and the blood of the people flowed. Firearms and bullets reigned everywhere. Some people associated the *tilegliz* movement with a political movement. All the members of the *tilegliz* became targets for the Macoutes.

And sometimes people called us "communist." Listen to me, little girl: Communist! What communist? For me, that's what living the gospel is. You should live in harmony with your brother, regardless of whether he's color X and you're color Y. It's linking hands with others as human beings to do what's good, to help others see better.

When things got so hot in 1987, sometimes a friend or a family member would come tell me, "Don't let your children go out into the streets. Go hide yourself somewhere, because the Macoutes are coming out to persecute." Then the Macoutes burned the silo at Allée and went up to Desarmes where I was living. My friends warned me, I ran away from my home, I left. I ran through the forests, through the woods and the bushes. I slept at different friends' houses along the way: one night here, another night there. Sometimes I had no food. Once, oh! I was so hungry. I went into a stranger's garden and pulled up a cassava plant. I took three cassavas. I said to myself, "Well, if they want to arrest me, now they can get me for stealing." I wore the same dress and same underwear for three days. I walked through the woods to Arcahaie, where I got the bus. I asked people along the roads for money so I could pay the fare.

Even when I got to Port-au-Prince, I wasn't safe. One of my friends sent a message for me not to go to the bus station because the section chief from my village, who was very hostile to the work we were doing in the *tilegliz*, was surveying the station. I used to go to the bus station regularly to get news of my children. I would meet with people going back home, and I would give them money for my family. But I couldn't go there anymore.

A friend came to tell me not to stay in Port-au-Prince because they were watching for me there. My friend took me to the border of the Dominican Republic, in Grand Bois. I hid at a priest's house for six months. The priest lodged me and fed me.

Finally I went back to work but in a different area. Then, in 1990, there was a massacre of the peasants of Piatte, where I was working. Because the peasants were demanding their land back, the army killed many, many people; I don't have the exact number. The army climbed the mountains in disguise. They burned the house I was living in. I lost all my things. I ran and hid myself in some rocks beneath a waterfall. I saw all the killing, everything they did. Every little while I stuck my head out to see what they were doing, and I took notes. I unwrapped the paper from a cigarette and wrote down everything. I folded the paper, put it in the plastic wrapping from the cigarette pack, and stuck it in a hole in the hem of my dress. Even if they had searched me, they wouldn't have found anything.

I slipped into the middle of the killers and moved right along with them. They thought I was one of them. People told me later they thought I'd vanished in thin air. It wasn't true! I took a chance and walked right in the middle of the crowd that had just committed the massacre.

I traveled through field after field and arrived at a priest's house in Montrouis. I told him, "Father, save me! They've burned everyone up there in Piatte!" The priest called Radio Soleil, and I kept going a back route, walking through the bush to reach Port-au-Prince. I couldn't travel by road because there were stone barricades on the road. I had nothing but the clothes on my back. I begged along the way so I could pay for my bus fare. I called out to one man, "Friend! I need to speak with you a second. Give me a dollar." The person looked at me and gave me two.

Here's what I'm telling you, now: I spent I-don't-know-how-many days with the same underwear on. When I finally got in Port-au-Prince, I went to the office of a group I was working with and told them about the event. My face was all swollen and bruised. They said, "What?" and they took me to Radio Haiti Inter where they interviewed me. When the slaughterers heard the interview on the radio, they regretted they hadn't killed me. They couldn't understand how I escaped, because they had encircled the village with fire.

The police didn't arrest me or beat me up. But I went into a life of hiding, moving from here to there, with one ear to the ground all the time. The police didn't find me, but I suffered a lot. I was on the move. I slept in terrible conditions! Sometimes I slept in the bush.

I can say I have never had harder experiences, but I felt joy in my heart doing this. I had a sense of purpose. Jesus, too, suffered all these things. Me, a lonely fisher, I didn't mind suffering the same thing because I was defending a cause. The persecution made me feel more committed.

VITA TELCY

Five Cans of Corn

Haitian women's history is such a long story, if we started talking about it, we'd have to stop midstream because otherwise we'd be talking all night. Despite all, they resist. For example, when you consider a woman who is working to feed the kids, feed the country, give the kids an education, go to the hospital with the kids when they're sick—and then at the same time prepare for the children's funerals—oh, these are things you can't explain.

But despite all the problems burning on their heads, they've found ways out.

Everyone understands resistance in her own way. I'll tell you how I understand it. By resistance I mean the ingenuity we use that allows us to live. Resistance is inside how we do the thing that lets us hold on and gives us a better way. It's in the very manner in which we organize ourselves to survive our situation.

Women resist with what means they have. For instance, me, I'm a farmer, but I can't get land to work. Farming is the mother of this country, right? But the land doesn't give you much anymore. But what little I find, no matter how small, lets me hold on. Rich people eat three times a day, me I can't. When I harvest five cans of corn, today my family can eat half a pound. Tomorrow if there's a cup, I'll cook it. I maximize those five cans like so: one can to send the children to school, one can to send my sick child to the hospital, one can for all the family to eat. With what's left over, I find seeds to plant to make sure I can grow next year.

This is how I see resistance with an economic face. It's small, but it's resistance in any case.

Women don't have jobs, yet they're working all the time. Women who work the earth—and I am a person who has lived that harsh life—watch the sky for small drops of rain because their land is too dry to till. Let me tell you, if it doesn't rain, they're completely lost. If it does rain—hmm!—what little they make, that's what they use for hospitals, for schools, for food for the whole family. Of course, the state doesn't give them any work so they could have something to live on. But women work together, on the farm, with the laundry, in solidarity with each other. This shows you the quality of their effort. If the woman subsists, well, it's with a lot of effort, risk, and skill.

Even if a woman is forced to prostitute herself, to sell her courage, that's her resistance. See? That's how she'll survive.

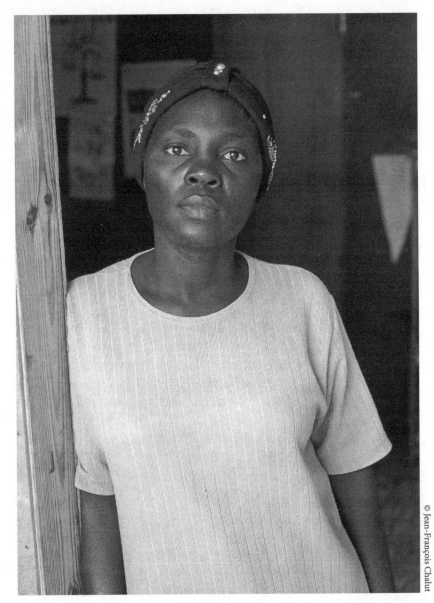

© Jean-François Chalut

Vita Telcy

On the political level, women use survival strategies against their bad fate. During the first battle for independence, women took actions to let them resist a bad life, and let the men resist, too. Well, none of that appears in the history of our country; their good work always stayed underground. Okay, a few names come up, but why didn't we learn about all those other women who were born on the earth so we could follow their examples, so we could have evolved from this other way of life those women created?

All right: let's take Jean Rabel, when the big Tontons Macoutes were controlling the area. The women were the ones who were behind the scenes on top of the hills organizing together. In '86 the game got worse. But the women kept on resisting, holding meetings right and left, discussing, reflecting, and doing work amongst themselves. The enemy couldn't understand the type of work we were doing.

During the peasant massacre in Jean Rabel in 1987, a lot of women died. Leonis and Man Djul were just two of the brave women who fell, ones who carried the women's struggle on their backs. They were peasants who couldn't read or write and who had advanced thinking. And because of this thinking they fell in the struggle.

Okay now: If we move on to the coup d'etat of '91, the section chiefs and army were hot on our asses to find out where we were and what type of work we were doing, to eliminate us from the terrain. But we found our own ways to survive. When the army appeared in the zone, how we fought and resisted them was to stay on top of the hills to control the situation. And we women, we did it. We didn't have the means to convince them or counter them. Our only tools were rocks to throw on them.

On the day of the coup, September 30, the army, Macoutes, and section chiefs of Port-de-Paix destroyed my two houses and everything that was in them. They dropped me with my six children at the feet of my parents. That same day, they arrested my mother-in-law and father-in-law. They arrested my brother and sister. Seventeen days they spent in jail.

Oh, we suffered. Look at *Madanm* Silaso, who had just had her baby one month before. The section chief took this woman, breast-feeding that tiny newborn, the poor little thing suffering so bad from lice—he took that baby away from her and took her right off to jail. Well, this is something that as a woman you can't explain.

Still, we as women resisted and forced the situation to change. Not in an isolated fashion, no way—this was done in an organized way. And each victory reinforced our courage because we saw that we were doing good work.

I was homeless, but despite all, I didn't leave the area. I slept one night here, one night there. I found a way to resist.

The small-scale resistance involves know-how that lets us survive. Maybe an underground way, maybe subterfuge. For instance, when times were good, the authorities knew the location of our meetings. But when the times changed, you changed, too. You didn't get up and say you were going to a meeting, no. You took your bag on your back and said you were going somewhere else. That way, the authorities didn't know. That's *teknik*, craftiness.

It's our resistance and sharing experiences, one woman with another, that will allow me to continue with the women's struggles. Look at my case as a community health worker. I do double work as a health worker and women's organizer. As you well know, the state has work it's supposed to be doing. But since it doesn't do it, you have to do more work than you should. And you work for nothing. I do prevention work that lets people in the community avoid illnesses like diarrhea, tuberculosis, typhoid, malaria, anemia. The state didn't train me, I was trained privately. And then I had to work in the community for free. Well, what did I do? I worked on a vaccination campaign. Before, there were a lot of children in the community who died shortly after birth. We didn't know the cause. But I learned that it was because the mothers hadn't been vaccinated when they were pregnant, and the children weren't vaccinated when they were born. Today I can say that in the community children don't die of tetanus or diphtheria or polio anymore.

I've continued to vaccinate children aged zero to four years. I also do nutrition education and potable water education with them. But I have to help them as an organizer, too, because to have health you have to be able to find something to eat. I'm organizing so that people will have a general idea of what's happening in their country: the education problem, the health problem, political and social problems. They arrive at identifying where exploitation comes from. Then they analyze and see if they should remain in their current situation, or if there isn't something they can do to get themselves out of it. For one thing, we must struggle to help the state take its responsibility.

The work isn't bad, but I should be given the resources to do it. Still, despite there not being any money, I'm not discouraged. This knowledge I share has allowed me to have more of a family. I've gained more friends, more sisters, brothers.

Without women there are things that just won't work. And because of this, I'm inflating my courage.

There's a proverb that says, *Timoun ki rele se li ki bezwen tete*. The child who cries is the child who needs the breast. That means that if you don't cry, you don't need the breast, but as long as you cry . . .

⤝MARIE JOSEE ST. FIRMIN⤞
Sharing the Dream

The basis of my life is this: My life and the struggle of the Haitian people are integrally tied together. This is because since I was born, I've seen misery and poverty all around me.

I was raised in a small privileged sector of society. When I was growing up, I could eat, drink, and sleep at ease. My parents could afford a house. Each day I put on a different outfit. I went to private school.

But as I got older, I saw that these circumstances were different from what most people lived. I grew conscious of the fact that other kids were going to school with ripped shoes on their feet, while I put on a different pair each day. This bothered me. Each day I asked my family, "How come some people are sleeping on the ground beside our house, while I'm sleeping under a nice sheet?" In high school, reality got even harder for me to grapple with. I was learning that this is a divided society of haves and have-nots. I was seeing that not everyone who was living and breathing had what might really be called a life.

Living under the Duvalier dictatorship, I also became conscious that a small group of people were making the lives of the rest of the citizens even harder. What I saw of this dictatorship in my youth was intolerable. When the president was in an area, for instance, people always died. Whenever Duvalier came to visit Les Cayes, he'd throw coins out the window of his car. Often when the poor bent down to the ground to pick up the coins, the cars in the motorcade struck them. Those people died without even being able to enjoy that fifty cents they'd just picked up. This would tie my insides up in knots, realizing that Haitians were dying for fifty cents.

I made a choice then. I said to myself that I must struggle so life can flower for all people.

I was becoming conscious, but I still didn't realize what dictatorship actually meant. Later on, as I was growing up, going to school, and learning, I started to take direct positions. I began doing radio broadcasts for the poor. I remember that the first radio broadcast I did was after the dictatorship had arrested a leader in the charismatic renewal movement, Gerard Duperval, in 1982, and I made an appeal to justice on the radio. This was my first public action. I asked, "Is struggling with the poor a barbaric act? Between dictatorship and struggling with the poor, which is the criminal act?" This question is more complex than it sounds, because in fact there is a higher cost to struggling with the poor than standing on the side of dictatorship.

I helped take care of the street children and *restavèk*—that was part of my social development. But I got directly involved in the political struggle in 1984 and 1985 when the repression got worse. My radio program focused on the discrimination in society. Even the songs and masses that I broadcast were a form of revolt and an appeal to conscience. We were calling on all people to reject the status quo, to send a clear sign to the perpetrators that their activities were wrong. As the struggle to overthrow Duvalier geared up, I participated in meetings and did all I could, though in Haitian society I was still a child. As long as you're living inside your family's doors, you're considered a child. I participated in many things without my family ever knowing.

In 1985, the politics heated up. On November 28, 1985, three youths in Gonaïves were assassinated. I was one of the main organizers of the student demonstrations in Les Cayes. One day I brought flyers for the demonstration to my high school class to give out to the students. The teacher made me understand that if I wanted to "get mine," this was the way to do it. I told him he was right; I would probably get it. But I would get it on my two feet and not on my knees.

The teacher threw me out of class that day. I went and joined up with a group of comrades and on December 2, we took to the street. That was in 1985, but I remember it as if it had happened today. The police dispersed the march and cracked open the head of a little girl in grammar school. We kept marching, though, to where we were going to have a final rally where I would deliver a statement. Further along the march route, a group of soldiers met us. They were trying to buy our consciences. The officer said to me, "Girl, a little girl like you could be my own daughter. We don't want to hit you. I don't want to give the order to strike you. You'd better go back home." I was with three comrades, three boys. One of them was from the bourgeois class whose parents didn't think he should be part of this action. The chief took that boy to a colonel's home and made the colonel beat him. They brought a complaint to my mother.

Because we were young, they tried to make it look like people had paid us to make us do these things, like we were being manipulated. But I stayed firm in the face of all these accusations. We kept on planning demonstrations and other events in Les Cayes, like other people were doing all around the country.

On February 7, 1986, Duvalier fell. We saw what they offered us in exchange—another form of Duvalierism—and we simply adopted new forms of struggle. Each person decided which form of action was best for him or her in the circumstance. I stayed in the political camp of the people, whom I'll continue to defend until the last blow of the bayonet.

I want to move quickly to 1990, the year of hope for all people who shared the dream. I participated actively in Jean-Bertrand Aristide's campaign for the December 1990 elections. I manned the Les Cayes office of the campaign. All sorts of people came and harassed me in the office. Once while I was sitting there, a man walked in and looked around. The office was small, just one room divided in two. He looked and looked, then turned around and walked out. Another person in the office who was supposed to be providing security didn't even realize what was happening. Later, the man who came into our office reported to someone else, "I was told something serious was going on there, but no. I don't need to commit a crime for nothing." He said he'd been given a grenade to explode in the office. But when he saw that there were no files, no papers, nothing—just me and a man sitting behind a table—he abandoned his intentions and left. We later found out that a powerful Tonton Macoute had given that man the mission. That meant nothing to me, because I was there to advance the struggle.

We saw the free elections of December 16, 1990, go off well. Then on January 31, 1991, an attempted coup almost prevented Titid's inauguration. This last-ditch attempt by the Tontons Macoutes to destroy democracy was defeated, and on February 7, 1991, we inaugurated our first democratic government—the most beautiful event Haiti could experience. What existed during the next seven months was hope, a people breathing the sweet air of night-blooming jasmine all day long.

One thing we learned during this year was that people can change. When Titid took power, we saw people who'd committed terrible acts, people within the Tonton Macoute structure, even people who'd created that structure, adopt a different vision. Some had grown exhausted of the endless changes of governments and death squads killing people at night. Even though Titid didn't represent an ideal president for them, they were ready for some stability. Even the Tontons Macoutes realized that the country had gone too far in its horror against human beings. Some began to participate, with all their hearts, in making the Aristide government work. Others only pretended to assist but in reality were preparing a trap.

With the coup d'etat of 1991, this rosy life that the Haitian people had started to know was lost. The enemies of democracy tore our beautiful experience from us. I compare the experience to a woman who's carried a baby in her womb, who has prepared long and hard for the birth of that baby. Then the day that she goes into labor, she loses the child. Women understand how searing that pain is.

I went right into hiding. The fear that I'd be discovered was constant. Many of us lived under that threat, but it didn't prevent the resistance movement from gaining strength. We all kept searching for ways to reject the coup d'etat.

Soldiers killed one of our comrades, Jean-Claude Museau, my dear friend. They arrested him one night in December 1991 when they found him pasting up posters of Titid on walls. The next day they beat and tortured him so badly. They even forced him to swallow a bunch of the posters with Titid's picture. Jean-Claude finally lost consciousness, and they took him to the barracks at the police post. He was held without any medical treatment, and none of us were allowed to visit him. Two days later, on January 8, 1992, he died.

Jean-Claude's friends and relatives gave him a funeral in the spirit of the struggle he'd led. I was responsible for organizing the church service, and I gave a statement during the ceremony about his life and work.

The military didn't hesitate to pursue all the people who were at that funeral and who'd worked with Jean-Claude. Their manhunt began right away.

One year after Jean-Claude's death in January 1993, his comrades organized a series of events to commemorate his life and work. Most of us were in hiding, but we found ways to work underground to sponsor a week of resistance activities. I came out from hiding to host a radio program about the repression and the political implications of the coup. I called on people to resist, to force respect for the election of December 16, 1990. I pointed the finger at those who had killed Jean-Claude, and said we wouldn't forget the assassins. We arranged a photo and poster exhibit and a demonstration. We sang a requiem mass in his honor at the cathedral in Les Cayes on January 8, 1993. A lot of people showed up for it.

Just after the mass, soldiers were sent out to get me. They invaded and ransacked my home, but I'd already fled. So they arrested my fifty-four-year-old mother instead. They took her to the police bureau in Les Cayes, interrogated her about my work, beat her, and tortured her horribly. She was denied medical care and wasn't charged in the period required by law. Later, she was transferred to another prison where they held her.

My mother had suffered for me before. This was the third time soldiers had invaded our home, though I'd been away each time. On the first two occasions, soldiers took her down to the station. They interrogated her about me and my work and accused her of working with communists.

But this time, the military actually imprisoned her for twenty-two days. The officers demanded I be turned in in exchange for her liberation. She refused to reveal where I was.

During her imprisonment, the political chief of the area came to our home again. He threw my three little children into the street. He stole everything he could, including a computer that he declared to be "material for communication." He locked the house and left.

Six international human rights groups were visiting Haiti at the time; they wrote letters to judicial and political authorities. Jesse Jackson and the special envoy to the United Nations also raised the question of my mother to the coup leaders.

Eventually my mother was liberated, but she was forbidden to leave town. One week later, three armed men invaded our home again, but she'd already abandoned it for her safety.

My mother was terrorized a fifth time during a sweep of arrests in Les Cayes in May 1992. I was in hiding at the time. Soldiers made my mother come down to the station, and again interrogated her about my political activities and my comrades who used to come to our house. The house was under constant surveillance.

After that, my mother fled to Port-au-Prince with the three children. But even there she received threats. Once she had to change her hiding place after a soldier recognized her in the streets and said, "Aren't you the mother of that trouble-maker, Marie Josée?"

Today my question is this: This society, which we are asking to change, can it truly change without an accompanying shift in mentality?

From day to day the struggle becomes more ensnared. But I'm more than ever certain that we must be accountable, that we can't sit with our arms crossed and do nothing. This determination is especially necessary for women because our struggle is all the more complicated.

For example: When my mother was in prison, her cell had a light in it. My mother shared this cell with another woman who never knew why she had been arrested. One day this woman said to my mother, "*Madanm*, I know you're not here for any valid reason. I don't know why I am being held, either. They say I killed someone, but I don't know who. I think you'll be released before me, and maybe then you could take some course of action to get me out."

These women got along so well that the men became jealous. The soldiers declared, "It seems these women think they're in their homes, sitting at ease in their garden rooms. They don't realize they're in prison." The women were just trying to resist the persecution from deep within their souls. They were trying to live. But the men decided my mother and the other woman were too well off in their cell because they had a bulb shining light on them and they could read their Bibles together. So the next day they transferred the women to a much dirtier and more horrible cell that didn't have electricity.

I tell this story to demonstrate that these men had no sense that women are human. They had no sense that women carried them in their wombs, raised them, and imbued them with life.

Every day I grow stronger in my commitment that where there are women, there's life. Not only do we carry life in our wombs, but we create life each day that we live, in all the work we do in the society.

I'll continue to struggle for the liberation of my people even if I have to give my blood for that. Even if I live in hiding and suffer because of my work—my country and its struggle hold life for me.

⇜ SELITANE JOSEPH ⇝
Chunk of Gold

There is a saying, *Yo pa bay libète. Se pran pou ou pran l.* Liberty is not given to you. Take, you must take it.

The life of the Haitian peasant woman is misery. Betrayal. Rage. We come from the hills carrying big baskets of meat, big baskets of plantains, great big sacks of grapefruit. Even when we're pregnant, when our bellies are big, we go up and down hills. Us, the women, we have no time for leisure, we have no time for rest. Our rest is when we're sick or, finally when it's all over, in the cemetery. We don't have doctors or health centers. Medicine is too expensive so we practice popular medicine, mixing different leaves and herbs. Even if you did have the money to go to the hospital, and you got there first, they'd see everyone else before you. But you've got to drag on. When we find the hills too hard and have to go to the city and work in the home of some woman—a woman like yourself!—they exploit us terribly.

Then the man: From the moment we're born, we're in preparation to go and be responsible for a man. There are times when they only sleep with us and give us a little money. That's why we have many fatherless children on our hands. And if you have a little job and don't let the bosses sleep with you, you'll find yourself unemployed. We have to gather our strength so one day we'll be able to answer back to men.

What bothers us even more is violence. There is not a woman who hasn't been struck. It doesn't matter who you are.

But we shouldn't remember this only on big occasions like International Day against Violence against Women. But each and every God-given day, because it's every day we're exploited. That's why today it's time, it's past time.

What did the big women's meeting in Beijing do for us Haitian women? We haven't seen any effects. Why don't they come and sit with us peasant women to see how we're living today? This is why we're launching an appeal to all women: the charcoal vendor, the plantain vendor, the meat vendor, the seamstress, workers in factories, the mountain woman and the city woman. We must get together so that one day we can destroy the system that's crushing us. We're the soul of this country. Don't forget that!

I sit with my children and reflect on the status of women. I show my boys that when they have a woman, they have to understand it's a chunk of gold in their hands.

I have hope that Haiti won't perish. It just has too many strong women.

Now then, my biggest problem with some women's organizations is that they think that women alone can wage the battle. It's not true! Men are exploited as well as us. We ask men and women to band together so we can overturn this bone-crushing system, this cursed system. We have to keep our eyes open because if women and men are divided, the place we want to go to—we'll never get there.

My dream is that the system change because the pot is boiling on only one side. One little group has the monopoly, has all the access. Electricity doesn't exist for the peasant. There are no roads. If we don't have the means to travel up to sixty kilometers on foot, we can't communicate among ourselves. That's why we can't have good organization. We're deprived of everything. We can't buy a radio, for instance, to hear the news. If today we said, "We market women, we're shutting down everything. We're not going into the city, we're not going to sell!" then the rich would have problems.

© Leah Gordon

As a peasant woman, thanks be to God, I had a chance to go to school. But I didn't spend a lot of time there because at seventeen I got pregnant. Afterward, I said, "Well, I myself will not sit and just bear child after child." I had to break off my relationship with that first man because he didn't have the same ideas as I do. But the other man I had eight children with, he's struggling along with me to change this system. That's why I can say for myself, I do it all. To have had nine children and survive in Haiti is no small matter. Plus I sew. I teach school. I make chocolate. I make things to sell.

But I don't forget the other women who are suffering in the hills. Every week or two I consecrate some time to meet with those women so we can reflect together on this society. I'm not afraid of that.

I belong to *Tèt Kole*, an organization of small peasants. We work with people who have no land, or just a little piece of land, or who are day laborers. I work with the women on literacy. I do this for free so that women who've always figured things out in their heads can tomorrow do their calculations on paper. Now they can figure out that if a cup of rice costs thirty gourdes, and they need six cups, how much that is. It gives me pleasure the way women are starting to write because sometimes even their men cheat them. Since they don't know how to count, the husband takes off with the money and when he returns, he gives her back what he wants to give her. But now he can't do that so easily. I train men and boys, too, because the struggle is for men and women.

One thing we do in *Tèt Kole*, we train women to make chocolate because that's a national product. Before, the powerful people got the big markets. But now we make a profit despite the fact that we have a lot of expenses like buying spices. But we're proud because it's us women who set the price. No one else fixes it for us. And we refuse to sell the cocoa for almost nothing. We transform it into chocolate and sell it locally and nationally.

Within my organization there's no gag on my mouth. When you're among men, sometimes you feel they don't give you much value, they don't really hear your voice. But in *Tèt Kole*, woman, she has all the power. She has the right to speak. She has taken the liberty. Because as I already said, if you don't, you're doomed.

Good evening. I am Rosemie Belvius who comes from Petite Rivière de l'Artibonite.

I grew up with my grandfather, my mother's father. I was in a small Catholic group. We stood by people and prayed with them. When I was praying, this organization that formed near my house said to me, "Wouldn't you like to participate?" That's how when I was very young I joined OGAD, the Organization of Agricultural Development Associations.

In each meeting, with fifty or so men, I was the only woman. Well, when I saw that, I sought out some of my friends and asked, "Hey, wouldn't you like to meet together and form a group of women?" They agreed, and we formed a small group of fifteen women. I called this group "Women Decided." When they asked why I gave the group that name, I said, "Because I was in the middle of fifty men and I *decided* to organize a women's group." We started holding meetings with these fifteen people, with me making sixteen. I told each woman to take initiative, get out there, and start her own group. That's how we came to have sixteen groups.

Let me tell you about peasants. As for working the land, we women know how to do that. But not every woman has land. For every hundred women, you'll find only ten women who do. Most women either marry a man who has some, or they find a man with a little piece of land and they work it. If you're not legally married but living with a man, and that man leaves you, forget it; you don't have land anymore. Also, most of the land is owned by the big landowners and the state. Us little peasants, we're obliged to buy a little from the big landowner or work it on halves: If you harvest one hundred canisters of rice, the big man gets fifty, you get fifty. This is even though *you* spent the money, *you* bought the fertilizer that sells for sixty dollars per sack, and *you* bought the labor for three dollars a day to hoe the garden. That means the landlord always has, and we're always losing.

Now let me tell you a little about how the women in the area do commerce. All the women in Petite Rivière de l'Artibonite live on *eskonte*, credit from the large landowners. When you take one hundred dollars from the landowner, you put one hundred dollars on top of that each month in interest. If you're a small vendor of rice, each Saturday you carry a can of rice, a liter of oil, or a cup of sugar to give him. It's like you're softening him up so that you can hold on to the money for three or six months until you can earn enough to pay him back. We call it *chouchoute l*, sweethearting him. You can see why we need to organize.

In 1987, around the time of the November elections, there was an uproar in the country. The Macoutes went after a collective grain silo we had put together that held six thousand canisters of corn. There was a large landowner in the area who used to buy all the corn from the peasants at harvest time, cheap. Then he would hike the price up to ten gourdes (U.S.$.66) in the spring when the peasants needed to plant. In the organization we were thinking, "We'll buy all the corn from the peasants and store it in the silo. Then at planting time, they'll get it at the same price they sold it, with just a little bit more to pay for the materials and the manager." We would buy it but we wouldn't sell it on the market. We'd sell it back to the peasants in the organization so it would benefit them. When we did that, the landowner couldn't find people to buy corn from him because everyone was buying from within the organization.

Now the big man, he wasn't making the profit. We were. So on November 29, he got the Macoutes to burn this silo and all the food in it. My husband, Jean,

Rosemie Belvius

he saw this. They were shooting, so Jean went behind a bush and lay down. He was lying there with bullets zinging all around him. The Macoutes filled their vehicle with corn and set fire to the rest.

Because of the work I was doing, Macoutes set fire to my house, too, with everything inside. While I was running away, I tripped in a hole and a branch pulled the dress off me. I left it and ran stark naked. I went and hid under a thorn bush. While I was hiding there, I saw a person passing and I made a sign to him. He came to me and said, "Is that your house burning down there?" I said, "Yes, it's my house. Save my life!" The man went to his wife's house. He came with a dress, gave it to me, and let me sleep at his wife's house.

Later that same night he borrowed a car and took me all the way to Port-au-Prince, to a safe house. I said to myself, "Huh! I'm a militant. I shouldn't have to sit in Port-au-Prince." So I said, "I won't hide. No! If I hide, leaving the women, the organization will break down. I'll stay here a few days, but then I have to return." Besides, I couldn't be in hiding here while I have my husband in hiding elsewhere. I had to look for him.

They were scared for me to return. But I said, "No way. Me, I won't run." Jean and I both returned to the Artibonite a few days later.

In 1990 Jean and I founded an organization called AGAPA, the Association of Peasant Groups of the Artibonite. We formed a little group of fifteen. We did it the same way as at OGAD: Each person took the initiative to form a group, and like that AGAPA came to have 5,000 members, with 1,210 members in its women's group. And we're still growing. We're working in soil conservation, and helping the women make art with pieces of wood. We do all this and we farm, too. Now we have a grain storage project and a mill.

AGAPA is a mixed-sex association. The women together, the men together. When a job asks for collaboration, everybody works on it.

Still, it's important for us to organize as women. When women are with men, then men take the posture of intellectuals and the women don't like to speak. And the women's power never comes to the fore. But women together looking for a solution bring fruit. We're reshuffling the cards.

In 1991 the coup d'etat took place and all the women dispersed. We thought we would grow weaker during that time, but instead we got stronger because of the way we had organized.

Now those three difficult years: While every man was in hiding, every woman was in hiding also. We used all our political tactics to survive. We held small underground meetings to see how we could escape this crisis. We women created a revolving loan system, whereby each woman who had ten dollars put it in until we reached one hundred dollars. Then we gave two women fifty dollars each. Those who could do a little grilled peanut business, did it. We didn't used to do commerce this way, but during the three years of the coup we needed a strategy like that. We also had food to carry to those who were in hiding, in the worst danger. Likewise, when we ourselves were in hiding, others sustained us, as well as our children that we had to leave behind. Like that, the movement grew.

Those three years left me with nothing. They killed my animals, they stole everything—my garden, everything. If you see while I'm speaking here that I hold my ear, it's because a soldier hit me there with the back of his rifle. The ear still buzzes loudly.

But I never get discouraged because I know that if we give up, we lose completely. We have a song in the organization that says,

> We will not give in, oh no.
> We'll never cede the battle.
> No we will not surrender
> To the assassins' power.

What gives me more chance than most to evolve like this? My husband and I have the same training and the same vision. Usually when a woman marries, if the husband isn't conscious of women's problems, then even if she has the capacity, she'll be prevented from becoming something big. Maybe, though, she still can do something small.

Why am I like this? Why are other women not like this? I don't know. There's a proverb that says, *Bondye bay chak moun pa li.* God gave each person her own. Maybe if it's not what she was granted, she can't lead well. Maybe that's the gift God gave me.

4 RESISTANCE FOR GENDER JUSTICE

The liberation of women comes through that of their people. The liberation of a people remains incomplete if it does not include that of women.
—Myrto Célestin Saurel

Haitian women have not benefited proportionally from the fruits of change that their mobilizations have helped create. Haiti's experience demonstrates that absolute improvement achieved by a national liberation movement does not necessarily yield relative improvement for women. Political and socioeconomic entitlement does not necessarily trickle down.

Many Haitian women have come to realize that their demands for justice and equitable distribution of resources will only gain visibility and clout through embedding gender into the debate and centralizing women's issues within the popular movement. Increasingly, women are redefining their advocacy to include gender-specific rights, access, and participation.

THE ROOTS OF THE HAITIAN WOMEN'S MOVEMENT

Haitian women's activism and achievement for their rights is, by global standards, notable. Like their engagement in broad political struggles, women's advocacy for gender empowerment extends far back in the country's development. Though their painstaking labors largely have been written out of history, recorded acts date as early as 1820. Then, a group of wealthy women changed the law that deemed all women minors.[1] The feminist movement was born in the 1930s with the birth of the Feminine League for Social Action. The group was founded by upper-class intellectual and professional women, and focused on obtaining rights that could increase their political and social mobility. The

League and other feminist groups that followed in its path succeeded in winning legal and constitutional gains for women, including the right to elective offices (other than the presidency) in 1944, and then full political rights, including voting rights, in 1950. Yet repression and electoral fraud denied women, like men, a *free* vote until 1990.

Haiti also has a good record, relative to world standards, of women holding high political office in appointed posts. Women have served as president (an appointed, interim one), prime minister, heads of cabinet ministries, and secretaries of state. Alternatively, there is a low incidence of women attaining elected offices, such as Parliament and local posts.

The feminist movement historically did not incorporate poor women, either as members or as a focus of their advocacy. And because poor women were so thoroughly disenfranchised, the political rights that the feminist movement won did not effectively include them. For example, for indigent and illiterate women the right to hold political office has been meaningless until very recently.

Under the Duvalier dictatorship, class distinctions between women were partially leveled because the regime denied political freedoms to *all* women equally. Losing access even to the rights that existed on the books, wealthy feminists could not enjoy the fruits of their recent victories.

The dictatorship also resulted in greater equality between the sexes, in a perverse way. Traditionally considered to be dependents and political innocents, women had been protected from state-sponsored violence. But when François Duvalier rose to power in 1957, state violence crossed gender lines. The first noted case of this was the kidnap, rape, and beating of a feminist, anti-Duvalier journalist in 1958. Under Papa Doc, *no* one was safe.

The loss of privilege and safety moved many middle-and upper-class feminists who previously had focused only on their own privileges into the national liberation struggle. By 1965, the autonomous women's movement had effectively merged with the antidictatorship movement.[2]

During the 1970s and 1980s, some women again began organizing around feminist issues. Once again, state repression was partially responsible, for it was in being forced into exile throughout the Americas and Europe that tens of thousands of Haitian women became exposed to rising feminist consciousness. In what sociologist Carolle Charles called the "transnationalization of Haitian women's struggles,"[3] the external feminist influence was passed back home.

While some feminist thinking assumes a unified women's profile, the *istwa* debunk these assumptions. Many of the *griyo* insist that "women" as a unit of analysis must be disaggregated. Evelyne Attis slaps a fly from her forearm and says, "They say they believe in women's rights, but look how they treat their maids. Those rich ladies have much more in common with their menfolk than with us poor women."

Claudette Phéné readjusts her youngest on her lap on the porch of her mother's mud home. She interrupts herself to shout at two of her boys who are throwing pebbles at a wobbly-legged puppy, then resumes:

> You see the bourgeois with their strollers. They press a button and *clap*! it opens. They press a button and *clap*! it folds down. Yourself, a little poor person, you don't even have a mat on the floor for your baby to lie on.

Nor do the women in such a polarized country share a cohesive set of demands. Indeed, peasant educator Gracita Osias points out, "In Haiti, not all women are exploited. Some are exploiters." Still, some from the middle and upper classes, including a few *griyo* in this book, have transcended their class

© Maggie Steber

interests and made common cause with the poor. And a broad group of women eventually came to benefit from the legal rights won by feminists.

Too, over time more philosophical and programmatic overlap has developed between the movements. As grassroots women's groups have made gender more central to their agenda, they have adopted increasingly feminist ideas. And many feminist groups now work extensively with poor women. This cross-fertilization spread during the coup years, when women representing peasant, worker, and middle classes joined together to end the violence and restore constitutional democracy. The slogan of the feminist organization Solidarity Among Haitian Women (SOFA) is characteristic of the new intersection: "The problem of women is the problem of the masses."

The dominant analysis among popular women's organizations is that class exploitation and repressive and unresponsive government, *combined* with patriarchy, form the bases of their oppression. By and large poor women do not perceive themselves as a class in themselves but rather as an especially oppressed group within the labor and peasant classes. The *istwa* reveal a belief common to women of these sectors that class and gender are interrelated sites of struggle; their absolute and relative status, therefore, will improve only as a result of changes in both areas.

Still, increasingly their experiences within the male-dominated movement are shifting the balance in the gender/class equation. More and more within the national liberation movement, women are emphasizing their own needs and rights.

GENDERING THE POPULAR MOVEMENT

Women's voices gained volume with the political opening of 1986. One of the first events of the post-Duvalier uncorking was a boisterous march of almost two thousand women in the remote village of Papaye. Immediately thereafter, on April 3, 1986, over thirty thousand women from all social sectors took to the streets throughout Haiti, rhythmically chanting their demands and carrying strongly worded posters. Both events called for justice for all Haitians, but particularly for women. Since then women have attempted to forcibly assert their own substantive participation, as well as demands particular to women, within the movement.

As discussed in Chapter 3, women formed their own groups to create room for their voices and leadership in the popular movement. Though the structures may have been created primarily for tactical purposes, in the course of organizing, women's awareness about both their importance as members of society, and the significance of gender in class oppression, have grown enormously. Listen to peasant organizer Selitane Joseph: "*Woy*, Jesus!" she exclaims vehemently,

> Women are the soul of the country. Don't forget that! . . . Without them, society could not survive. There are many women who don't yet recognize their own value. This value, the man takes it and hides it, he stomps on it. But today, we women, we have value just like every other member of society.

Autonomous organizing has opened doors for women to develop solidarity, independence, and identity. When the process first began, a sharp distinction marks the women's presence at mixed-gender meetings, where they sit silent, and at their own meetings, where they dance, laugh, and sometimes shout to be heard as everyone gives their opinions at once. In her *istwa*, Claudette Werleigh describes how organizing independently of men has allowed women to learn faster, occupy leadership positions, and develop a public voice. Kesta Occident says, "When women's groups began forming, we started discovering the worth of people whose voices we'd never heard. Those people really started taking the initiative in their communities."

The history of women's marginalization in the popular movement is, therefore, also the history of their growing consciousness, political development, and leadership.

Some men continue to suppress women's roles and presence in grassroots organizations. Still, women are breaking down the male domination. As one indicator: in 1987 I attended the First National Congress of Democratic Movements at a church hall in Port-au-Prince. Of the approximately eleven hundred participants, only a couple of women had visible roles as speakers or organizers. Of the two or three women's groups present among the more than one hundred organizations, one was confined to the kitchen with the task of preparing food for the conferees. On the last day, they came to the kitchen doorway for a brief moment so that other activists could applaud their cooking.

One decade later I returned to that airless, cinder-block hall next to the uneven soccer field. This time it was for a conference of the National Association of Haitian Women, where peasant activists from throughout the country had gathered for a lively exchange. I told the women about my last experience at that same venue. They were outraged.

GENDERING THE AGENDA

Regarding domestic, social, and economic relations between the sexes, women are shifting political debates in vital ways. One key development is that the perceived spaces between individual and collective, and private and political, are collapsing. Traditionally, men's lives have been viewed as public and political while women's have been designated as private and personal, thus excluding their concerns from the priorities of the liberation movement, power centers of civil society, and government. Slowly such critical social issues as the welfare of children, health and reproductive rights, spousal abuse, and unequal distribution of labor are taking their places on the national political agenda.[4]

Still, just as women have had trouble inserting themselves as equal actors in popular organizations, they have had trouble inserting their gender-specific demands. While some men in the movement have been strongly supportive of women's empowerment, generally women's social conditions and needs have been pushed to the background. The needs and interests have been viewed as ancillary to the global call for justice, or worse, as a wedge dividing and distracting from a loftier goal. Lise-Marie Déjean pensively taps her pencil on the glass-topped table, then says:

> There was a mentality that women's problems are secondary. "Let's take care of the problems of the country first, and we'll deal with women later." As though women's problems aren't the country's problems!

This mentality is changing. Women are slowly moving toward center not only as political participants but also as a claimant group. There are two primary arenas of women's gender-specific claims: one toward men and patriarchal systems for power and access, the other to the state for legal guarantees and protections specific to women.

As discussed in the *istwa*, women's demands of men now include child support; greater control over household earnings and property; the rights to leave the home, to associate freely, and to speak; and an end to psychological humiliation and physical abuse.

The *griyo* also speak to the importance of receiving respect. Fanning herself with a red rag, Selitane Joseph says, "I show my boys that, when they have a woman, they have to understand it's a chunk of gold in their hands."

From the state, women's organizations are advocating equal rights for themselves and their children, protection against rape and domestic abuse, financial support from the fathers, recognition of *plasaj*, rights for offspring born of those unions, government investment in a social infrastructure that better serves women and their children, an end to state-sponsored violence against women, access to credit, and better protections to land and other property.

Women won important gender victories under the Aristide administration. The government implemented basic needs programs that benefited poor women and their children, redirecting spending to health and immunization, education, potable water, electricity, judicial reform, and rural infrastructure such as roads. A minor increase in the minimum wage impacted thousands of female factory workers, though it still did not bring them a living wage.

Under this administration, six ministries, including the prime ministry, were headed by women. Toward the end of his term, Aristide created the Ministry on the Status and Rights of Women. Then, in a gesture whose symbolism was missed by none, Aristide transferred the former General Headquarters of the Armed Forces of Haiti, a forbidding structure across a boulevard from the National Palace, to the new ministry. The edifice's renovation into a lavender ribbon- and flower-bedecked place where women from the poor classes can go to give testimony and bring complaints was a slap to the traditional sites of power. The headquarters' reconsecration, says the first head of the Ministry of the Status and Rights of Women, Lise-Marie Déjean, was "the second reason why there is so much antagonism toward us among certain nerve centers. The first reason is that we exist at all."

The ministry's priorities were to: (1) respond to violence again women; (2) help women gain credit, education, and good working conditions; (3) support women's organizing initiatives; (4) launch a consciousness-raising program on women's and girls' rights; (5) generate women's rights and equality; and (6) establish strategic programs in education, culture, economics, work, the law, communication, and protection against domestic violence.[5]

Women's advocacy is beginning, in small increments, to shift control of wealth, resources, and power away from a male-exclusive domain. The changes confirm the Haitian expression, which Selitane Joseph recalls solemnly: *Yo pa bay libète. Se pran pou ou pran l.* Liberty is not given to you. Take, you must take it.

⋘ LISE-MARIE DEJEAN ⋙
Minister of the Status and Rights of Women

When I was minister of the Status and Rights of Women, I always used to say to the women that they are a force. They have the power to make and unmake, politically. The question of our sitting at the table—men are not doing us a favor. It's our right because society rests on our backs.

One of the big demands that we made in '91 when Aristide came to power was that not only should women participate to change the color of this state, we must also be around the table where the decisions are made. That's how we came to participate en masse in the elections. We participated in the campaigns to such a point that men felt the necessity of putting women up for offices of mayor around the country.

We wanted a ministry to serve the needs of women. Given that women had borne the victimization of the coup so heavily, we felt we had all the more need and right to change the state into the one we wanted. Also, we wanted the ministry not only to point fingers at problem areas but to force the transformation of the state.

We were lucky; we had the global winds behind us because during that time the Fourth World Conference on Women in Beijing was being prepared. It allowed us to show the urgency for women to participate.

Titid asked me twice to be minister of Social Affairs. I refused him. After that he asked if I wanted to be the assistant minister of Social Affairs. I told him, "Well, Titid, I know two things. I am a doctor and I am a woman." I must say that after we held the demonstration to demand a women's ministry in March of '91, Titid met with all the women. But most of the women who participated in that meeting were against the establishment of the ministry.

The opposition was based on the idea that the government didn't have money. And there was a mentality that women's problems are secondary. "Let's take care of the problems of the country first, and we'll deal with women later." As though women's problems aren't the country's problems!

So the plan didn't work then, but Titid asked me to be the minister anyway. When he made me that proposition, I didn't see myself as a minister, you see. I said, well, I must learn how the state functions. I thought there were other people who could occupy the place, with the support of their organizations. That was my vision. But the last time Titid called to ask me to be a part of the

Lise-Marie Déjean

Ministry of Social Affairs and I said no, he told me, "Next time I won't ask you. I'll just appoint you."

I was at a meeting of SOFA when the prime minister phoned me to ask if I would agree to be minister. While he was talking with me, I wrote down what he said, and underneath it I wrote "Yes" and "No." Then I held it up to the women at the meeting. Since everyone agreed, I said yes.

The government installed the Ministry on the Status and Rights of Women on November 8, 1994. We were installed as minister two days after, on the tenth of November. When I say "we," speaking of the minister, I'm speaking of the team. I didn't just see myself as the minister.

They moved us to four different offices. All the moves were tied to their underlying conceptions of the ministry. First, they gave us a room inside the Ministry of Social Affairs. The day after they installed us, there was a meeting of ministers. The first thing I said was that our ministry is not an appendage of Social Affairs. It was a totally separate ministry, so we had to have our own space. We spent ten days there.

The second office they gave us was behind the prime minister's office. We were better off there, certainly—it was a nicer building—but it was just a transient locale. We were borrowing the office of the director of Public Relations, who was temporarily gone. They were searching for a headquarters, as were we. Each time we asked them for a building, they said, "No, such-and-such is wrong with it," or some excuse. Finally they gave us a space that was the annex of former Prime Minister Malval's office. It wasn't a bad space but it was really remote. It was like we were something they wanted to forget, like they were sending us off to our own little corner to be forgotten. But we tried to make the space lively, anyway.

Then, luckily for us, the army became practically dismantled and, in a presidential decree, they granted us the military headquarters. Well, everyone said, "What! Aren't you ashamed to go to a place with such a bad reputation?" But our argument was, "What makes the reputation of the place? It's not the place itself because it's just a building. It's the people within a building who give it its reputation. The people who were there were sowing death, so the building symbolized death. But since women give life, the building will be the symbol of life." So with all of our enthusiasm, we took over the building.

Getting the military's building was the second reason there was so much antagonism toward us among certain nerve centers. The first reason was that we exist at all. When we got there we were shocked because the building, which appeared so nice on the outside, was destroyed and plundered inside. The whole computer system, the whole electricity system, had been sabotaged. They had even taken the toilet bowls out of the bathrooms with them when they left. The office of General Cédras leaked. The building was practically a ruin. If you treat the place where you're working like that, and you have the folly to think that you are running a country, it doesn't surprise me that the country is broken like it is. I can't understand something like that, especially since the army's budget had been $210 million (U.S.$70 million), more than 40 percent of the national budget! We had to make a request of the United Nations Educational, Scientific, and Cultural Organization (UNESCO) to fund the repairs.

The day Titid gave us the building, we had all the telephone lines changed. That very same afternoon, we started receiving threatening calls. The women used to intercept the telephone calls so the threats didn't get to me, I only learned of them afterward. That increased the question of security for us. Later I started getting threats at my home. I had to have security with me all the time. When you're a minister, your personal life is reduced to three times zero.

One of our first steps was to visit the people in all nine departments and meet with the organizations there. We asked each department to choose two people who would represent them, and to send them to us for training so they could know how to represent the ministry in their own area. We gave them legal training and training on women's health and psychological screening, to arm them—no, I don't like the word *arm*—to equip them to train *other* women. We always underscored that. We didn't want to create an elite.

Since women's organizations reinforce women's rights, we established a service for organizations. We also had a service for complaints, so the women could determine what they want, so that you're not thinking for them. If you want decentralized power, you must begin by sitting with people and listening to them. This let us sharpen our programs to be in touch with the women and respond to their needs.

One of the first things that we saw was a fight against poverty. This would allow women to begin to enter into economic power. A primary thing they were asking for was credit. We searched out a line of credit for women in the banks, so they could enter the macro or formal economy. One of our dreams was to establish a sort of Grameen Bank, a bank of the poor in Haiti. We even spoke about that to Mrs. Danielle Mitterrand, wife of the former prime minister of France, who was very close to the head of the Grameen Bank.

The other thing women wanted most was justice and reparations for the abuses against them. We worked with the minister of Justice and participated in the training of a new police force, showing how they should deal with violence against women.

We put a lot of emphasis on health. Programs related to women's health have always been oriented toward them as mothers, so we wanted to at least provide decent maternity care throughout the country. We spoke with the Ministry of Public Health about it.

Also we insisted, along with the minister of national education, that the training of girls change profoundly. Should the girls learn how to sew, cook, et cetera, while the little boys don't have the right to cook? If he cooks, he's a fag, so they say. Schooling in Haiti reinforces these ideas.

Something that really pleased us was that one woman who was effectively against women's issues came to bring us the complaint that she took her child to school, and what did the child come home knowing? The old song that says,

> A little man not much bigger than a rat
> Beats his wife with a wooden bat.

Kids learn this in school and there is a little dance that goes with it, where they fall down and get up again. It continues,

> *Madame*, that will teach you square
> Not to eat my apples when I'm not there.

That means that the things in the home are not hers, and that the little man has the right to beat his wife because she ate some food while her husband was out. I learned the song as a kid, too, and really liked it. When that person came to complain to us, that made the presence of the ministry useful. It was one step toward transforming society from the bottom to the top.

While I was minister, there were two big demonstrations against the ministry. Some people couldn't understand why that pleased me. But we don't have the solution for everything; it's normal that people question us. That allowed us to reevaluate ourselves.

In the first demonstration women were saying, "We heard there's credit for women, the president promised credit. Where's the credit? What did you do with the money?" That pleased me because, in fact, I was running after the money. Every time I went, they told me, "Go to this place. No, go to that place." That demonstration gave me more strength to put pressure on and get the credit. Then when school was going to start in October, the mothers held a big protest because they wanted to send their children to school. As a woman minister, what were you doing for them? When that happened, it gave me power to say, "Oh yes, we need the children in school. The educational system must open up for them." A woman in the ministry said, "We're just firefighters here." But being firefighters allowed us to get more than one thousand enrollment scholarships.

Unfortunately, a lot of our plans came down to the budget. That blocked us. But we planted a good seed for the next generation.

Some people in the state don't want the ministry to continue. Each time there's a budget vote in the Parliament, they discuss whether or not to close the ministry. Have you seen a cat with a mouse? This is the game they're playing with us. They want us to believe that keeping the ministry open is a favor, and that in fact we are nothing. When women enter into power, we must guard that place. We need to fight to make Parliament know they're not doing us a favor. We need to organize ourselves so the results of our battle won't be taken from us.

We have an expression that says *Nap kontinwe lite jouk mayi a mi*. We will continue to struggle until the corn has ripened. But corn is never ripe, you see; you harvest it green and then you cut the kernels off, you grind it, you do what you want with it, but it's never really ripe. That means that until we cannot go another step, until the bitter end, we'll fight. We won't cede so much as a fingernail. *No pasaran*. They will not get past.

These days I am evaluating our success in the ministry. Since I've returned to my former job as director for social medicine in the Diocese of Grand-Anse, I've been hearing testimonies of women. Even if the work of the women's ministry was blocked, a certain sensitizing took place. Women are beginning to represent themselves as people with rights. It's a beautiful gain. When a person is psychologically ready to defend herself as a human being, that's a big victory. She won't get lost, she won't allow anyone to walk on her. I believe that's the most positive result, when adult women tell you that they are happy they didn't die before they experienced that.

GRACITA OSIAS

The Marriage Question

My mother and father didn't marry in the church, but they lived together a long time and had nine children. My father, he loved a lot of women. He had twenty-five children with about six mothers. But he met my mother and he said, "This girl, that's it, definitely," and they moved in together. But he cheated the whole time. Even when he became an old man, he kept on cheating. When I was twelve, he went to cheat with a young girl that could have been his daughter and he had a child with her. Then he abandoned us.

My mother wasn't happy, but I believe the person that was least happy was me. I couldn't handle that at all. My father always had a special affection for me. I was the one who always made his food, who did everything for him. I spoke with him, I said, "You can't leave my mother with all us children. You have to go get the child you just had and bring him to my mother's house and after that, leave the girl. You already have nine children here. You can't abandon us." He said, "My child, what you say is true. I hear what you're saying." I got happy, I knew I was going to be all right.

Instead, he totally disregarded our cause. He didn't take it seriously. He half left the house; well, he came and went. Oh, my heart broke.

He didn't completely neglect us, but economically he did. My mother was forced to carry the whole load. But not one day did my mother ever argue with my father. She truly has a lot of dignity. She simply ignored it all, she never argued. My father abandoned us and she just left it at that.

When I entered teaching school, my father paid for three years. When I got to my last year, he didn't want to pay for me. Now my mother, when I was crying over this, she borrowed money to help pay the tuition for me.

There are so many cases like that, where men make children, but it's the mother who has to fight to carry the load, to pay for education and support the household. My mother had to struggle, struggle, work, work, to pay for the children's schooling until they all grew up. As soon as I finished school, I had to start working right away because my mother had other children who couldn't go to school because of the tuition. I started to pay for their schooling out of my salary teaching at a religious school, where I earned 125 gourdes (U.S.$8.34) a month. Only now that her last child is twenty-six years old and all the kids are responsible for themselves, do she and I have some relief.

It's *the* question of the Haitian woman's life: the marriage question, the mistress question. Have other women spoken to you about this? When a woman is married, the man has the right to humiliate her and beat her, and then he abandons her with the children to carry the load. So one of the issues that women discuss a lot in their organizations is how women and men can have equality. That's why one of their principle demands is that, in the household, we must have respect. We're not the same, we're two different people, but you can have one complementing the other.

In Haiti, a girl that doesn't marry doesn't have value. If the girl isn't married to her man, she can't sing in the church choir; sometimes she can't even be a teacher. And if a teacher gets pregnant and she's not married, *poof!,* she's fired.

My cousin, that happened to her. She was working in a religious school and got pregnant. The director fired her, put her out to dry—but not the man who made her pregnant. He kept teaching. And he didn't even take care of my cousin. He said the child wasn't his, but when it was born, that child resembled him to a T!

All women are dominated by problems in the relationship between men and women. It touches the bourgeois class and the poor class. But it's true—the women in the poor class here are exploited twice as much.

Sometimes I have to ask myself why I didn't go through a wedding and get formally married. But I say, what is marriage? You see people who are doing very well, they're living together, they're good friends. As soon as they marry, problems come along to change things. The man begins to think he has rights over the woman, he can beat her and do what he wants to her. That's always stayed in my head. I'm fine the way I am.

After I had two children with the man I'm living with, we wrote up a paper as a civil act. Even when I got my civil papers, I never truly valued that as marriage. We get by very well. The only thing I need is for him to respect me, and I respect him also. Marriage isn't what would create that respect. His sister always says we must marry, but signing papers doesn't have any importance.

I don't need a man supporting me economically. I don't make big money, but what I make, I live with it. I always looked to the example of my mother. If she could support us, then I must always look for a way to support myself. When a man in Haiti—in general, not for everybody—supports a woman economically, that gives him power over her.

In all my talks with my sisters, I always tell them: Your first duty is to learn to be responsible for yourself. Don't count on men! Because the day he dumps you, you'll be able to carry yourself economically.

Walking with My Little Coffin

During the years of the coup d'etat, I worked with raped women. But it wasn't easy at all, at all. A true Calvary. But if I had heard of all these things happening and didn't do anything, wouldn't I be an accomplice? I couldn't just say, as the expression goes, "A sheep's problems aren't the business of the goat." I'm a woman, too; they could have done the same thing to me.

We used our own tactics to gather information about the rapes. We used street theater. This is the way we did it: If we knew that a woman in a specific courtyard had been raped, my friend would go and sit in that courtyard. Later on, I'd pass by. My friend would call me, "Hey Louise, where are you going?" I would answer, "Oh, I'm rushed, rushed, rushed! I can't stop." Lie! That was a big lie because that person's house was exactly the place I was going. And then the conversation would continue, like this:

My friend would say, "Louise, where are you going?" I'd say, "I've got to go visit some friends who've been raped! I'm going to see how they're doing and take them to the doctor." Lie! This was another lie, I was headed straight for that woman's house so she could give me information. When I'd arrive in the court-yard, the woman would be ironing. She'd hear what I said, and she'd stop and look at me sadly. And then she'd say to me, "Why don't you sit down for a little bit?" I'd answer, "No, no, I can't stay. I'm going somewhere else." She'd tell me, "Sit down. Please. If you sit down, I'll explain something to you." So I would sit down. She'd put the iron up and begin telling her story. The woman would say, "You know, they raped me, too. They broke into my house at two o'clock in the morning. Three men raped me, they beat me, they raped my younger sister."

I'd say to myself, "Ah-hah!" She would start to cry. She'd put her head on my shoulder and cry and I'd rub her back. I'd say, "You shouldn't be ashamed. It's those guys who should be ashamed! They're savages. Only beasts could do such a horrid act." I'd tell her, "Love is something that's too good, too precious, for you to feel ashamed when you've been a victim." I would tell her not to cry be-cause we're there for her. We're there!

Cheri, the women told me everything, how it all happened. I gathered infor-mation from many women, house after house. And then the women spread the news to each other. They trusted me so much that if they learned of another woman, they would run to tell me. They would bring that woman to me. I would say, "Thank you, my sister." Then I would meet with her and help her like the other ones.

The FRAPH men would rape the women until they bled. They told the women, "We're going to beat you so hard, when Aristide comes back he'll just find your scraps." The worst story was the one of that little baby, one year old. The rapists couldn't rape her. So they raped her mother and when they were finished, all three ejaculated into that baby's mouth. Listen to me well! They said, "You're a woman, too." A one-year-old baby, you hear? Poor little thing! She got all the germs from their semen, and then, of course, her intestines weren't prepared for that kind of thing. This baby is still sick. This week, the diarrhea stops; the next week, the diarrhea comes back. Her mother is in our group and we're still working with her and her baby.

When I was getting information, I couldn't write anything, absolutely nothing, in front of them. My head had to be clear. When five or ten people were telling me the story of their rapes, I had to remember all the names, all the details. I'd take the information and I'd say, "Okay, I'm going to leave now, but I'll see you soon, hear? I'll come back to see you." And as soon as I got on the road, I'd look for a place I could stop. I'd sit down and write down everything the women told me. And the next time I met with them, I'd bring my notebook. They'd think it was a personal notebook. I'd question them again, trying to review my earlier notes very subtly without their knowing. Then I could verify that the previous information was correct. If I missed something, I could add it. *Cheri*, that was very difficult work but I had to do it. I did it because I needed the information.

I wrote up the information and gave it to the institution I was working with and they put it on file. With it, they could start lawsuits and accompany the women through the judicial process. Because the women wanted justice! Also, a lot of international human rights organizations came and I gave them the information. I got together the facts for a complaint some American lawyers were bringing before the Organization of American States Inter-American Commission on Human Rights. We're still working on that.

My work didn't stop with gathering information. Meeting with them as victims of rape wasn't enough. When we finished taking their testimony, we needed to get them together and get them to form a women's organization. We helped them understand their rights. Also, we wanted to help these women be the owners of their bodies. No one else may have control over their bodies. Nobody may have authority over them.

But my life was in danger. If the rapists had known I was doing this, they would have shot me in the streets. It was like I was walking with my little coffin under my arm. But even if they had beaten me, it wouldn't have mattered. It would have been because I was part of something just and noble.

I didn't want to have a heavy heart when I was going to bed at night because my conscience was troubling me. Where is God? He's in my heart because I have a conscience. I know right from wrong. With a conscience, when you do wrong, you know it. You can't sleep at night. When you do good, frankly, you feel well. You lie down and say, "Dear God, I feel good," and then sleep carries you away. So I always asked God for strength and courage so I could struggle.

Ah, but it was hard, hard! Now I have another problem: I can't make love to any man. I had a boyfriend when I was doing this work. I called him one day and told him I was coming over. When I arrived at his place, he was lying on the bed with the intention of making love to me. I lay down next to him, but when he started to caress me, I pushed him away! I pushed him away because I had only one thought in my mind: he could have a gun under his pillow. That was all I could think about.

It wasn't true, of course. Not at all! It was like I was experiencing all that the women had explained to me. Listen, I spent those three years of hell. Hell! It's been one year since I've made love with a man. I don't need men. They disgust me.

Imagine a man breaking into your house. You don't know him, he's not your boyfriend, he's not your friend. Even if he were your friend, he would have asked you. It would have been an agreement between the two of you to make love. Now not only does the person beat you, he makes you have sex with him, he forces you to suck him, he stinks! You can understand how bad that situation is. And the men know you but you don't know them, because they have masks on their faces. You might be in the streets and they'll mark you. To this day, the women feel embarrassed when they're walking in the streets. They've almost gone crazy, they've been so disturbed by what happened to them. And a lot of them got diseases in their vaginas, they even got gonorrhea. When we found that out, my organization gave me money to bring them to the doctor. I've visited every single doctor in Port-au-Prince, I've been to every single pharmacy in Port-au-Prince to help the women get rid of their disease.

Lady, I'm telling you . . . During those years of hell, people disappeared. Some girls were raped in front of their mothers or fathers. And if one of the parents talked, the attackers would beat them, kill them, or take them away. The rapists always threatened the women. They said, "Don't you go tell the radio about this or we'll come back and kill you." And I recorded all this information in a notebook.

So imagine: If the rapists knew I was doing this, they could have shot me in the streets. Sometimes when I met with the women, people climbed up the walls to listen to us. My life was in danger. I could feel good during the day but when the night came, I had trouble. When I heard they were forcing sons to have sex with their mothers, I got scared. I have a twenty-one-year-old, and I kept saying to myself, "Will they come to my house one night and force my son to have sex with me?" He said to me, "Mama, don't worry. You have two sons. If they try to force me to sleep with you, I would rather they shoot me. You'll still have another son." I can tell you, at night, whenever I heard the noise of a straw breaking in the yard or a dog barking, I sat up in bed and lit a cigarette. I was shaking, I was so scared.

Every time I was going out, honestly, I would kneel down. I would talk to God and to my kids, I would stroke them and kiss them. Tears would roll down my cheeks. I'd tell them, "If I come back, great. If not, know that pigs have eaten me or that my body's been dropped off at the dumping grounds." I told them, "If day and night go by and I don't come back, wait for the next morning and alert my co-workers." I was never sure if I was going to come home. That pained me.

The way you see my hair now, that's not how it used to be. I used to have dreadlocks and wear African clothes and tie a scarf around my head. But when I went out in the streets, everyone looked at me. I was very suspicious and nervous. Sometimes I'd be walking and I would suddenly imagine everyone was looking at me. I would get so scared I'd jump onto a bus. Still, I would have preferred to die with a clear conscience instead of not doing what I had to do.

So I changed my look. Some people asked me, "Louise, what's going on?" I went to a friend's beauty parlor and asked her to put a permanent in my hair. My hair got long and I had all kinds of hairdos. Every time I went out, I put on makeup, I combed my hair a different way. Some friends were surprised to see me like that. They said, "Wow! Look at Louise!" Because they knew me with a different style, an African style. I told them, "Well, you know, I want to feel like a young girl again." I joked about it. But, in fact, I was scared. A few days after, I would go back to the beauty parlor and have my hair cut again. My kids said, "Mama, what in the world are you doing? You're getting a new hairstyle every day." My oldest son said, "Hmm. Mama is feeling young again." But that was only my strategy.

In the struggles happening, I devoted myself entirely to the cause. I gave myself, my soul, even if I was afraid all the time. I didn't menstruate for a long time. I had many health problems. It was trauma that caused that. I tell you, sometimes suddenly I had those panic attacks. I was scared, I was so scared! Sometimes I could be lying down in my bed with the lights off and I'd feel the presence of someone in the room. It wasn't true. It was just an illusion, a creation of my mind. And I haven't even been raped.

But when you sit there, and people tell you about one thing only . . . all the women tell you stories of rape, the same stories over and over again, and you listen to them, and you write the stories. . . . Ah, my dear . . . all these things remain engraved in my heart.

During those horrible days, I was fighting against two different forces: the force of my fear of being hurt and the force of my conscience that was pushing me to do that work. I would have felt very badly if I weren't doing it. My conscience wouldn't have been in peace. I heard that people were suffering and I knew that God would have asked me, "What did you do when you heard that? Did you use all your strength and your intelligence to strengthen the voice of those who couldn't speak?" So I said to God, "Here I am!"

CLAUDETTE WERLEIGH
Women's Business[6]

I've just come from a meeting in Stockholm of women who were either current or former prime ministers or presidents.[7] One of the interesting things they were saying is that when they got together as women, things went just fine. There wasn't any competition and they felt at ease. It was quite different from their meetings with men, and they enjoyed it. While they were saying that, I was remembering the mixed-gender courses we used to have at the popular education center where I was the director. Whenever there were just one or two women in with the men, they listened, but they didn't talk much, they didn't participate. Whenever there were five or six women, even if they were still a minority among thirty men, then the women had confidence in themselves and it was a whole different story. They just opened up, they blossomed. They gave the meetings a whole new atmosphere, there was more dynamism. The women put out flowers, they sang. Everything became energized.

It was interesting that very high-level women, in top levels of government, were saying the same thing that grassroots women in Haiti were saying. That was good to hear, because it meant that we women have a certain way of working together, of sharing the burden, and at the same time, coping with life through laughter and a joy that we don't experience when we work with men.

This special spirit is something that we women have to bring not only to everyday life, but to political life. Women need to find ways to shape politics to make it vibrant, make it joyful, make everybody work together without competition and without the negative aspects that currently dominate politics.

In Haiti, we say women are the *poto mitan*, the center pole that supports all buildings, supports the whole structure. But when I first started to work, I wasn't really conscious of gender. I remember the first time the issue was raised to me. I was secretary general of Caritas International. A man from England interviewed me and asked me how I could do what I was doing, as a woman working with men. I was doing it as Claudette, as myself. But after that, in about 1979, I participated in a meeting with women and that's when I started to focus on women and their particular life in Haiti: what they're doing, how they do it, what they're saying.

A Haitian proverb says, *Tout fanm se fanm, men tout fanm pa kreye egalego.* All women are women, but not all women are created equal. When we're speaking about Haitian women, we need to refer to the cultural and socioeconomic environment to which they belong. Haitian women's lives are distinguished by their economic condition, their origin, and their social position, rather than just their identity as women.

Many distinctions mark the lives of poor women, but all share certain conditions. They all have an insufficient salary for a hard job, usually in dangerous conditions or toxic atmospheres. They often far surpass normal workday hours. They have no job contract or respect from their employers for conditions such as illness or pregnancy. They have no access to day care for their children, cafeterias or snack stands at the workplace, adequate transportation, or medical care. After their workday, they're expected to do housework.

In a sense, women are muzzled, their words have no voice. Their work doesn't count unless they exhaust themselves from four o'clock in the morning until late at night. Many women speak of sexual relations as a chore, a night job, or even a matrimonial obligation done when the man feels like it. The percentage of women who get beaten is quite high.

But women aren't only oppressed by men; their oppression has been instilled within them. It's not unusual to knock at a door and hear a response from a female voice, "There's no one here." It's not uncommon to hear a woman say, "I don't work," while she's really wanting to say, "I don't have a job that I'm getting paid for, but I work sixteen hours a day cleaning house, cooking meals, washing, and caring for children."

In the women's groups that have proliferated, they feel more at ease talking about the humiliation that's been inflicted on them by men and society. And anyway, it's easier for them to learn very quickly the different roles: president, treasurer, or secretary. After learning those roles, they usually feel more comfortable going into mixed groups.

But in some places, women feel it's more difficult to work in women's groups. When they try to organize, the men are very aggressive. Sometimes they throw stones at the women or the places where they meet. I don't know why this is, but the men think the women are getting together just to criticize them. In those places, the women prefer to work in mixed groups. The essential thing is that they realize they have to express themselves and take an active part in a group, not just carry water and prepare the food. They have to discuss what's going on and give their ideas.

When people repeat insistently that "women don't do politics" or that "political business is not women's business," they're speaking about politics in the strictest sense of the word—the direction of the state and determining its activity. But of course, women have always been very involved. For example, during the dictatorship, women traveled from one place to another, bringing food and doing marketing. Because they were traveling back and forth, they knew what was happening, so they could bring the news to other people. They knew how to be careful, what to do and not do. During that time, they were very involved in stimulating resistance to the dictatorship with their songs and their determination.

I've heard some men say, "Wait a minute, how can we not get involved when the women are so involved themselves?" Men would feel ashamed, or that they were less human, if they let women be totally in charge. It seems that they would feel like cowards if they didn't get involved while women were active.

Haitian women participate in politics. There are, however, important issues to consider. We should clearly define, first of all, the type of women we're referring to. Until all women in Haiti, not only the elite class, have access to the decision-making process, we can't say that Haitian women *really* participate in the country's politics.

Participation in the political agenda means that merchant women should be involved in commercial politics, factory workers and the unemployed in labor politics, and renters and homeless in housing programs. The women who ensure that their homes and children are clean and in good order should be able to extend their skills and experiences to a broader community. Also, women who are the main providers of health care in their homes and communities, using herbal teas and massages, should have access to other techniques and be integrated into health policy in order to make primary health care accessible to the poor. Women involved in agriculture certainly have something to say about agrarian policies and the price of agriculture products; women vendors in the marketplace, undoubtedly, are more knowledgeable about inflation than most male politicians.

Another important consideration is the final goal. While it's important for more women to be concerned and to get involved in the decision-making process, their involvement shouldn't just be a matter of their presence, but of their ability to offer an alternative course, or to bring about something that's lacking. The struggle for a woman to achieve posts of distinction is fine and good, but more important than her position is her agenda. Will she seek to ensure that the market vendors at the roadsides, the charcoal merchant, and the peasant woman living in the hills can participate in decisions that determine their country's policies? Will she use her experience to maintain roads, employment, and health? She is biologically the holder of life, but will she have a politic in favor of life? Will she choose to spend public funds for education and housing, instead of buying guns and other military weapons that kill people? More significant than whether women should have access to the highest political posts is that all women can participate in setting up a new society rooted in justice and the satisfaction of basic needs of the Haitian population.

The political field, in a way, is dominated by intellectuals behind the curtains. By that I mean that plans and decisions are made in little rooms, in politicians' offices, without taking enough consideration of the real life outside. Currently, the whole world is organized so you have political parties, you have a president, and you have specified ways for people to play their roles in politics. We have to find other ways that women can participate. We have to find ways to bring the qualities that women have in other fields into political life, to make things work better.

Despite women's full participation in society and the economy, there are some very curious contradictions. For example, Haiti has never had a woman minister of commerce even though in Haiti, ninety to ninety-five percent of the trade is actually done by women. This even happened when I was prime minister. It was only after I wasn't prime minister any longer that it occurred to me that the person who is traditionally appointed in Haiti as minister of commerce is a man. We should have to refer to the women, since they know better than anyone else how things go in the market, how to do their own marketing, how to fix prices, et cetera.

I mentioned the case of the minister of commerce. That's just one illustration of the contradictions. Haiti is a country where we've already had a female president, we've had a female prime minister, cabinet ministers, secretaries of state, and women parliamentarians. Of course, the number of women in high office is still small compared to the number of men. But what I want to express here is that, at the same time, it seems natural for women to serve in politics. For instance, when I was prime minister, perhaps others were against me, but I never heard anyone say or express that I couldn't do the job because I was a woman. But at the same time, women aren't in political life enough that we can say that women are shaping the politics in Haiti. In real life, every other aspect of the society and the economy of the country is carried out by women. But this is not the case in formal politics.

One of the challenges that we have to face is how we can involve women so much that they can imbue politics with their creativity, with their determination to struggle and to fight, with everything they've brought and keep bringing in ordinary life. Haitian women are becoming increasingly aware of their responsibilities, and what's interesting is that they aren't just fighting on women's issues or just for equality with men. Most of them are also fighting for a better society. Women are the ones who sustain life. If we could bring all that strength into politics in Haiti, maybe we could shape not only politics but also a new country.

Support for the Children

I have seven children. I have a big young man, twenty-eight years old, who's not working. All he does is take cigarettes: he smokes, he smokes, he smokes. He has no weight on him. He says, "It's me who should be giving you what you need, not the reverse. But I can't find work. Here's the thing, Yolande: When people tell me not to smoke, why don't they give me some work to do?" Go to my house now, and you'll find him still lying in bed. He says he feels like his head is empty inside.

This makes me feel like I'm dying. *Woy*, I'm dying, and I don't know what to do. The children's hunger is the big problem. The children are getting even skinnier in my hands.

My children have three different fathers. I'm at the point where I wish they didn't have one. It's too hard for me. As for one of the three fathers, they killed him. This happened at a demonstration on Fifth Avenue. When the police arrived, they shot him and a food vendor and they both died.

Another father, then, he's alive but he has his back against the wall. Sometimes, during the embargo, he gave the children ten gourdes (U.S.$.67). The children got by on that, you understand, and on what I added when I could. But I must tell you: that man just doesn't have anything. He can't take care of the children. One of his little ones is twelve years old. And I'm just now putting him in school for the first time. What can I say? I'm resigned to it.

Well now, I have two more children whose father is also still living. He doesn't give them even one gourde, not one cent! Recently I felt too despairing; this had gone on too long. I went to court to send a warrant for him. I got to the court and said, "I've come to demand my women's rights." I sent a first warrant, then a second warrant.

My grown son said, "Yolande, it's not worth all this effort. You're putting too much effort into trying to get him judged in court. You know he won't give you anything." Another of my sons said, "Mama, it's a waste. Stop now. Don't go asking from others. Ask him to give you five gourdes, he won't give it to you. Ask him for ten gourdes. . . . What are you going to get in court? You know he won't give you anything. If he was going to give anything, he would only give to his two children anyway, not to you or the other kids." He said, "Yolande, you don't need to go judge him before the state. Leave it alone. Since the children were small you've been battling to see if maybe he'll want to give them something. Today you're still battling. But he won't give anything."

Sometimes I see this man in the street and he says, "Oh, I don't have any money. Why don't you go do something to make some money for them?" Well, I don't need to repeat what he tells me to do to make money for the children! I say, "Huh! I'm already old and now I'm going to go do *that*?"

All women like me should stand up to say a word. I ask for support for our children. I ask for justice for women because we've suffered a lot.

YANIQUE GUITEAU DANDIN
A Country's Problems, A Woman's Problems

I started to learn the reality of the country when I went to nursing school. I did internships, went into the hospital, went to Cité Soleil, went to the countryside where we did community work. I said: "*Vwala*! Aha!" I started to see that the country was one big problem.

I realized that, to be a nurse, I had to struggle for the people's health care to change. I decided I had to study anthropology to complement my health knowledge and have more tools for the resistance. It helped me tie all the pieces together.

I plunged myself into the battle for change, not as a woman on the basis of womanhood, but with the consciousness of a citizen.

I started working with the League for Women's Action, an old organization that had gotten women the right to vote. The women were closely tied to Duvalierist power. We wanted to do literacy work with factory workers and maids, but to do that in the old days you had to pass via the groups the dictatorship had established. If not, you would have been considered a subversive and been killed. Plus, these were the only groups there were. But we always searched out the sympathetic people to help us get around the problems. This wasn't easy. With the League, we had to watch out so other women didn't become aware of what we were doing.

I wanted to create neighborhood committees. With my health training, I could enter neighborhoods and talk with people easily. I didn't have obstacles that other people had because I wasn't really talking "politics." It was the health program that let me meet women and their children. It was a trip to see how much even nonpolitical politics could create change. I found women sitting in their homes because unemployment is very high in the shantytowns. They were the ones I usually dialogued with—more on global issues than on women's issues per se. Finally, the League prevented me from doing anything further.

Women were less involved in those days. Don't forget the women's movement didn't really take off until after 1986. Back then, the women were in the midst of a bunch of men who had ideas for change but were nonetheless very antidemocratic in their behavior toward women in the movement. Before women had their own autonomous groups, the men couldn't really understand how the women could resist the same way as them.

Something every woman experienced during those days was being seen by the men as a sex object. That created a lot of problems in the resistance, breaking down organizations with all kinds of—how can I put it?—emotional issues. I'll bet there aren't many people who'll admit that, but it was really significant. There was always a message that, well, you had to fool around with them a little.

The work I did in the shantytowns was urban resistance. Nursing school helped me understand the city. Then things got even more interesting when I realized the country is not urban, it's rural. That's where I said okay, the path to change is not about sitting around in the city. So I asked to go to the country-side for my internship. And that's where I really began to discover my true country. Actually, I'm from the countryside, but I emigrated when I was little. When I had gone back before, it was always on a picnic.

It was essential that organizing be done in the mountains. The towns already had lots of troops; it was much harder in the countryside. And in rural areas, women's issues weren't spoken about at all.

I had two tools in my hands: anthropology and medicine. Granted, under the dictatorship, there was nothing you could do besides help people with little development projects. Still, I was trying to reorient development work into re-sistance. My part was figuring out the health systems people used to survive, and then seeing what alternative systems we could construct together. We cre-ated some isolated projects, but I realized that as long as the global system of the country didn't change, those would remain small and marginalized. For me personally, though, they were very interesting experiments because they helped me theorize about a lot of issues.

Prior to 1986, people who were working on women's issues saw the problems primarily in terms of relations with men in the household, violence against women, et cetera. But in rural areas it was hard to perceive the problems in that sense. Issues specific to women were not the order of the day at all. And when I tried to organize on broader political issues, the women were com-pletely absent.

I had always considered the struggle a global one. But little by little I came to realize that women's issues were a reality we had to pay attention to. I decided I'd have to try and understand what would mobilize women.

I observed that there were natural groups of women. For instance, there were groups of market women, especially among the youth. They were so organized they even wore the same style of clothing and had the same schedule to go to the marketplace and the corn mill.

I have to tell you that in my research group, I was the only woman. It was quite a battle to tell the others, "Listen, we have to organize groups for the women." Because so many of the issues we were dealing with were central to women, like the tax the government demanded in the marketplace. Well, declaration of war! But we started searching out the women and figuring out how to help them in their work and their analysis. Finally, by 1986, the idea of creating a women's grassroots movement in rural areas started to become a reality.

All the work gave way to a first result: Duvalier was ousted and the grassroots scene opened up, still with a majority of men but with some women.

There was an explosion of the women's movement, too. The first new group, Women of Haiti, had all social classes in it. The first big women's demonstration had people from all classes, as well. More groups started to form within the various sectors. Some were centered on women who lived comfortably, while others said, "Most women are from down under, from the mountains and the slums; let's orient the women's movement that way." As I told you, I hadn't been directly involved in the women's movement before 1986, because my impression was that it had mainly been oriented in battles against men. I started realizing that women's autonomy from the point of view of organizing was indispensable, but I never saw it in a feminist sense.

I was still working in the countryside, but with a few other women I decided to form a nurses' union in 1986 to see if we could create structures to make democracy a reality.

We didn't construct it as a women's organization—it was a professional organization—but along the road we realized that women had a problem. For instance, the nurse who was director of the Nursing Division of the Ministry of Health was paid $1,200 Haitian (U.S.$400), while all the other directors, who were men, were paid $1,500 (U.S.$500). She was at the exact same organizational level as them. When I asked for an explanation, they had none. I said, "Absolutely, there is a women's problem here." Don't forget that the doctor's profession is dominated by men—not just in Haiti, but everywhere. Nurses' problems are closely tied to the fact that their profession is composed of women. Every single nurse in Haiti is a woman. And the relationship between doctors and nurses is not professional: it reflects male-female inequality. We made it clear that the nurses' battle was a battle of professional *women*, not just *professionals*. At our last nurses' congress, we amended our by-laws to inscribe the nurses' struggle within the women's struggle.

I must point out that in Haiti's whole health profession, we are the only combative organization. Plus we are the only union of professionals. We said to ourselves, "Ah! If we lead this democratic struggle well, it will be a big contribution for women's struggles. It will affirm women's capacity in the eyes of society. It will show what women can do to change Haitian society."

We've been fighting the Ministry of Health. The minister said he wouldn't sit down with our organization. The women said, "*Vwala*! If it had been doctors, he would have sat down with them." The moment doctors say "Ah!" they sit down to negotiate. We spent a month protesting and no one paid any attention to us. The women were indignant.

So we occupied the office of the Health Department. Whenever people passed by and saw us, they said, "Oh my God! It's three women!" You understand? They meant that it was so extraordinary that *women* were causing all this disruption. We got this same response in all the publicity, press, and public reaction.

When everything else failed, we said, "Okay, we'll do a hunger strike." Six of us refused all food for a month. People said, "Wow! That minister is harsh. Here you have *women* doing this and he still won't respond!" You understand? The public said, "Boy, those women are tough!" And after three days the ministry ceded.

Little by little I've come to feel that my resistance is as a woman. There's a lot of work that women's groups are doing—like women's radio programs and publications—that have opened my eyes about women's roles in establishing a democratic society. And in the world that's being redefined, we need to find our place not only as women, but also as Haitian women.

I hope all this talk can push the battle for democracy further.

MARIE JOSEE ST. FIRMIN
Deciding My Life

I'm the only girl in a family of five children. My whole childhood was spent with boys. I learned all the games that boys play and lived like they lived. My house didn't have the discrimination that men are *kòk chante*, crowing roosters, while women should work all day.

But the social message that was visible in society around me was that certain kinds of work were women's work. Men say, "I'm a man, so I can't pick up the broom. I'm a man so I can't baby-sit the kids." It's ground into all women's heads, too, that if they go beyond staying in the home, cleaning house, taking care of kids, they'll lose their role as women.

At first, that message didn't bother me. I didn't have to worry about it because I was hanging around with both boys and girls without personally feeling any discrimination, except that sometimes when my brothers went out, I had to stay home. Also, when I started to grow up and develop, I wasn't allowed to play soccer. I sometimes wondered about these things, but for me they weren't very important.

As I was growing up, though, I shared experiences with some women friends who talked about their problems and difficulties as women. Eventually I became more sympathetic to the problems of women. I got inspired to begin digging into the history of my own country. I learned that women worked as hard as men in achieving our independence in 1804. There was no discrimination of, "You are a woman, and you are a man." I learned that women have an important role to play, and so I started questioning the discrimination.

I went to secretarial school. But I got pregnant and had to abandon my schooling. I had to raise my child by myself. I didn't get any understanding from the baby's father or from society.

Though a woman with a child needs a lot of assistance and care, she usually bears and raises that child alone. Society pillages her, then treats her worse than a dog. I was made to suffer like that.

I had my son Daniel in October 1989. I was still involved with the baby's father but we didn't have enough of an understanding between us to get married. So I left him when Daniel was one month old. I've never tried to communicate with him about myself or the child since.

I made that decision but society marginalized me because I was an unmarried woman who had a child. If you're not married, you're not a human being. You're finished in the eyes of society. Even your family will abandon you.

But I said to society, "I'm going to have this child. You will accept me. You'll accept me because I'll stay under your skin until I change you, since you're the one that's wrong, not me." Instead of letting society marginalize me, I put society on the margins. I dealt it a blow.

I was raised in a society where people beat each other for no reason and no one says anything. I was raised in a society where men mistreat women in the house, in the street, on the job, in their small commerce and other professions; society says nothing about that. So society has no right to say anything to a woman who decides her own life. In my own head, I deal society that defeat.

OLGA BENOIT
Assuming the Title "Feminist"

When I was one and a half months old, my father was forced to leave the country because of Duvalier's repression. We thought he had died. We never heard from him again until I was sixteen years old. So I wasn't raised under the dictatorship of men. I was raised with my mother and a little sister. Later my grandmother came to live with us. The childhood I had with my mother and my grandmother made me believe in women.

My mother deprived herself so her children didn't lack anything. I was never hungry or naked or out of school. It was her courage and intelligence that brought me to this point. This has given me confidence in women.

One of the things that's been most important for me as an activist was when I entered into a women's organization, Solidarity Among Haitian Women (SOFA). We made a choice to work with women who are most marginalized in this society—women who live in the slums and who are market women or unemployed or work in others' homes, and peasant women. Now I know how they live, how they think, how they sleep, how they reflect, and how the problematics of women in society affects these people.

There must be more solidarity developed between women because we were raised in a society where each person is taught to focus on his or her own interests. These problems are deep and no magic is going to make them disappear. But I think everyone who wants to change society must struggle within him or herself each day to surmount all the old values this society has instilled. There are many bad values, and if we aren't conscious, we'll reproduce them.

Many people say that the problem of gender doesn't break the barrier of class, that class is a much greater unifying factor. But the reality is that you find victims among all women. Women of the upper and middle classes can wage their battles in solidarity with poor women.

Our organization is very committed to tying the women's struggle to the people's struggle. That's our slogan: "The women's struggle is the struggle of the masses." This isn't just a nice phrase we throw around; we believe that a society that doesn't respect people's rights can't respect women's rights.

I always present facts, arguments, and information about women. I remember a friend pointing out that the only books I read now are on women. It's not

Olga Benoit

that other battles aren't interesting or important; I participate in them too. But I need to be clear on where I want to go.

I can't hide, I always present myself as a feminist. For me, as another woman said, "Becoming a feminist means becoming a woman politically." I like that language, that's what feminism is to me. And I deplore the women who are organized but who can't assume the title "feminist." They say, "Well, feminists are just women leading struggles against men." People come with all sorts of accusations, saying that the women's struggle is dividing the people's struggle. Or they say, "Okay, we agree with you as long as you don't start articulating the problem in terms of womanhood." Well, I say, I'm not going to paint it with any other word. It's the action I engage in, the way that I struggle, that will show that feminism isn't what other people believe it to be.

I believe we must have men with women, joining hands to advance in this society. We must do sensitivity training, with men so that they can be conscious of the problems, but especially with women, because people who are sick need the cure most.

Women must define what quality of life we want. The plight of women didn't begin with capitalist society; it began long before that. In all different models of society, you find that since men are always accumulating power, they define things according to their own eyes, the way they see it. But now it's time for us to develop the capacity to define things according to how we see it. That's what makes me see myself as a feminist activist who believes in the battle of women, who believes in the battle of the people.

One International Women's Day—I don't remember the year—there was a big demonstration involving thousands of Haitian women from all walks of life, demanding and defending their rights. A journalist interviewed two women, one from the bourgeoisie and the other from the popular class. The poor woman from the popular class understood women's issues a thousand times better than the former. She knew exactly what the needs of women are. She knew what it would mean to liberate women. She knew what has to happen to advance the cause of women, what people need for their kids, their responsibilities—she knew it all. She could enumerate what her rights were—the right to life, health, education for her children, rights at home, respect. This from a woman who couldn't read or write! The upper-class woman who had gone to school, who had read this and that, couldn't articulate what she meant by "women's rights."

That reinforced my conviction that the evolution of the women's struggle must be based in the grassroots. These people understand the struggle. They are the ones who truly need liberation.

The background to the work I do is this: I spent many years abroad during Duvalier's regime. First I studied in Europe, then I spent six years in Africa working with women in the Congo. I worked in the Ministry of Social Affairs there in a training center for women and in social centers with women.

Then I spent eighteen years in the United States in voluntary exile because I didn't agree with what was happening in my country. I raised my kids and worked with a group mounting international pressure to overthrow the regime.

I always said that the work I did in the Congo, in a country that wasn't mine—even though I trace my roots to Africa—was the kind of work I wanted to do at home. So when my husband and I returned to Haiti in 1987, I tried to dedicate myself to that kind of work.

I must tell you that the way I speak today has not always been the way I spoke. When I grew up in the middle class, I was incapable of seeing certain things even though they were in plain sight. It was a closed circle. To be from the middle class means you go to good schools. You have certain privileges that others don't have. You have access to work, generation after generation, and

Josette Pérard

therefore to the good things of life that the majority don't have. This occurs to the point that you take these things for granted and fail to realize that the poor majority aren't entitled to the same things.

The change in me was gradual. In my work with grassroots organizations and women's groups in my country, I got in touch with militant women who during the coup years were jailed, but who as soon as they were released, had the guts to distribute pictures of Titid, hidden in their bosom, at two o'clock in the morning. I worked with people facing real hardship who split whatever they had—a mandarin orange, for instance—and gave part to someone even poorer. I met people who, despite their utter misery, had a sense of hope.

In the sphere I grew up in, there was no interest in defending the right of the majority. People were busy defending strictly personal interests. Well, I changed. I gained a different sense of the truth. I saw the truth residing in the majority. Now, for instance, Tatanne, a woman from one of the peasant groups I work with, calls me this morning. Not to really tell me anything but to ask how I, her *cheri*, is, because she hasn't heard from me in a while. This is because I've had a relationship of trust with her that overrides class interest. I'm defending the same things she is; we're on the same side.

This is the biggest change in my life. I can't think of not doing what I'm doing. When I leave the office of the Lambi Fund at four o'clock, I'm not through. All the time in my head I'm thinking about what I'll tell that woman I'll be meeting tomorrow. The groups I work with have become my life. It's my duty as a citizen and a woman. It's not just my job.

Recently a group of peasant women visited the office and we talked about agrarian reform. I regret that I didn't have a tape recorder. It was extraordinary to hear what they had to say. One said, "Agrarian reform, okay. But if they're just going to distribute tiny little pieces of land here and there, they're going to make the situation worse. There's already a rivalry over land and they're going to distribute land when there's not enough for everybody. They should make cooperatives, where peasants will be paid a salary for their work and the state will distribute their production."

At that moment, I saw the wisdom in our midst. I remember making the joke that I should invite the director of the agrarian reform program to come and listen to these women.

Someone else said that the state shouldn't impose the program but that they should discuss it with the local people to see if it's good for them, if they want it. This sense of democracy is innate. The urge for democratic change comes from within. It's not going to come from elsewhere, not from me and not from you; it can only come from the common sense of people who can't read or write. As Titid used to say, *analfabèt pa bèt*, the illiterate are not ignorant. They may have much more common sense than many people with diplomas.

I was so impressed in that meeting, where the women gave their opinions on national issues. They talked, for instance, about state-sponsored education, about a law in Parliament that would provide state scholarships to kids. One said, "I don't have anything against that; I would love to see it. But I would prefer the state repair the schools and build more schools so more kids can go to school. A scholarship might last only one year and after that the kid would be stuck." I am not inventing this—it came out of that same meeting, that wisdom related to everything that was discussed. This is why I have hope in the grassroots.

I remember once an American group came to Haiti to investigate the food aid being sent here. I was walking with this group in a shantytown—all white folks, with me as the only black person. A woman passed by and looped her arm though mine. I looked at her; I didn't know her. She said to me, "My sister, let us walk." As we continued walking, she said, "Don't look to your right or to your left, but there is a FRAPH group here with arms. Take your white people out of the area because anything can happen. But I have a little message for them. Tell the foreigners we don't need food. What we need is Titid back in the country." And she left. You see the sense these women have?

Here's another example: Possibly a few months after Titid's return, a group came from the United States to look at some projects we were running. One of the Americans asked the members of a grassroots women's organization that had joined us for the occasion, "I don't see that your situation has improved. Why are you still supporting Titid?" One of them answered, "Foreigner"—that's what she said—"I'll tell you. Had it not been for Titid, you wouldn't be sitting here talking with us, poor women who can't read and write, who have dirty feet, about what we think about the political situation in Haiti." She said, "Titid made this possible. Titid came back to make changes. He can't give me food and I don't expect him to, because it's up to me to work and feed myself." The visitor simply shut up. I love telling this story.

You see what I mean. This is why I say that the people, the grassroots groups, peasant associations, women's groups, poor people's groups, well, they are the future.

When I look at the courage of women in the grassroots, the struggles they go through, and I compare them with women of other classes, it's night and day. Upper-class women can't do it without them. But the grassroots women can win the struggle alone because they are the majority. Now the carriage is leaving and upper-class women run the risk of being left behind unless they realize what's going on and join forces with the majority to defend their rights.

5 RESISTANCE TRANSFORMING POWER

WHEN SHIFTING THE BALANCE OF POWER IS NOT ENOUGH

The most elusive part of the popular movement's agenda is that true liberation involves more than a shift from wealthy to poor, right to left, men to
women, privileged to marginalized. The goal extends beyond shifting the
margins of power to democratize government and civil society and to redis-
tribute resources. It involves actually changing the character and application
of dominant power. The goal, in short, is to take power in order to transform
power.

The *griyo* speak here of creating new economic and political structures and
of forging new human and social relations. They demand that politics be put at
the service of the people. They dream of forms of power geared to enhance, not
diminish, the full humanity and participation of every citizen. This prophetic
movement stands on the conviction that broadly and equitably shared power is
the prerequisite for dignity, quality of life, and justice.

RECONSTRUCTING POWER

The paradigm of power governing Haiti, like virtually all nations, is known
as realpolitik. Within it, power operates on a zero-sum basis, meaning that like
the finite number of pieces in a pie, there is a determined quantity of power
within society.

Realpolitik accommodates only the few who can access power according to
its logic. It thus fails in serving anyone who cannot compete by its rules, as the
desperate conditions of women in Haiti prove. *How* realpolitik is exercised is

equally devastating to the losers—through domination and coercion at all levels: political, economic, community, domestic, gender, and bodily.

A second failure of realpolitik is its theoretical underpinnings. That there exists only a defined amount of power in society is not a given.

Intrinsic to the ideology of certain sectors of the radical Haitian movement is that breaking the monopoly on power by the state, elite, security forces, and patriarchy could open the way to a positive-sum schema. In this schema, shared power and its fruits are expanded to include civil society, women, children, and all those who suffer the effects of disenfranchisement. This vision mandates that a new model be owned by, and serve, the destitute majority. This power-sharing would benefit collective interests as well as the individual members.

Power could then become a liberatory force, holding the potential for human rights, democratic voice, and economic well-being for all. A positive-sum model could become a force toward enfranchisement and justice.

The new praxis for which Haitian women and men strive requires not just a new set of people making the rules but a dramatic conversion of the rules. Recent experiences with so-called democratic government in the island nation have proved that new ends cannot evolve from the old means the oppressors used. As Audre Lorde noted, "The master's tools will never dismantle the master's house."[1]

Haitian activists refuse to accept that their vision is too idealistic to be realized, since they cannot accept that their poverty and marginalization are inevitable. Over the *cling*! of her heavy bracelets as she brushes a few dreadlocks from her eyes, Myriam Merlet says, "The more people dream, the more likely that power can change. The more people share in the same dream . . . the more likely we will achieve it collectively."

More than a dream, Haitians are putting their philosophy into practice, realizing alternative systems among themselves. The movement for transformation is struggling to create models of horizontal power[2] in a multitude of ways, from peasants having an equal chance at elective office to workers controlling their own means of production. And reaching beyond class and national and international systems, women in the popular and feminist movements are attempting to force the boundaries of change to encompass gender as well.

The Haitian experience draws on lessons from around the world: among others, from Tanzanians, South Africans, Cubans, Nicaraguan Sandinistas, and Mexican Zapatistas. At the same time, the Haitian people offer their own vision of metamorphosis to the world. What they have accomplished gives hope to others who believe it cannot be done.

A NEW PARADIGM OF POLITICAL POWER

In political domains, the Haitian resistance movement is struggling to achieve the transformation through participatory democracy. Going far beyond the periodic elections of liberal democracy, in this model civil society shares power with the state in shaping the policies that influence citizens' everyday lives. This positive-sum approach opens political systems to oppressed classes, not just the elite, and to women, not just men.

A broad coalition of groups is demanding a say, on a national level, in everything from budget allocation decisions to the scope of foreign investments within the country, from the organization of elections to the determination of factory wages.

Some groups have already expanded the power base in their communities. Under repressive regimes, vigilance committees seized back control from death squads by organizing defense systems to stop the squads from entering their neighborhoods. Using prearranged signals, lookouts notified neighbors of the entry of suspect people into their areas and arranged escapes for those targeted. And there are many ongoing successes, as well. Some peasant associations have raised local ruckuses and gotten on the radio. They have traveled many hours by decrepit flatbed trucks to descend on the Ministry of Agriculture where, the men in their straw hats and the women in the best dresses they owned or could borrow, they have sat on hallway benches for hours to present their cases. By so doing, they have won back their land and agricultural profits from the landowners. Some organizations and sectors have forced their way to the table of national government to join the consultative process. Many grassroots groups have gained ascendance through local government, electing to office their own "people's candidates," thus overturning the old system where those with money bought political power. For the first time, communal counsels and some seats in Parliament are filled with the perspectives and voices of peasants and workers.

It is not enough for civil society, or even formerly marginalized sectors of civil society, to gain a share of the power. Power circulates at different levels; the poorest and most downtrodden man still has power over his wife and children at home.[3] Thus, women, and especially poor women, must continue to evolve as active stakeholders in the widening of power. As Edèle Thébaud explains, "If women are kept outside of the process, we'll never really have democracy."

A NEW PARADIGM OF ECONOMIC POWER

Pushing her wire-rimmed glasses up on her nose, Claudette Werleigh quotes the late president of Burkina Faso, Thomas Sankara: "Water for everyone instead of champagne for a minority."

On a national level, the economic justice movement has outlined that the new strategy would, as articulated in a statement of Haiti's main environment and alternative development networks, "be based on the valorization of individuals, refusing the logic of commercialism and capitalism; make a rupture with the logic of the predator which is pillaging our natural resources; accord priority to the struggle against poverty, prioritizing basic needs; favor development of a local market, based on appropriate and healthful technology; open the possibility of self-sufficient and sustainable development; be based on food sustainable agricultural production and protect the many endangered animal and vegetable species; [and] privilege modern technologies which have a continuity with the values of traditional Haitian culture."[4] The plan would include that the state maintain ownership of the main utilities and industries. New marketing networks, neither fettered by middlemen nor undermined by foreign goods, would yield for producers maximum profits. Domestic-led development would allow people to feed and sustain themselves, rather than be used as cheap labor for foreign markets and new consumer outlets for overseas goods.

The movement is demanding a shift in the control of resources and productive capacities not only between rich and poor sectors within Haiti but also between Haiti and rich countries. Activists are working to broaden the base of power so that Haiti can have a new relationship to the global economy. As it currently stands, Haiti's decision-making maneuverability is limited by foreign aid and loans, which amount to 85 percent of the government's investment budget and 45 percent of its operating expenses,[5] though the popular movement is not in consensus about abandoning that assistance. Still, activists are advocating greater autonomy within that relationship: for control of their own development path, against the suffocating conditions attached to the aid, and against repayment of the foreign debt (roughly U.S.$1 billion), most of which was incurred by the Duvaliers.[6] Haitian alternative development organizations also propose greater integration into Caribbean markets, which could be based on equal negotiation instead of the exploitation of Haiti's so-called comparative advantage in the global market.

A radical shift in power needs to address gender-equal control over production, property, and wealth. Because Haitian women and their children carry the heaviest burden of poverty, women demand that a transformed economic system incorporate their ability to control economic resources.

A NEW PARADIGM OF SOCIAL RELATIONS

The commitment to transformation extends to new social relations, creating the possibility for a "revolution from the inside out," to quote Nicaraguan poet Gioconda Belli.[7] The analysis that power can be broadly shared and liberatory opens possibilities for a humane society. This means a society in which every citizen has the ability to eat as well as to live with dignity and meaning. This means government policies that are based on an affirmation of life and human integrity. From her bright office filled with posters advocating for children and women, Myriam Merlet encapsulates the vision: "Individuals should have the opportunity to be complete human beings, women as well as men, youth as well as old people, the lame as well as the healthy."

American writer and social activist Suzanne Pharr echoed the philosophy underscoring this agenda: "It may be that our most important political work is figuring out how to make the full human connection, how to engage our *hearts* as well as our *minds*, how to do organizing that transforms people as well as institutions."[8]

The movement for transformation is not soft or sentimental. Its prophetic aspects are merged with hard experience, critical pedagogy, and fierce ideological rejection of the established order.

Haitians often say, *Genyen tout yon sosyete ki pou chanje.* There is a whole society to be changed. This expression challenges a traditional premise of the political left that the nation-state, private capital, and the security apparatus are the most important, if not the only, sites of power contestation. Haitian women's voices and involvement widen the premise to include issues of household, community, and gender.

A society based on mutual respect and concern would facilitate poor women's entitlement within the home as well as in the popular movement and the larger political economy, and would facilitate their ability to contribute their gifts and skills to better the country at all levels.

The women working for a new society insist that compassion and love must be foundational components. Hissing a scrawny dog out of her cactus-fenced yard, rural midwife Denise Laurent says:

> We women have to change this country to make it a better place to live. We know how to love and care for people; otherwise none of us would have survived. We need to make the whole society reflect that love, so we can all take care of each other.

In the face of legacies of hatred, greed, and violence, it may seem that the agenda for social transformation is a utopian dream. But, in fact, the agenda has wrought concrete change throughout Haiti's history, dating back to the slave insurrections. Moreover, the principles of transformation guide the movement's very real progress for a new society.

EXPERIENCES IN TRANSFORMATION: *LAVALAS*

Despite some victories in transforming political and social structures, the full potential for fundamentally new power relations had always remained thwarted by the state and the elite.

Then the December 1990 election brought to power the people's platform embedded in *lavalas*, the popular movement reflected in the imagery of a flash flood, which, rushing down from the mountains, leaves the land clean of detritus. With Reverend Jean-Bertrand Aristide —famed for his fiery, pro-poor oratory and defiance of the government-army-bourgeoisie alliance—as its standard bearer, the movement surged with the hope that it could now realize the changes that had eluded it throughout history.

The vote that brought Aristide to office itself represented a new form of power, the result of expanding electoral participation to the poor for the first time. Wizened elders and illiterate youth, their registration papers carefully wrapped in bandannas, stood in long lines before small huts or church halls that bustled chaotically with electoral workers. Years of grassroots organizing, topped by a volcanic last-minute campaign of education and mobilization, produced the overwhelming victory for the people's candidate.

The ascendance of *lavalas* and the Aristide administration sparked hope for transforming power. The president articulated the potential as follows:

> The rules of this society are not the same as the old world, which requires tools of domination for victory. . . . We are not machines, and we have the vision and options available to us to rise above and beyond in the power of love.[9]

This period offered two tremendous advantages for the development of a new civil society and politic. The first came from the top, with government committed to a partnership with civil society. Advocates and organizers were recruited to government posts, and moved their operations to the sparkling white National Palace at the heart of the teeming capitol city. Popular and civic organizations were formally included in policy consultation. The administration also worked to incorporate the neglected majority who live outside what is known as the Republic of Port-au-Prince into decision-making. Decentralization initiatives included empowering local government.

Beyond participatory process, Aristide's government moved forward with policies reflecting the *lavalas* agenda. It began creating a development strategy intended to increase the quality of life. It made priorities of health education and services, immunization, increased literacy, women's economic empowerment, agricultural production, reforestation, road construction and maintenance, improved water quality, and electrification. Government policies tried to stimulate local development and prioritize women's business with credit and microenterprise. During Aristide's seven-and-a-half months in office in 1991, he raised U.S.$511 million from the international community, much of which went to these pro-poor policies. This was up from U.S.$241 million raised by the preceding government during all of 1990.[10] Though succumbing to pressure from industrialists and the United States to lower his initial goal for a new minimum wage, he succeeded in raising the wage.

The government attempted to reorient agricultural policy to promote peasant production and the natural environment on which it depends. It created a Ministry of Environment. It sought to develop such programs as the marketing of cooperatively grown goods to socially responsible networks. [Then] Minister of Agriculture François Séverain outlined the scope of the new vision, which far transcended economistic changes:

Marketing must be humanized. You have something to buy, yes, but the peasant has something to sell. If you come here as a person or a purchasing nation, you must respect the peasants and my country. My country produces beautiful mangoes, true, but it has something more. A humanized view of relations. That's what Haiti has to offer.[11]

Reflecting the citizen movement's priorities, Aristide urged a more compassionate society. He was an outspoken advocate for the rights of children, the homeless, and the handicapped. The palace hallways, like Aristide's personal residence, became the stomping grounds of dozens of boisterous orphaned and abandoned boys, and the palace gardens became the venue for feasts for beggars and street people. The head of state moved to back up his commitment with policies to protect the human rights of all citizens, including working to ratify and implement international human rights conventions and to establish an Office of the Protection of the Citizen to address rights violations.

As long as the Duvaliers' legacy remained, it would maim government and grassroots attempts at a humane society. So the administration committed itself to destroying the corruption, mismanagement, waste, and nepotism on which the legacy thrived. Aristide took a step toward demilitarizing the country by separating the police from the military.[12] He destroyed a key source of brutality and corruption, the good-ol'-boy rural sheriff system known as the section chiefs, planning to replace it with rural police. He set up a commission to explore reform of the corrupt, paralytic judiciary and began to overhaul the inequitable tax system. The government made attempts to crack down on drug trafficking.

Despite Aristide's intentions and continued popular pressure, the initiatives were erratic and met with limited success. One reason was that some departments and agencies remained under the leadership of the *ancien régime*. Too, the same small elite still held the trade and financial reigns, blocking change at the macro level. Because Haiti remained dependent on foreign aid and loans, the administration's choices were further circumscribed by foreign antagonism to the *lavalas* program, antagonism that ran high among the United States and most other donor governments. The combined result was that the brief term of the Aristide administration was ineffectual at changing the socioeconomic face of Haiti or abating policy levels.

The main blockage to the reforms was the coup, which came quickly. The old forces of power in the elite and their foreign friends united behind the military to curtail the threat to their power. The coup overturned the policies and programs that Aristide had made up to that point, and set the country on a course that, when the government was restored three years later, it could not reverse—political and financial actors, both Haitian and international, were too strong. One can only speculate on how far Aristide's administration would otherwise have chosen, or been able, to go.

Nevertheless, during the nine-and-a-half months between the election and the coup, civil society was free from repression and had the space to widen the horizons of justice exponentially. These advantages offered the second possibility for a new politic that the moment offered: pressure from the ground up.

The image of *lavalas* captures the rushing momentum of the period, which swept citizens from diverse backgrounds along toward collective transformation. Formerly silenced people claimed their civil freedoms and interjected themselves into the democratic process. The media claimed its right to free speech. *Tilegliz* groups, community-based collectives, and Haitian and foreign development institutions established new social programs to develop human potential through popular education, skills training, literacy, and child care projects. For the first time, women were able to impose their empowerment agenda onto the overarching political program.

As well, Haitians urged each other to act out a different social construction of power at microcosmic levels. They initiated a struggle for new human values, including compassion and respect. Gesticulating emphatically, human rights activist Marie Josée St. Firmin says:

> One thing we learned during this year was that people can change. . . . We saw people who'd committed terrible acts, people within the Tonton Macoute structure, even people who had created that structure, adopt a different vision.

Despite the coup and all that came after, many communities have not relinquished their political or social program, nor have they ceded the moral ground. Guitele Miradieu squints toward the stiletto stalks of the sugar cane, shimmering mirage-like under the sun, and says,

We saw people being killed like flies, violence and rape and bar-
barism everywhere. But we know that we have a morality inside
ourselves that we have to hold on to. We're better than that.

EXPERIENCES IN TRANSFORMATION: WOMEN IN THE MANAGEMENT OF POWER

Women's growing political participation is helping expand Haiti from a liberal to a participatory democracy. Under the Aristide administration, women
broke open the narrow margins of patriarchal government, obtaining space for
their participation through the Ministry on the Status and Rights of Women
and numerous high-level political posts.[13]

Women's leadership in government changed the face of power. More than
most male officials, the women who served in the early 1990s as prime minister
and as ministers of Foreign Affairs, Education, Commerce, Social Affairs and
Labor, Information, and the Status and Rights of Women brought special attention to the needs and rights of the poor, and implemented programs on
their behalf. This priority is revealed here in the *istwa* of three such women,
each of whom notes that what is important is not that women ascend to elective power but *how* they use that power for the good of all. They point out that
a second critical question is *which* women can participate in power, and insist
that the political system must be opened to ensure that it is available to all
women, not just the elite.

Women's organizations typically have adopted a positive-sum approach to
power at a grassroots level, too. As an example, when the prime minister
phoned Lise-Marie Déjean at a feminist meeting to ask her to be minister of
the Status and Rights of Women, she recounts in her *istwa*, she made him wait
while she put the question to the other women in the room. Reflecting the
shared decision-making common in these groups, only when they came to
consensus did she accept. The voices and leadership of all, not just the officers
of the groups, are typically encouraged. Tasks are completed more through vol-
unteerism than through imposition of authority.

The experience of both mass women's organizations and women ministers
has demonstrated an emphasis on promoting the collective instead of the individual. This is true vis-à-vis not only participants and decision-makers but also
beneficiaries. Yolette Etienne rests her head against the flowered vinyl couch on
the gallery before saying, "You accomplish for yourself and you accomplish for

the country, so that all of us can live together for the collective good." Haitian women's organizations commonly strive to give the most marginalized the tools they need to garner more power, by changing their perception of their abilities and by practical skills-building programs.

Women in the state and in community organizations have encouraged others to challenge realpolitik in Haitian society. Educator and former government minister Myrto Célestin Saurel says in her soft, measured way,

> Women shouldn't use their placement and position to reproduce dominant power. They shouldn't go from being dominated to being dominant. They want to take up the challenge and exercise power differently.

The prevailing experience of women's exercise of power in Haiti is not a result of biological essentialism, but of their social placement and acculturation process. Women's collective interest may stem from the fact that they have suffered political exclusion based on social category. Many women in Haiti, as elsewhere, have speculated that another factor may be that females are encouraged to be nurturers, based on their being assigned responsibility, as mothers, wives, and sisters, for others' well-being.

Not all women share these predilections or think like Myrto. For example, the head of the Tontons Macoutes under François Duvalier was Mme. Max Adolphe, who wore the Macoutes' terror-inspiring uniform of denim suit and sunglasses, a machine gun rarely absent from her hand. And throughout the *istwa* are mentions of privileged women acting only in their class interests and exploiting women lower on the ladder.

Former Prime Minister Claudette Werleigh summarizes the potential of women at their best: "If we could bring all that strength into politics in Haiti, maybe we could shape not only politics but also a new country."

EXPERIENCES IN TRANSFORMATION: COLLECTIVIZATION

"Listen to this!" ebulliently exclaimed Josette Pérard one morning during the days when the elected government appeared likely to return from exile soon.

> A radio reporter went to the bustling strip in Port-au-Prince named Kuwait City, where merchants fought over who would sell

their black market gas to journalists, U.S. officials, and the local elite for as much as U.S.$40 a gallon. "*Madanm*," the reporter commented to one of the women, "When Aristide comes back to Haiti, the embargo will be lifted and you'll lose your business." He meant that the gas market would be removed from the hands of street vendors and placed back under the control of the multinational gas corporations.

"You got a problem with that?" she asked him.

"But *Madanm*. The gas will go back to the pumps. You won't be able to sell it anymore."

"And you got a problem with that?"

The journalist tried once more. Finally the woman spelled it out for him. "Isn't that what we've been working for?"

This same philosophy of prioritizing the common good over personal advantage is reconstructing the every-man-for-himself local economies into something quite different.

Haitians have always had to depend on each other for survival activities. In just one example, *konbit*, work exchange teams, have planted and harvested each other's land in fields and on rocky mountainsides for centuries.

Since the 1980s, collective practices have burgeoned. While the grassroots movement has not been able to reorient the macroeconomy, new systems of economic power are at work on local levels through small-scale communal initiatives.

The work is inspired by socialist struggles throughout Latin America and Africa and informed by the logic of the proverb, *Men anpil chay pa lou*. Many hands make the burden light.

Within agriculture and small industry, citizens are merging capital and labor and sharing ownership and income. There are now local- and national-scale, collectively run networks for credit, production, and marketing. Associations are establishing and managing microenterprises, bottom-up development projects, and new land use policies. Eliminating rapacious middlemen, the groups are putting income back into their communities. They are increasing their output, profits, standard of living, and autonomy in their lives and work.

For example: Women in the Artibonite Valley run a grain mill that has displaced the former power of the large landowner and the men in the community. Not only are the women raising their incomes and becoming socially empowered together, but also the mill benefits other peasants by grinding corn at a lower cost than the landowner charged. "This is *ours!*" a woman told me proudly as she removed a burlap sack of corn from her head and placed it in front of the mammoth grinder. In another case, a national lending institution is building direct links between peasant producers and market women. When the system is in place, supplanting old power networks, farmers will no longer be forced to sell their crops for too low a price to middlemen, nor will small vendors have to buy for too high a price.

Farming collectives have been especially successful, aided by the fact that peasant production has always been adept at maximizing available resources and pooling risks. The collectives foster environmental sustainability through appropriate technology and innovation. On local levels, they are disproving standard predictions about Haiti's incapacity to feed itself. When farmers have tenure security over their land, and the finances to secure the necessary inputs, some cooperatives have been able not only to adequately supply the local population with foodstuffs but also to create surplus. Some groups have merged to create regional cooperatives for exporting. Combating the imported goods currently flooding Haiti, this system enhances instead of displaces domestic production, while taking advantage of global markets to increase income. Mimose Jean, a small producer from one of these collectives, proudly told a 1998 national women's meeting, "In my area, there isn't a shred of hunger anymore!"

The cooperatives accomplish other purposes. United, citizens have amassed more social power against corrupt local government, landowners, and employers, helping to level the asymmetrical relation of forces. They have stretched their meager economic resources by sharing them. And they have created a shift in mentality from individualist social Darwinism to community-minded collaboration.

Where the cooperatives are mixed-gender, the usual caveat applies: women usually cannot participate as meaningfully as their male counterparts. Nor have they benefited equally. But women have established many collective associations of their own since the 1980s. Their proliferation and success come in part because women control so much of the informal economy and in part because their survival networks have always emphasized collaboration.

EXPERIENCES IN TRANSFORMATION: *TILEGLIZ*

Another experiment in changing the practice of power is found in the *tigleliz*, "the little church" or Christian base community. An expression of spiritual convictions based in liberation theology, the *tilegliz* claims a preferential option for the poor. It is a church *of* the poor, who nourish the hope of overturning their degradation as "the wretched of the earth," and fostering their humanity as children of God.

In the 1970s, religious and lay activists in Haiti, as throughout Latin America and other parts of the world, stepped forward to advocate a new society in which heaven could be realized on earth. Some clerics and laity began to challenge the traditional Catholic Church, with its close ties to the Duvaliers and the ruling elite. Religious youth groups and the national association of Catholic clergy began publishing stinging challenges to the church hierarchy. A defining image of the early 1980s is of priests and nuns, dressed in their vestments and habits and carrying crosses, marching through town streets to protest the regime. According to former nun Myrto Célestin Saurel, "We could not stand back with our arms crossed and say, 'God is good,' and wait for Him to send down change. We had to roll up our sleeves to force the system to change." Faith in a God who cares for the poor propelled the vast Catholic population into the resistance that brought down the dictator. Thousands of *tilegliz* communities have continued their social and political engagement since that time, despite attempts by the Vatican and Haitian bishops to suppress the movement.

Tilegliz followers are inspired by the belief that they have a biblical mandate to transform the world to one that reflects Jesus' teachings about justice and love. This belief compels followers' social involvement, for the message is that to be a true Christian, one must confront the barriers that prevent Christian principles from flourishing—that is, violence, tyranny, economic misery, and all other injustice. For the wealthy and powerful, liberation theology invokes Jesus' teachings that encourage them to work with the oppressed. Louise Monfils clutches my arm as she explains,

> What does living the gospel mean? . . . Imagine someone on a Sunday morning saying to a sick person all alone and in need, "Oh, today I can't help you, I have to go to church." No, you've got to use this morning to help that person. . . . You're taking a better communion that way. It's not opening your mouth and taking the host, answering, "Amen" to "The Body of Christ."

Like the cooperatives, the *tilegliz* has explored ways that resources, like power, can best be shared to maximize their advantage for everyone. The church communities have organized alternative socioeconomic structures and engaged in advocacy and activism so that the influence spreads and the impact grows.

Though women's public strength and leadership have suffered under the patriarchal structures of the official church, many women have been active members of the *tilegliz*. Some, like Kesta Occident and Marie Sonia Dely in this book, are prominent leaders in the movement.

EXPERIENCES IN TRANSFORMATION: CONSCIENTIZATION

The inequities of power in Haiti are reflected in the old adage *Tout moun pa moun*. Not everyone is someone. A new slogan that symbolizes the spirit of *lavalas* is *Tout moun se moun*. Everyone *is* someone.

This new philosophy has largely evolved through the conscientization movement, first developed by the Brazilian Paolo Freire, which has provided the pedagogic strategy for change. The process of developing critical consciousness of oneself and the world, as discussed in Chapter 1, conscientization has fostered transformation of the poor and society in Haiti as well as around the world.

While its roots in Haiti go back to the 1960s, the conscientization movement has spread broadly there since the 1980s through popular education, also called adult education. The education is conducted through collective analysis of individual and community experiences, which is then applied to action for change. Claudette Werleigh explains, "We start with what we already know: praxis, discuss it, analyze its components, look for causes and consequences: theory, and try to find out how together we can improve their living conditions: improved praxis."[14]

In the evenings after returning from the fields, or on Sundays after church, members of community groups have taken strength and sustenance from long exchanges about rights and responsibilities in a democracy. On rickety benches under shade trees, and in dark and dusty cement-block classrooms, they have analyzed local and global power and how to change it.

Conscientization has destroyed the belief among many impoverished Haitians that they are fated by God or circumstance to be poor. Claudette Werleigh says, "This is a new phenomenon in Haiti: poor people who used to accept poverty and squalor as 'God's will,' now have a very clear sense of their rights." The process has helped the Haitian majority move from objecthood to subjecthood, becoming protagonists in their own destiny.

Conscientization has had a special focus on women's empowerment and equality. "Not only must we avoid reproducing things as they currently are, we must also eradicate from ourselves what was indoctrinated within us that isn't correct," asserts Myrto Célestin Saurel.

Transforming beliefs and ideology is not the same as transforming systems and structures, but it is a critical step toward dynamized movement in that direction. Feminist economist Myriam Merlet says, "We must begin seeing things differently because, after all, things change first in one's head."

TOWARD TOMORROW

Piti piti zwazo fè nich li.
Bit by bit the bird builds her nest.

—Haitian proverb

Some organizations continued their work at discrete levels during the coup. Many more have resumed their programs since the coup was reversed. All, however, continue to be hobbled by those three vicious years. The military destroyed tightly knit networks throughout the nation. Thousands of activists are now dead or remain in foreign countries. The regime also destroyed community infrastructure, and many groups have not had the money to rebuild. Pressure from the conservative Catholic hierarchy in Haiti—backed by the Vatican, the only government in the world to formally recognize the coup regime—succeeded in weakening the *tilegliz* movement.

Populist administrations since 1994, which the poor had hoped would free them from their misery, have not met the high expectations. Aristide's second administration, beginning in February 2001, is not as engaged with broad sectors of the grassroots movement as was his first. There exists a different structure of power within the polity, and citizens have not been offered the same potential to participate in the structure or to benefit from it.

Some local governments continue to be dominated by carry-overs from the Tonton Macoute system, who collaborate with the local oligarchy. And although the army was disbanded in 1995 and respect for human rights has ascended, the new police force has engaged in instances of brutality reminiscent of the old modus operandi. Activists and government critics have again been targeted for violent attack. While such incidents are rare, that they occur at all indicates that the old roots still hold life.

Haiti remains the hemisphere's poorest country. National policy has consistently failed to prioritize the well-being of the poor, privileging instead the elites and international capital. The World Bank, International Monetary Fund, and U.S.-imposed structural adjustment and free market policies have led to greater concentration of wealth than at any time in modern-day Haiti. Farmers are having a tougher time selling crops they struggle to grow while foreign food imports render Haiti more dependent.

All these factors indicate the entrenchment of the ruling powers and institutions, despite the years and lives given to defeating them. To an observer, Haiti may seem hopelessly stuck in its oppressed condition, the idea of profound social transformation but a quixotic dream.

That analysis would be faulty, however, for several reasons. First, although the coup destroyed many programs, it could not eradicate deeper levels of change in popular values and ideology. Such nonmaterial change should not be underestimated; it is the foundation of the new society many Haitians are determined to build. The lessons from recent history cannot be destroyed; they remain vibrantly alive within collective memory. Holding two emaciated children on her lap outside her ten-foot-by-twelve-foot cardboard shack in the shantytown of La Saline, sweatshop worker Jesila Fils-Aime coins the best reason for hope for Haiti:

> I know what it is to hold my head up now and be treated as a human being. I'm not going to bow my head again. I might be hungry today, but if I keep my head up and keep calling out for justice, maybe tomorrow that will change, too.

Second, recent history has proved that resistance by the poor *is* capable of overturning power paradigms. Between Duvalier's departure in 1986 and the coup of 1991, very real transformations occurred. Subsequent backward steps do not negate the victories of the new power models that the people created. Nor do current regressions undermine future potential. As Shakespeare said, "What is past is prologue."

Third, Haitian history has shown that resistance is cyclical: each ebb has subsequently given way to a rise. Haitian women frequently say that resistance is *nan trip nou, nou te fèt avè l.* It is in our gut, we were born with it. The seeds of protest, evident since slavery days, are still germinating, as demonstrated by recent forward movement. As of this writing in 2000, there is a burgeoning of new grassroots activism. Farmers, workers, unemployed, youth, and market women are again grouping to strengthen internal democracy, fight for jobs and living wages, guarantee stable and healthy food sources, and increase their quality of life. The popular movement continues to advocate its needs and demands, while attempting to change the relation of forces that have kept those needs and demands from being met. Prophetic components of the movement continue to work for liberation through new social models, applied religious faith, respect, and love.

Seated under a crucifix in her convent's spare salon, Kesta Occident declares,

> There are people who are tired, who are weary of fighting. There are those who lost all their utopia. . . . But at the same time you feel that God gave the poor what they need to not give up. They have something that's still nourishing their hope. If it weren't for that, you'd have an apathetic people who would sit and do nothing, awaiting all the plans that have been prepared for them.

The challenges of the next stage are immense. For the Haitian people, especially women, negotiating and transforming power will be a long and painful climb along a switchback trail. But while the people have not consolidated victory, neither has the opposition.

The day after the coup was reversed, Aristide leaned back in the white armchair in his office in the National Palace and told me, "We were supposed to have all been dead already. But as you can see. . . ." He raised his palms heavenward, shrugged, and laughed. And as Marie Sonia Pantal concluded her *istwa* with a discussion about the strength and viciousness of the enemy, I asked her if she was saying that the resistance movement had lost. *Ki sa?* What? she asked in disbelief. She shook her head side to side. "Lost? Now, *cheri. That's* a different story!"

CLAUDETTE WERLEIGH
Lighting Candles of Hope

Let's face it: Working for change implies rejection of the present order. Working for change in a country where 1 percent of the population owns 49 percent of the wealth means working for the benefit of the poor. As the late president of Burkina Faso, Thomas Sankara, put it, "Water for everyone instead of champagne for a minority."

Working for change also means to struggle. This is because there is no place in the world where people have surrendered or shared their power, privileges, and wealth joyfully and spontaneously.

This is a new phenomenon in Haiti: Poor people who used to accept poverty and squalor as "God's will," now have a very clear sense of their rights. They say they, too, have human rights and political freedoms. They also recognize they have economic rights, such as the right to a job and the basic necessities of life. They claim the right to life, since for many of them it's an everyday struggle just to survive and keep their families alive. They say they have the right to participate in decision-making, and to shape the destiny of their own country. And they have the right to be treated with respect, like human beings.

Real and profound change in Haiti is still a long way off. We are not so conceited as to believe that we can immediately solve all the problems, especially the economic crisis and our ecological catastrophe, and change the face of Haiti. What we do hope for, though, is to help raise the awareness of the population so they themselves decide their lives and shape their own future. Our job is like lighting candles of hope.

MARIE SONIA DELY
Sharing the Breadfruit

The Word itself tells you, "You must get involved." The work of the first Christians was to meet among themselves in their families, in their homes, in their neighborhoods. They pooled some of their income to help each other and did what God tells us, which is to see how to change the situation.

I live in the community of Bizoton. I took the initiative as a Christian who saw that there was a need in the community. That need led me to work in the *tilegliz* movement, involving myself both in the church and in society.

This faith we have in God has shown us that one must be in solidarity with another. I wasn't born in order to have for myself only. I was born to give to others what I have. Otherwise, what meaning would life with God have? It's not right to say God is up there. I must bring him into the reality of *this* life. This is how we work in the *tilegliz*. This is the root of our life.

We are already in a country that doesn't offer us anything. If we don't act in solidarity with each other, how will we survive? In the *tilegliz*, if I have a problem in the house, they must come give me aid. Imagine, my father hasn't worked in twenty-two years. I have to eat, I have to drink, I have to dress myself. If there weren't familial relations among the people in the area, how could I live?

Also, I'm obliged to go give help. If it's a problem of illness, I have to go to the doctor's with them. If there's a person who needs a little medicine, we must get it. If today I have fifty cents in my pocket, and I see that someone doesn't have any money to buy food, I'll take twenty-five cents to buy food for my home; the other twenty-five cents I must leave for her because she's a member of my family, too. If her children aren't clean, I come and I wash them. She has something else she'll share with me. If I leave her to die, down the road who will help me?

Aristide said something to us over the radio from exile during the coup d'etat: "I know that the embargo is getting worse. Don't forget that if you have a little can of rice, when you cook it, let all your neighbors eat it." That happened, truly. In the neighborhoods that's how people survived. "So-and-so, you don't have any food today? We have boiled breadfruit, yes. You know that Aristide said that if one person boils a breadfruit, it's for all of us. We'll eat today. Another day if God wills, someone else will have a breadfruit." That's how many people were spared from dying of hunger. If one has, she'll send a plate of food to give to another in the neighborhood.

But in the *tilegliz* we were used to doing that. That's how we work. We consider the community as if it's one big family. This family has the same importance as the little family I have at home—my mother, my father, my brother, my sister. It needs my attention. It needs my support. No matter my circumstances, I'm obliged to do things for it. It's not like in some foreign countries where everyone takes care of their business for themselves only.

If we didn't have this hope, didn't have this familial solidarity, I don't believe we would all be alive. There would not be one member remaining because we would have all despaired.

Our faith makes us believe that Jesus Christ accepted dying to show us another model where there can be life. So what's the presence of God among the poor in Latin America, when there are people just across from us living in a little paradise, while we have nothing to survive on? Does God live just for people who are rich? We don't think so. We say despite our difficult situation, God is present in our situation because he gave proof: Mary was not a woman who had any money. She was a person who was humble, you understand?

God doesn't have a preference either for the poor or the rich. He loves us all. He simply asks that we make an effort to be in solidarity with each other, you see. That lets us find more strength to combat and to struggle.

LISE-MARIE DEJEAN
The People Say Jump

We established the Ministry on the Status and Rights of Women with the idea that not only the decision-making, but the programs we were going to establish, would permit a new form of power, because the men's power was always exercised through coercion; it was a power of domination. We wanted a more egalitarian power. We believed that if we invaded all domains of government, it would change the form of the state.

When women truly join the decision-making table, it begins to change. That has to be nuanced, though. There have been women on the inside, for instance, women in Duvalier's government. But the power they exercised? It wasn't the kind that encouraged women to sit at the decision-making table, too. And their understanding of power? Was it power to serve the people? It was part of the same bad imposed force, which doesn't change anything in people's lives.

For me, power is a service. When I'm in power, I'm in a position that lets me serve the most people possible, create an opening to let women—especially the poorest and the most disdained—change their status. I don't conceive of power as a privilege. You yourself may be at the table, but you're at the service of the people, you see. You're educating people to let *them* participate in power.

There's a game we used to play when I was doing popular education to let people develop their conception that *their* speech, the speech of the people, counts most. One person says, "The people say, jump," then you respond. Whenever the command is preceded with "The people say," you have to do it. But if the person doesn't start off with "The people say," you can't respond. Today if the minister says, "Stand," they stand. If the minister says, "Step forward," they step forward. This is the concept of authority, you see. It hasn't yet left the mentality of people. You have to teach people that they are human beings the same as you.

The exercise of power we used in the ministry was based on a perception of power that would set women on the road of change so future generations could harvest the transformation. This will give them a point of comparison to be able to say, "When I was young, it wasn't like this. Now as I'm getting older, I see things changing. Hence, they must continue to change."

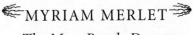

MYRIAM MERLET

The More People Dream

I was born in Haiti but I lived abroad until I was twenty-nine. There people tended to see Haiti through a series of clichés: Papa Doc, Baby Doc, black, illiterate, hungry. I had to always explain, "No, not Tahiti."

I got my degree in economics from Canada and studied women's issues, political sociology, and feminist theory. But while I was abroad I felt the need to find out who I was and where my soul was. I chose to be a Haitian woman. I couldn't see myself being forever a nigger in the United States, an immigrant in Canada, or a stranger in Europe. I felt the need to be part of something. This couldn't be the black cause in the United States or the immigration cause in Canada. It could only be the cause of the Haitian people. Thus, I decided to return to Haiti.

One would think that a Haitian women can only be a illiterate black woman from Cité Soleil. Well, no, I am a Haitian woman who is a professional with a university education. We must be careful not to be fixated on a prototype.

This is one of my struggles: for the community to consider all types of people within it. Everyone has to be able to live without discrimination. But society functions according to stereotypes. People see your color, they assess your style of speaking, they focus on your background. Society has decided what I am and how I should behave. If I don't do exactly what it wants, it marginalizes me. I was reading Nietzsche the other day and he was discussing the same principles. By what criteria, anyway, are we going to decide who is a good Haitian and who isn't? If we accept a legal criterion, everyone with a Haitian passport is part of the community. We can't keep on excluding certain categories of people. I say there are different types of Haitian women. I'm part of the whole, too. I refuse to justify myself. I have my place here.

My entire background has led me to where I am today, where my biggest research question has been to look at how power relations are put in place. My main focus of involvement has been about this and about interpersonal relations, which are in fact usually power relations.

Conventionally, power has been thought of in terms of one's power over something else—over another individual, another category of people, another class. It's men over women, women over women, men over men, social class over social class. This is how power is typically exercised in this society.

Myriam Merlet

As a result of my own reflection and evolution, I have a different concept of power. I've come to accept a concept that is not relative—a power fundamental that depends on the individual, what he or she is, knows, can do, brings to the table, or wants to be.

I look at things through the eyes of women, very conscious of the roles, limitations, and stereotypes imposed on us. Everything I do is informed by that consciousness. So I want to get to a different concept and application of power than the one that keeps women from attaining their full potential.

The basis of my work with women is to open them up to other things, give them new tools, give them new capabilities. This is what is called, in English, empowerment. The idea is to give women the opportunity to grow so that we may end up with more complete human beings who can really change things.

I want this society to get to a different theory and application of power in all aspects. It's not easy because we're so deeply affected by traditional concepts. Look where we are as we move into the twenty-first century: we have so many problems, clearly the current approach is not working. More people must be willing to conceive of things in a different way, be it in Haiti, the United States, or globally.

In a new society, individuals should have the opportunity to be complete human beings, women as well as men, youth as well as old people, the lame as well as the healthy. People should have the opportunity to be what they want to be and not what others would impose on them. It's not because I was born with a female biology that I must be a certain way. This characteristic shouldn't oblige me to do certain things like have children. Likewise, my blackness shouldn't confine me to certain activities. In some societies, if you're black, you're considered to be good only at dancing, singing, or sports, but not able to perform intellectually. One should be able to realize and express one's full potential and not only one's social condition. This is fundamentally the basis of the new society.

Of course, it's a utopian dream. But the more people dream, the more likely that power can change. The more people share in the same dream, as in Martin Luther King's "I Have a Dream" speech, the more likely we'll achieve it collectively.

Often I ask myself if it's possible to make this dream a reality when it's not shared by others. One may try to act so as to make oneself a model life, but the environment doesn't always allow it. More people must be willing to take a different course, though some might call them crazy. The dominant model is not creating viable development or the blossoming of the individual.

How do you explain that in spite of the fact that the Haitian people have been clamoring for participation since 1986, still no mechanism has been put in place to allow this? It's not simply a matter of negligence. There is a reticence— an unconscious one, I hope—on the part of the leaders to share the power they have, to use it in a different way. The only model is the Macoute model; that's all they know. They have yet to question the issue of power so we can progress.

We must understand what's behind the rot and implement changes in everything that we do. For instance, in working within women's organizations it isn't enough for us to complain about problems; what is fundamental is to determine why things are as they are. Why, for example, would a soldier rape a woman? What explains such behavior? It's not because he's a devil; there's conditioning behind such an act. Unless we crush that conditioning, it will be repeated: Yesterday, it was the Haitian army. Today it may be the National Police. Tomorrow, for all I know, it may be the People's Volunteers.

I've reached the conclusion that one should just proceed, and to hell with the others. This means that I won't play the game. It's hard and frustrating because you find yourself alone. At times you question your sanity, your ability to function while being so different from others. If you have children, it becomes a huge dilemma. In my case, I have a fifteen-year-old daughter to whom I try to impart certain principles. But when she faces a social model with its own conditioning so different from mine, especially at that age, she's tempted to side with the stronger party.

We're a country in which three-fourths of the people can't read and don't eat properly. I'm an integral part of the situation. I am not in Canada in a black ghetto, or an extraterrestrial from outer space. I am a Haitian woman. I don't mean to say that I am responsible for the problems. But still, as a Haitian woman, I must make an effort so that all together we can extricate ourselves from them.

YANNICK ETIENNE
You Can't Eat Gumbo with One Finger

I really believe in organizing because *yon sèl dwèt pa manje kalalou.* You can't eat gumbo with one finger.

In spite of the poverty, the humiliation, and the fact that people are treated as subhuman, the spirit that we encounter everyday in Haiti holds a pride. A human pride to transform life. That's what's guiding me in spite of all the sad times and the frightening moments.

Today we're reconstructing the popular democratic movement. The working class movement is becoming more powerful, especially against structural adjustment. The work is based on the fact that the umbilical cord of this country is tied with the international capitalist system. One of the things we're dealing with today is the campaign against worker exploitation in sweatshops manufacturing for Disney; this clearly demonstrates the problem of the economic orientation we're being forced into: the "New World Order." This is what the popular democratic movement has to contend with. So, we need to build organizations in which the popular masses have stronger control.

Our antislavery struggles gave way to a state that still serves the exploiting classes. Even though slaves won the battle, they never got the victory they were seeking. And those who took over leadership only had Europe as their model. So in fact nothing changed. Even though we no longer had slaves, we still had an economic system of small farmers without land tenure. We weren't able to do what we had hoped, so we must do it now.

The Haitian people have a lot to contribute to the global movement for change. Haitians have this creative, innovative aspect; they bring new alternatives. The Haitian praxis of struggle is unique. Others can learn from us and advance in their own struggles. Our history allows us to assert what we are and what we're worth, and to challenge the New World Order through our revolution. I have a profound belief in the Haitian people.

It's from this experience of battling against the rotten state machine, which does nothing for its people, that a totally radical, revolutionary orientation will come out. I'm hoping that these current struggles will give way to an entirely new vision. I don't have a precise schema in my head of what this might be. I think we'll find the form in the course of leading the battle. But we must be radical.

Yannick Etienne

MYRTO CELESTIN SAUREL
Rocks in the River

I'm thinking about the issue of power, how I see my involvement with it, and how a transformation might take place. To put the question in its proper context, I believe from February 7, 1986, when Duvalier went into exile, until December 16, 1990, when Aristide was elected, democracy was in gestation in Haiti. Popular political life was burgeoning. There was a ferment of ideas and a great deal of mobilization to prevent the dictatorship that had been overthrown from reemerging in a different form. It was the resistance to dictatorship that enabled us to give birth to democracy.

Right after Aristide came to power, I became director of the Ministry of Education. Shortly thereafter, I became minister of Social Affairs. It's from this experience that I say that we can think of the first nine months of our stint at democracy—from the day Aristide was elected to when the coup d'etat took place—as the first nine months in the life of a baby. The baby is fragile, the baby requires a lot of care, attention. The baby is brand new with no experience of life. It's powerless in the face of an enemy with far more experience and the capacity to do wrong. Maybe my imagery is exaggerated, but in my opinion, all these people involved in the daily management of power during the first nine months were like babies in democracy. They didn't know how to run a country because they had had nothing to do with the prior Duvalierist government. In a global framework, ours was a society without reference or political tradition. On an individual basis, we were faced with people with no experience or practice in the management of power inside a state structure, yet who had the responsibility to deliver. It was a difficult training period.

There was no national solidarity because those with the power of money did not support those with political power. The rich sensed that the government had a different vision of society not in accord with their own. They felt very insecure for they considered themselves as *wòch nan dlo ki pa konnen doulè wòch nan soley*, as we say. Rocks in the river that don't understand the misery of the rocks in the sun. The rich were scared that the rocks in the sun would take revenge on them. This was heightened by the turbulence they saw when Duvalier fell. The people with their newly acquired political consciousness were pressing for justice, fairness, and a better division of the cake, as they should have. We had underestimated our powerful internal enemies who kept unraveling what

Myrto Célestin Saurel

we were creating. We thought that the power of the people could stand up to them and block their way.

Additionally, we faced real economic and financial problems during the months of democratic governance that made it difficult for the government to respond to the demands of the population.

There was also a lot of reservation and obstruction at the international level. The international bourgeoisie believed that politics must be the preserve of the educated, and feared that the old economic order and traditional politics would be subverted by the people's participation. In the financial arena, "the people" as an entity—especially an illiterate people—is not considered a good thing. Maybe if we had realized the strength of our enemies, both inside and outside, we might have avoided the coup d'etat.

All these problems, including a poor choice of partners and poor management of relations of power between the political groups, tore up the fabric of democracy. This is the way I see our management during the first phase of our democratic experience.

After the coup, we didn't sit back; the government was reconstituted in exile. Each person assumed a piece of responsibility to help carry the whole responsibility.

Our approach while in exile was to speak with pride, to speak with conviction that the country wouldn't be destroyed. We didn't want Haiti to be discussed only in terms of the dictatorship, the military, the coup, and then be forgotten, so that the people at home didn't all go into body bags and into the morgue. And while asking for international solidarity, we stressed that it was our right as a member of the United Nations and of other international organizations to have the international community show their solidarity with us.

I attended human rights and labor conferences all over the world. Everywhere we went, we raised the Haitian flag high and asked that the impunity of human rights abuse no longer be tolerated. They received our presentations with much applause. But we were interested in more than just applause. We wanted to make sure that the voice of the Haitian people was heard where it needed to be heard.

Our presence in the international arena contributed to the final outcome of the crisis. All these efforts strengthened the insistence that justice must prevail. They constituted blows to the coup d'etat.

Afterward, a certain healing took place. Yes, we took beatings; we were wounded and the scars are visible and ugly. You'll always be able see the scars, but that won't prevent us from going into a new phase. It's like someone who experiences a serious illness, and who either fails to recover and degenerates into a precarious life, or overcomes the disease and the suffering, and blossoms into a new beauty made of maturity and transcendence.

If we want democracy to gain strength in Haiti, the most important challenge is a new understanding of politics. This is our new point of departure. What is political power? When an individual or a team achieves power, what do they do with it? How do they manage it? What does it mean to them? As a sociologist, I know that power is not made without your realizing what forces you have at your disposal, and identifying what forces oppose you.

But power is not simply a matter of relation of forces. Power is a space where one defines, builds, and manages a whole. Managing not for yourself and your own self-interest, but for the interests of everyone. Because the system works well only when all its elements function well.

The management of power must be tied to the people's situation. As a woman, I believe that as long as we don't succeed in translating this attitude into our practice, the people will always be left out of the political equation, no matter how strong their demands are. One can succeed as a leader only when there is a dialogue going in both directions. One can be smart, one can be astute in politics, in economics, but one cannot be a lone ranger. A lone ranger will always fail.

The relationship of women to power, if it sits within a framework of women's experiences, is different from men's relationship to power. What experiences do women have? They have the experience of people always being in a minority position, of their voices not being heard, of having someone's foot on their heads. Women have the most interest in change because they don't come from a privileged position sociologically. That's what gives us hope that change can come from women and will be made in favor of the majority who are victims of traditional power and domination.

Women must educate themselves to a different perspective of authority, not where one flexes one's muscle—what I would call male power. I don't admire strong power or dream of using it. From our experience as women, from the education we receive as women, from our readings, our self-criticism, from reality itself, not only must we avoid reproducing things as they currently are, we must also eradicate from ourselves what was indoctrinated within us that isn't correct.

Women shouldn't use their placement and position to reproduce dominant power. They shouldn't go from being dominated to being dominant. They want to take up the challenge and exercise power differently.

For me, the issue of power management from the perspective of a woman is really management with sensitivity. In traditional power throughout the world, the more cynical and manipulative one is, the better the political man. I use the word *man* advisedly, though a political woman might act this way, too. However, women rarely use authoritarian power. To the extent that a man accepts his sensitivity as a human being, then we're dealing with a complete man, a correct man, one more likely to have a balanced behavior. By the same token, whenever a woman denies her sensitivity, rejects the approach I have described, well, she'll end up with an atrophied vision and practice.

One new dimension that we women can introduce into the management of power is our practical abilities. These include the ability to separate what's important from what's not, to listen to what's essential and shut out the rest, to push forward only what deserves to be promoted and, especially, to never lose sight of the final goal. And that goal is not personal but collective. Also, the priority that we place on people: people are the heart of our preoccupation. These are elements that women can bring to the exercise of power.

There must be women in all the structures of the state to take charge of the country's future: as communal council members, senators, deputies, cabinet ministers, general directors, members of the Electoral Council. This is not about women's personal quest for power. It has to do with a need for balance.

One problem is that since women don't normally speak loudly, we run a high risk of not being heard. We women must make the effort to know what we want, to affirm ourselves, and to approach power with all our honesty and all our pride. Because of my perspective as a woman, it's my duty to be stronger and be more assertive to ensure that what I must say is said, that my vision is implemented. But our partners in power must make a special effort to listen to those who do not shout.

A Stubborn Hope

Before, we believed that the poor in various countries would triumph, and right away. Now we're facing a new conjuncture in the world, and we must assume something very different is surging up. Even if sometimes we question our strategies and approaches, we are convinced that this system—producing more and more poor countries, and more and more poor people even in the richest countries—is in decay.

And at the same time, something new is germinating. The excluded people are demanding land, housing, water, services. They want to be part of the decisions that affect their lives. They know that their voices and their votes can make a difference. They know that they can bring their cries for justice and for life beyond their borders, even if it comes at the expense of their own lives.

This is a major shift in the struggle for liberation. Global is the oppression of the free market: The same machine that produces more poor in Haiti is producing more poor in Detroit, in Rwanda, in the Philippines, all over the world. Global must be the force that can challenge it.

Transformation is still possible with the combined strength of the oppressed and excluded throughout the world, joining hands across borders and creating new relations.

But the question is, how can we help build these bridges of solidarity all over the world? How are we going to pull ourselves together to create that alternative? Change that really comes from the grassroots evolves from their understanding that if there's misery, it's shared misery. If there's poverty, it's shared poverty. The grassroots will look beyond their individual situations; they'll overcome their individual and national isolation to embrace a community, the community of all the pariahs of the world. They have the power of numbers, of solidarity, of community-building. This doesn't mean anybody will give them their rights right away, but they can gain more space.

A collective international conscience is developing more than before. Our labor unions are meeting with labor unions from other countries. Haitian peasants are meeting with Latin American peasants. Haitian women are in touch with African and Caribbean women. At the church level some strong networks have been built these last years. What a beacon of hope!

I believe in the future even if we have to fight against a strong and powerful empire. I believe in all grassroots alternative efforts: social, economic, political. I believe in all the initiatives, small but great, for a better organization of civil society. We are rooted in a culture of resistance and stubborn hope. We believe strongly in life. We choose to risk our own lives in search of a better collective life.

More than before, I think, if we are really Christians, our role is not only to maintain hope but also to help connect people for a real world community of brothers and sisters. We're fighting not only for bread but also for roses. We're fighting for dignity and beauty. Our struggle for a better life has to be rooted in a deep spirituality. This spirituality is the personal and collective conscience that helps us not give up in adverse situations, but to go on with stubborn determination, to find new ways to build communities, to build sorority, fraternity, to build justice, peace, and beauty for all.

We Haitians always give ourselves reason to live, reason to believe that one day our lives will change, even if not for ourselves, then for the generations after us. If they kill a woman with misery or hunger, she'll die with the hope that her kids will live better.

Fighting for life nourishes our hope and keeps us alive. We know it's a knot that you and I are making on the cord of life, so the cord will resist more firmly and not break. We won't let it break.

EPILOGUE

RESISTANCE AS SOLIDARITY

Elvia has increased the peril to her own life by telling us her story. But she has not taken this risk for nothing; she is asking us for something in return. She is asking us to take a stand, as she has. She is asking us to speak out, as she has. She is asking us to take risks, as she has.
　　　　　　　　　　　　　　　　　　　　　　　　—Medea Benjamin

The Haitians' message is the opposite of the pity-filled "Read it and weep." The women's testimonies entreat us to "Read it and act." To quote American activist Suzanne Pharr, "Tolerance, sympathy, and understanding are not enough, though they soften the impact of oppression by making us feel better in the face of it. Our job is not just to soften blows, but to make change, fundamental and far-reaching."[1]

In solidarity is embedded another model of power: the weak uniting to de-center dominant sites of power. When strongly organized, grassroots civil society can assert itself as an effective political actor, displacing the set of actors usually limited to domestic and foreign capital, domestic and foreign governments, international governmental bodies, and international financial institution. Within civil society, women can employ solidarity to displace the hegemony of patriarchy. Solidarity is a means through which people can help each other negotiate the margins of power to attain a more compassionate society, a people-centered government, and a development path of their own choosing.

Voices throughout *Walking on Fire* invite us to take risks and join with them in resisting inhumanity and in creating a new world. The *griyo* ask our solidarity and support as they struggle to expand their democratic space and to transform the power structures that oppress them. They ask the reader to ally with them as they build a new society, economy, and polity. Indigent market woman, coup-era rape survivor, and freedom fighter Mesinette Louis urges, "My friends in other countries, I am praying for you to have strength and courage to work with us and with other women who have problems."

In keeping with Martin Luther King, Jr.'s dictum that no one is free while others are oppressed, solidarity also contributes to a mutual conversion. It has a boomerang effect: In collaborating with Haitians as they fight detrimental U.S. policies and influence in Haiti, Americans can also shift power within the United States. Through working for more just foreign policy toward Haiti, we are also building democracy and accountability at home.

An additional component of solidarity lies in the bidirectional nature of its benefits. Solidarity is often presented in terms of what Americans, and others in the disproportionately influential global North, can offer Haitians. Less acknowledged, but vividly real, is what Haitians have to offer us. Haitian women—and more generally, the Haitian people—can teach and inspire us with new concepts and models for our own struggles for fully participatory democracy and the enrichment of humanity. Perhaps the ultimate lesson that Haitians' solidarity offers is that transformation is possible.[2]

As former Mozambican president Samora Machel said, "The foremost . . . objective [of solidarity] is to aid in the development of humanity to the highest level possible."[3]

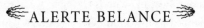

ALERTE BELANCE
Get Up, Shake Your Bodies

I would like people who are reading this to put Haiti in their consciences. It deserves to have the rule of law and democracy, so that the children of Haiti can speak, the children of Haiti can work, the children of Haiti can go to school and know how to read.

Some countries bigger than Haiti are hell-bent on Haiti's falling into the sea. That's their vision for the people of Haiti: that they fall into the sea and drown. Each time they hold a coup d'etat, the people are forced to get on a couple of planks of wood and take to the sea and perish there. I would like everyone who reads this to help us so the sea doesn't drag us deep under.

Haiti is my country, but it didn't put me in this wretchedness. That was the people who got a little blood money. I would like activists who are hearing me to help us so there will be no more Alertes in this situation, never ever ever. If you do this, you'll help me and God will bless you.

I only have a stub where my right arm used to be, and the fingers of my left hand have been severed; I can't close it. That hand can't do anything for me. That's why I say to you: consider that I always lift my face up, I speak out. You, then, who have two arms and two hands, should say, "Oh, let me help this woman carry the cause."

Look at my martyrdom from when the wicked ones kidnapped me and took me to the killing fields of Titanyen. I believe it was the will of God for me to live, so activists of conscience could become aware and say: "If Alerte Belance is in this state and she's still speaking for change in the country, we who still have our two hands and our two feet must take off our shoes and hitch up our pants. We must jump over the water to the other side, to a state of law."

That's why, activists of conscience, I would like you to help me shoulder this burden. Even though my body isn't intact, I still carry this burden on my back. God let me live so I could lay this burden at the feet of activists and concerned citizens. Come help me and the others so we can see our way free of the biggest country that has put its foot on our neck and is squeezing us. That's why I give you this message—see if you can help carry the burden on Haiti's back.

Me, if I found justice, I would tell God thanks. But we need activists of conscience to help us get it. If they all stood up, we'd get justice, and Haiti could move toward a state of law. Justice, that's exactly what we need.

People of conscience, hear me who is trying to wake you up. Hear my story, what I have experienced as a woman. Get up, shake your bodies, wash your faces, put democracy on its path. Plunge your feet into the waters. Hot will not feel hot, cold will not feel cold.

I send this call especially to women, because we're all sisters, regardless of whether we're black or red. We must open our eyes to torture, because they're torturing women all over the world. I know there are many activist brothers struggling with women, too. Though when torture does occur as in the case of Alerte Belance, it's men who commit the act.

Women of Haiti and of the whole world, let's enter into strong solidarity with each other and stop those men who are betraying us. Let's get our voices out.

Killing Alerte Belance was supposed to mean that Alerte Belance couldn't speak of a better life. Contrary to their stopping me, I'm progressing because I'm still bearing children. They tried to take my life away, but not only couldn't they do that, I'm producing *more* life. I know that if it's the will of God, this child I am bearing now will always move to action like me, will speak about the cause of the people, the cause of women.

Those who would like to help us get out from under this situation, look at me, a victim, still standing on my own two feet. You who are not victims, you should lend a hand. Because many hands make the burden light.

NOTES

Preface

1. I am grateful to Ruth Behar for raising this concept—she used the Spanish word *historia*—to describe the narrative of a Mexican *campesina* in *Translated Woman* (Boston: Beacon Press, 1993), 16.

2. Lila Abu-Lughod, *Writing Women's Worlds: Bedouin Stories* (Berkeley: University of California Press, 1993), 36.

Introduction

1. Nicos Poulantzas, *Political Power and Social Classes* (London: NLB, 1968), 104.

2. See broader discussion in Steven Lukes, ed., *Power* (New York: New York University Press, 1986).

3. As articulated by James C. Scott. Discussed in Danny Yee, "Anthropology Informs Political Economy: A Book Review" (www.anatomy.su.oz.au/danny/book-reviews, 1994).

4. James C. Scott, *Domination and the Arts of Resistance* (New Haven: Yale University Press, 1990), 17.

5. For a broader discussion of this topic, see Bina Agarwal, *A Field of One's Own: Gender and Land Rights in South Asia* (Cambridge: Cambridge University Press, 1994), and Scott, *Domination and the Arts of Resistance*.

6. James C. Scott, *Weapons of the Weak: Everyday Forms of Peasant Resistance* (New Haven: Yale University Press, 1985), 236.

7. For a more thorough discussion, see Paul Farmer, Margaret Connors, and Janie Simmons, eds., *Women, Poverty, and AIDS* (Monroe, Maine: Common Courage Press, 1996).

8. For a more thorough discussion and many illustrations of this characterization, see Robert Lawless, *Haiti's Bad Press* (Rochester, Vt.: Schenkman Books, 1992), and Paul Farmer, *The Uses of Haiti* (Monroe, Maine: Common Courage Press, 1994).

9. "Histoire des caciques d'Haïti" (Port-au-Prince: Editions Panorama, 1894), quoted in Carolyn E. Fick, *The Making of Haiti: The Saint Domingue Revolution from Below* (Knoxville: University of Tennessee Press, 1990), 288.

10. Fick, *The Making of Haiti*, 22.

11. See the declassified documents from the presidential libraries, such as U.S. Department of State, "Declassified State Department Document 79 D" (Washington, D.C., 1964), and U.S. Department of State, "Memorandum to the Latin American Committee, 80 B" (Washington, D.C., 1964).

12. For a more in-depth discussion, see Josh DeWind and David Kinley, *Aiding Migration* (Boulder, Colo.: Westview Press, 1989).

13. Though the singular "movement" is used, it is not a monolithic entity, having varying and sometimes conflicting ideologies and agendas.

14. The allegations, based on a wealth of evidence, were provided to the author by two cabinet ministers and three other very high-level officials. The names and exact posts of the informants must be withheld due to ongoing security concerns.

15. From an interview of a defected *zenglendo* to Haitian human rights organizations, Port-au-Prince, 1993.

16. Tim Weiner, "Haitian Ex-Paramilitary Leader Confirms CIA Relationship," *New York Times*, December 3, 1995; Allan Nairn, "Haiti under the Gun: How U.S.-Backed Paramilitaries Rule through Fear," *Nation*, January 8–15, 1996; John Kifner, "Haitians Ask If U.S. Had Ties to Attaché," *New York Times*, October 6, 1994; Allan Nairn, "Behind Haiti's Paramilitaries," *Nation*, October 24, 1994; Marcia Myers, "Claiming CIA Ties, Haitian Sues over Detention in U.S.," *Baltimore Sun*, December 12, 1995.

17. The U.S. military seized these photographs, along with rosters of FRAPH members and thousands of other pieces of evidence, from the FRAPH offices at the time of the multinational invasion. The Haitian government has repeatedly requested that this documentation—the property of the Haitian state—be returned to aid in its legal proceedings against FRAPH. Years later, the U.S. government has continued to refuse.

18. Inter-American Development Bank, Integration and Regional Programs Department, *Haiti: Basic Socio-Economic Data* (Washington, D.C.: Inter-American Development Bank, November 1994).

19. "Files Contend Haiti Ignoring Trafficker," *Miami Herald*, April 4, 1993; Douglas Farah, "U.S. Shares Anti-Drug Data with Haiti's Military," *Washington Post*, October 24, 1993; "Interview with Senator John Kerry (D-MA)," *Reuters Transcript Report, Fox Morning News*, October 28, 1993.

20. See, for instance, Government of Haiti, "Strategy of Social and Economic Reconstruction," also known as the Paris Plan. Unpublished. August 22, 1994.

21. See, for instance, Plate-forme Haïtienne de Plaidoyer pour un Développement Alternative, "Economie Haïtienne, le mirage de la croissance" (Port-au-Prince: Plate-forme Haïtienne de Plaidoyer pour un Développement Alternative, 1999); Camille Chalmers and Jonathan Pitts, Institute for International Relations, "Haiti: Responses and Alternatives to Structural Adjustment" (London: Catholic Institute for International Relations, June 1997). A few indices are telling. The coefficient of food dependency has risen from 26.2 in 1990 to 36.5 in 1998. The importation of grain has risen from an average of 236,000 tons per year during the 1980s to 350,000 tons in 1998. United Nations Development Program, *Human Development Report 1998* (New York: Oxford University Press, 1998).

22. United Nations Development Program, "Gender-Related Development Index," *Human Development Report 2000* (http://www.undp.org/hdr2000/english/book/back2.pdf, 2000). Statistics are from 1998.

23. Inter-American Development Bank, *Economic and Social Progress in Latin America: 1990 Report* (Washington, D.C.: Inter-American Development Bank, October 1990), 211.

24. United Nations Development Program, "Gender-Related Development Index," 2000.

25. UNDP, 2000. Figure is from 1998.

26. Ibid.

27. Estimates of the number of female-headed households range from 30 to 60 percent. United Nations Development Program, *Human Development Report 1995* (New York: Oxford University Press, 1995), 80. Mary Catherine Maternowska's study indicates 60 percent. "Coups d'Etat and Contraceptives: The Forces of Fertility in Haiti" (unpublished, 1996), 89.

28. Reported to author by anthropologist Jennie Smith from her study of rural Haiti in the 1990s.

29. Simon Fass, *The Economics of Survival: A Study of Poverty and Planning in Haiti* (Washington, D.C.: U.S. Agency for International Development, Bureau of Development Support, 1980).

30. United Nations Development Program, "Gender-Related Development Index," 2000.

31. Ibid. Statistic was compiled between 1995 and 2000.

32. Studies by the World Health Organization, discussed in Frances Moore Lappe and Rachel Schurman, *Taking Population Seriously* (San Francisco: Institute for Food and Development Policy, 1990), 25.

33. For more discussion, see Julia Cleeves Mosse, *Half the World, Half a Chance: An Introduction to Gender and Development* (Oxford: Oxfam, 1993), 195; Lynne Brydon and Sylvia Chant, *Women in the Third World: Gender Issues in Rural and Urban Areas* (New Brunswick, N.J.: Rutgers University Press, 1989), 210.

34. United Nations Development Program, *Report for Cooperation and Development* (New York: Oxford University Press, 1998).

35. Inter-American Development Bank, *Economic and Social Progress in Latin America*, 224.

36. The conversion is calculated at an exchange rate of 25G:U.S.$1.00, based on December 2000 rates.

37. United Nations Development Program, United Nations Development Report 2000 (http:// www.undp.org/hdr2000/english/book/back2.pdf, 2000).

38. Centre de Promotion des Femmes Ouvrières (CPFO), "Legal Education and Legal Assistance Program for Haitian Women Factory Workers" (Port-au-Prince: CPFO, October 1990), 4.

39. Verbal account from anthropologist Catherine Maternowska to author. Figures collected from Cité Soleil, 1994.

40. Maternowska, "Coups d'Etats and Contraceptives," 88.

41. Centre Haïtien de Récherches et d'Actions pour la Promotion Féminine (CHRE-PROF), *Violences exercées sur les femmes et les filles en Haïti* (Port-au-Prince: Les Imprimeries Henri Deschamps, November 1996), 11.

42. U.S. Embassy of Haiti, "Confidential Cablegram" (Port-au-Prince, April 12, 1994), 2–3.

43. This figure may include some double reporting of the same cases.

44. Commission Nationale de Verité et de Justice, *Si m pa rele* (Pétionville, Haiti: Commission Nationale de Verité et de Justice, 1995), 59.

45. Carolle Charles, "Gender and Politics in Contemporary Haiti: The Duvalierist State, Transnationalism, and the Emergence of a New Feminism 1980–1990," *Feminist Studies* 21 (Spring 1995): 136.

46. Stephen J. Williams, Nirmala Murthy, and Gretchen Berggren, "Conjugal Unions

among Poor Haitian Women," *Journal of Marriage and the Family* 37, No. 4 (November 1975): 1026.

Chapter 1. Resistance in Survival

1. Lest the stories paint a super-human view of Haitian women, it should be noted that the interviewing and production processes contain implicit distortions. Selection is implicit at every stage: in the women I opted to interview, what those women chose to present, the interviews I culled for inclusion, and the material I drew out in the editing process. While I attempted to intervene as little as possible in the substance of the texts, I have emphasized the ways these women fight back. Other women not included here have chosen to acquiesce, or to appear to acquiesce, for their own strategic reasons. And while the women represented here have heroic traits, some of them occasionally oppress their own children and each other.

2. I am grateful to Robert Maguire for this analogy.

3. Paul Farmer, Margaret Connors, and Janie Simmons, eds. *Women, Poverty, and AIDS* (Monroe, Maine: Common Courage Press, 1996), 369.

4. Dr. Howard Thurman, quoted in Katie G. Cannon, *Black Womanist Ethics* (Atlanta: Scholars Press, 1988), 161.

5. United Nations Development Program, *Human Development Report 2000* (http://www.undp.org/hdr2000/english/book/back2.pdf, 2000).

6. Quoted in Marcelo Suaréz-Orozco, "A Grammar of Terror: Psychocultural Responses to State Terrorism in Dirty War and Post-Dirty War Argentina," in *The Paths to Domination, Resistance and Terror*, ed. Carolyn Nordstrom and JoAnn Martin (Berkeley: University of California Press, 1992), 220.

7. Margaret Randall, *Our Voices, Our Lives: Stories of Women from Central America and the Caribbean* (Monroe, Maine: Common Courage Press, 1995), 156.

8. Quoted in bell hooks, *Yearning: Race, Gender, and Cultural Politics* (Boston: South End Press, 1990), 40.

9. Titanyen was originally a potter's field that, since the days of Duvalier, has been sporadically used as a dumping ground for military and death-squad victims. During the coup, the death squads dumped bodies at Titanyen on a nightly basis.

10. The conversions used throughout the *istwa* are 15 gourdes, or Haitian$3, to U.S.$1. This was the rate of exchange in 1996, at the time when most of the *istwa* were compiled.

11. Little Haiti is a neighborhood in Cité Soleil.

Chapter 2. Resistance as Expression

1. James C. Scott, *Domination and the Art of Resistance* (New Haven: Yale University Press, 1990), 162.

2. No one can say with certainty what percentage of the Haitian citizenry practices vodou. A common estimate is 85 percent.

3. Special thanks go to Danielle Georges for helping with the translation of Alina "Tibebe" Cajuste's poetry.

Chapter 3. Resistance for Political and Economic Change

1. James C. Scott, *Domination and the Art of Resistance* (New Haven: Yale University Press, 1990), 192.

2. This is what Antonio Gramsci described as moving from a war of position to a war of movement. For a fuller discussion, see *Selections from the Prison Notebooks* (New York: International Publishers, 1978).

3. Carolle Charles, "Gender and Politics in Contemporary Haiti: The Duvalierist State, Transnationalism, and the Emergence of a New Feminism 1980–1990," *Feminist Studies* 21 (Spring 1995): 140.

4. Claudette Werleigh, "Democracy and Political Empowerment," a talk given at the Thirtieth Anniversary Forum of the Ecumenical Program on Central America and the Caribbean, Washington, D.C., October 24, 1998.

5. Mary Catherine Maternowska, "Coups d'Etat and Contraceptives: The Forces of Fertility in Haiti" (unpublished, 1996), 94.

6. Tim Weiner, "Haitian Ex-Paramilitary Leader Confirms CIA Relationship," *New York Times*, December 3, 1995; Allan Nairn, "Haiti under the Gun: How U.S.-Backed Paramilitaries Rule Through Fear," *Nation*, January 8–15, 1996. John Kifner, "Haitians Ask If U.S. Had Ties to Attaché," *New York Times*, October 6, 1994; Allan Nairn, "Behind Haiti's Paramilitaries," *Nation*, October 24, 1994; Marcia Myers, "Claiming CIA Ties, Haitian Sues over Detention in U.S.," *Baltimore Sun*, December 12, 1995.

7. Government of Haiti, *Country Presentation*, prepared for the United Nations Conference on the Least Developed Countries, 1990. Quoted from Lisa McGowan, *Democracy Undermined, Economic Justice Denied: Structural Adjustment and the Aid Juggernaut in Haiti* (Washington, D.C.: Development Group for Alternative Policy, 1997).

8. For a more thorough discussion of Haiti's structural adjustment program, see McGowan, *Democracy Undermined, Economic Justice Denied*; Camille Chalmers and Jonathan Pitts, *Haiti: Responses and Alternatives to Structural Adjustment* (London: Catholic Institute for International Relations, June 1997); and Plate-forme Haïtienne de Plaidoyer pour un Développement Alternatif, *Justice Economique*, no. 6 (February–June 1998); no. 7 (July–September 1998); no. 8 (October 1999).

9. "In countries undergoing structural adjustment, when there are cuts in government spending, especially social services, these mainly affect women, who must provide many services in the home and community formerly provided by the government. As food subsidies are cut and prices rise, women spend more time working to buy the same amount of food. Increased hunger and ill health usually affect girls and women the worst. With transport fares higher, women also spend more time walking and are less able to access jobs and markets farther away from their homes. With mothers working harder to help the family to survive, their daughters take on added responsibilities, which further limit their ability to go to school. With cuts in male workers' jobs or simply because of lower wages, economic pressures on women to earn income and buy food for their families grow even more. Yet women's rates of unemployment are much higher than men's, pressuring women to accept exploitative jobs or lower job benefits. The gap between men's and women's wages usually grows wider. Even where women get jobs in export industries, these tend to be temporary and unsafe. When

agricultural exports are promoted at the expense of local food production and rural credit is concentrated among large businesses typically run by men, the peasant household—often run by women—suffers. When land ownership titles are granted, women do not usually gain access to property and women's traditional land rights are weakened. In the home, women are often subjugated to more domestic violence and stress under the pressure of growing poverty." Plate-forme Haïtienne de Plaidoyer pour un Développement Alternatif, "L'Avenir Economique d'Haïti" (Port-au-Prince: PAPDA, 1995), 8.

Chapter 4. Resistance for Gender Justice

1. The law deeming women minors was subsequently reinstated, and remained until 1979.

2. Carolle Charles, "Gender and Politics in Contemporary Haiti: The Duvalierist State, Transnationalism, and the Emergence of a New Feminism 1980–1990," *Feminist Studies* 21 (Spring 1995): 137–38.

3. Ibid.

4. Carolle Charles, "Feminism and Power: Haitian Women, Political Struggles in Haiti and the Diaspora, 1930–1990" (unpublished, 1990).

5. Ministère à la Condition Féminine et aux Droits de la Femme, "Message on the Occasion of the Inauguration of the Headquarters of the Ministry on the Status and Rights of Women" (Port-au-Prince, 1995).

The subsequent administration all but dismantled the Women's Ministry.

6. Claudette Werleigh's oral history was substantiated by articles she authored: "Socio-Cultural, Economic, and Political Portrait of Haitian Women" (unpublished, April 1989), and "Working for Change in Haiti," *Justice Paper* 12 (London: Catholic Institute for International Relations, July 1989).

7. Claudette Werleigh was prime minister of Haiti from 1994 to 1996.

Chapter 5. Resistance Transforming Power

1. Audre Lorde, "The Master's Tools Will Never Dismantle the Master's House," in *This Bridge Called My Back*, ed. Cherrie Moraga and Gloria Anzaldua (New York: Kitchen Table/Women of Color Press, 1983), 99.

2. Other experiments in radical change, such as Sandinismo and Leninism, have been based on the premise that tight vertical power is the prerequisite to challenging old power systems and distributing resources.

3. For a broader discussion, see Alain Foucault, *A History of Sexuality* (New York: Random House, 1990).

4. Collectif Haïtien pour la Protection de l'Environnement et le Développement Alternatif, Plate-forme Haïtienne de Plaidoyer pour un Développement Alternatif, and Multinational Resource Center, "Resolutions from the Colloquium on the Environment" (Port-au-Prince, June 1998).

5. Camille Chalmers, "Haiti's Latest Coup: Structural Adjustment and the Struggle for Democracy," *Multinational Monitor*, May 1997, 23.

6. Camille Chalmers and Jonathan Pitts, *Haiti: Responses and Alternatives to Structural Adjustment* (London: Catholic Institute for International Relations, June 1997), 8.

7. Margaret Randall, *Risking a Somersault in the Air: Conversations with Nicaraguan Writers* (San Francisco: Solidarity Publishers, 1984), 150.

8. Suzanne Pharr, "Transformational Organizing," *Ark* (National Organizers Alliance), No. 4 (Winter 1995), 11.

9. Jean-Bertrand Aristide and Beverly Bell, "Epilogue: Stronger than the Gun," in Jean-Bertrand Aristide, *Aristide: An Autobiography* (Maryknoll, N.Y.: Orbis Books, 1993), 166–67, 169.

10. Center for International Policy, "Mobilizing Resources for Development: A Retrospect on President Aristide's Economic Strategy for Haiti and His Administration's Record with Aid Donors," *International Policy Report*, May 1992, 3.

11. Interview with author, Port-au-Prince, February 13, 1995.

12. In 1995, after returning from exile, Aristide entirely destroyed the military.

13. Patriarchal hegemony in the subsequent administration reversed most of the gender-related progress from Aristide's government.

14. Claudette Werleigh, "Working for Change in Haiti," *Justice Paper 12* (London: Catholic Institute for International Relations, July 1989).

Epilogue

1. Suzanne Pharr, "Taking the High Road," *Ms. Magazine* 7, no. 1 (July/August 1996): 65.

2. I am grateful to Scott Wright for sharing this idea. From Scott Wright, *Promised Land: Death and Life in El Salvador* (Maryknoll, N.Y.: Orbis Press, 1994), xxxi.

3. Quoted in Medea Benjamin and Andrea Freedman, *Bridging the Global Gap* (Cabin John, Md.: Seven Locks Press, 1989), 5.

GLOSSARY

All terms are in Creole unless otherwise noted.

Abse sou abse Abscess on abscess.

Afrik Ginen Mother Africa, the spiritual homeland, the source

Analfabèt pa bèt. The illiterate are not ignorant.

ancien régime (French) former regime

bat tenèb to beat back the darkness

bay tè a blanch to clear or level the field

blakaout electrical blackout

blan foreigner

Bondye bay chak moun pa li. God gives each person his/her own.

Bondye si bon. God is so good.

bouk cluster of huts

chapo ba hats off

chèche lavi to search for life

cheri sweetheart

chouchoute l to ingratiate or subtly bribe

dechoukaj uprooting

defavorize marginalized

degaje innovate, do the best one can

eben well, oh well

eskonte credit given at excessively high interest rates

fanm vanyan valiant woman

Fòk sa chanje. This must change.

FRAPH Revolutionary Front for the Advancement and Progress of Haiti, the most active and violent death squad of the coup regime

Genyen tout yon sosyete ki pou chanje. There is a whole society to be changed.

Ginen see *Afrik Ginen*

gratis ticheri a special treat or incentive

griyo honored storyteller of a family or village, recipient and transmitter of history and wisdom; refers in this text to the narrators of oral histories

Haïtiennité (French) Haitianicity

itswa   story, history; refers in this text to the oral histories

kanpe djanm   stand strong
kenbe fèm   hold strong
kenbe la   to hang on, hold the line
ki sa?   what?
klas defavorize   marginalized class
konbit   collective work exchange team
kòk chante   crowing rooster
Kote gen lespwa, gen lavi.   Where there is hope, there is life.

lakou   yard
lavalas   literally means "flash flood"; refers to the popular movement that prompted the ouster of the Duvalier dictatorship, forced through many political and social reforms, and brought to power the Aristide administration in 1991.
lòt bò dlo   literally, the other side of the water; refers to going abroad or in exile
lwa   vodou spirit

machin enfènal   hellish machine
Macoute   see *Tonton Macoute*
madanm   madam, ma'am; term of respect for addressing a woman
medanm   ladies, women
manbo   vodou priestess
marronage (French)   marooning, refers to slaves escaping from plantations and living in communities in the mountains, from where they launched guerrilla attacks on their former masters. In current usage, means both going into hiding or internal exile, and the practice of evasion.
mawonaj   marooning; see *marronage*
Men anpil chay pa lou.   Many hands make the burden light.
Mèsi anpil.   Thank you very much.
Mizè yon fanm se mizè tout fanm.   The misery of one woman is the misery of all women.
msye   sir, man
Mòn Pitimi   Millet Mountain
M reziye m.   I resign myself.

N ap kontinye lite jiska mayi a mi.   We will continue to struggle until the corn has ripened.
nan trip nou   in our gut
No pasarán. (Spanish)   They will not get past.
nom de guerre (French)   pseudonym
Nou lèd, nou la.   We are ugly, but we are here.
Nou pa gen lechwa.   We don't have a choice.
Nou te bite, nou pat tonbe.   We have stumbled but we have not fallen.
Nou te fèt avè l.   We were born with it.

oungan   vodou priest

peze souse   literally, squeeze and suck; a popular snack of frozen soda in a plastic bag
Piti piti zwazo fè nich li.   Bit by bit the bird builds her nest.
plan lanmò   death plan; Haitian term for the structural adjustment program

plasaj　　common-law marriage

plase　　to live with a partner in common-law marriage

poto mitan　　central pillar

Pou w kapab konprann sa k ap pase joudi a, fòk ou konnen sa k pase anvan.　　To understand today, you must know the past.

rara　　pre-carnival musical street celebration led by vodou societies

rasin　　literally, root; music and culture influenced by vodou and Rastafarianism

restavèk　　literally, "to stay with"; refers to the street children and children of indigent parents who are turned over to work for friends or relatives. They become live-in servants, who are for the most part unpaid, underfed, unschooled, beaten, and often sexually abused.

sanba　　bard, caller

santim　　penny

Se lavi.　　That's life.

section chiefs (English)　　corrupt and violent rural sheriffs who controlled local power and resources in the countryside during the Duvalier reign, under subsequent Duvalierism, and then again during the coup d'etat; responsible for extortion, land grabs, arrest, abuse, and repression of dissent.

si m pa rele　　if I don't cry out

Si pa gen lapè nan tèt, pa ka gen lapè nan vant.　　There can be no peace in the head if there is no peace in the stomach.

SOFA　　Solidarity Among Haitian Woman, a feminist organization

sòti nan lamizè pou n rive nan povrete ak diyite　　from misery to poverty with dignity

sou fòs kouray　　literally, on the strength of your courage; implies carrying on with nothing but sheer personal determination

structural adjustment　　A set of policies promoted and imposed in developing countries by the International Monetary Fund and the World Bank, especially since 1982. The policies usually include government budget cuts, removal of import and export restrictions and tariffs, privatization of government-owned industries and services, elimination of subsidies for basic consumption, financial liberalization, and promotion of exports to earn hard currency.

tap-tap　　flatbed truck

teknik　　subterfuge, subtle craft

tèt ansanm　　unity

Tèt Kole　　the abbreviated form of *Tèt Kole Ti Peyizan Ayisyen*, Heads Together Small Haitian Peasants, a national peasant organization

Tèt Kole Ti Peyizan Ayisyen　　see *Tèt Kole*

teledjol　　literally, tele-jaw; a highly efficient means of oral communication

tilegliz　　literally, "the little church"; liberation-theology based church of the poor or Christian-base community

Timoun ki rele, se li ki bezwen tete.　　The child who cries is the child who needs the breast.

Titanyen　　A traditional potter's field used as a dumping ground for victims of military and death squads since the days of Duvalier.

Titid　　Little 'Tide, nickname for Jean-Bertrand Aristide

Tonton Macoute　　see *Tontons Macoutes*. The singular form refers to an individual in the security force.

Tontons Macoutes   Armed militia created by François Duvalier in 1958, accountable to no law or no one except the Duvaliers; served as the main perpetrators of violence until its official disbanding in 1986; have since reappeared as political and repressive force.

Tout fanm se fanm, men tout fanm pa kreye egalego.   All women are women, but not all women are created equal.

Tout moun pa moun.   Not everyone is someone.

Tout moun se moun.   Everyone is someone.

Viv Aristide! Men bounda m, vin ban m baton.   Long live Aristide! Here's my ass, now try to whip it.

vodou   voodoo

vodouizan   vodou practitioner

vwala!   aha!

Yo debouche boutèy la. Yo pa kapab bouche l ankó.   The bottle has been uncorked; the cork cannot be put back now.

Yo pa bay libète. Se pran pou au pran l.   Liberty is not given to you. Take, you must take it.

yon alemyè   a better go of it

yon pi bon demen   a better tomorrow

Yon sèl dwèt pa manje kalalou.   You can't eat gumbo with one finger.

Wòch nan dlo pa konnen doulè wòch nan soley.   Rocks in the river don't understand the misery of the rocks in the sun.

woy   oh! wow!

zenglendo   armed thugs who functioned as part of the paramilitary network under the coup regime; name is derived from a term for shards of shattered glass.

zye vèt   literally, green-eyed; refers to Haiti's light-skinned elite

FOR FURTHER RESEARCH AND INVOLVEMENT

Batay Ouvriyè, Workers' Struggle, B.P. 13326, Delmas, Haiti, (509)222-6719, batayouvriye@hotmail.com. This association organizes and supports workers in the multinational assembly sector. Batay Ouvriyè denounces poor wages and working conditions and lack of labor rights in the sweatshops, provides assistance to those trying to organize and fight back, and generates international support.

Center for Economic and Policy Research, 1015 18th Street, N.W., Suite 200, Washington, D.C., 20036, (202)293-5380, cepr@cepr.net. Among other work, CEPR provides research and analysis on global economic issues, with a focus on the role and effects of international financial institutions in poor countries.

Center for Economic Justice, 144 Harvard Drive, S.E., Albuquerque, NM, 87106, (505)232-3100, info@econjustice.net. Center for Economic Justice seeks to build the strength of global South struggles for economic justice. One program is the Haitian Economic Justice Project, which generates support for the Haitian people's fight against internationally imposed development and for humane and just economic policies and programs.

Fondasyon Kole Zepòl (FONKOZE), Shoulder to Shoulder Foundation, P.O. Box 53144, Washington, D.C., 20009, (202)667-1277, fonkozeusa@cs.com; #7 Ave. Jean Paul II, Delmas, Haiti, (509)22-7631 or 221-7641, fonkoze@aol.com. FONKOZE is an alternative bank for the organized poor, making available saving accounts and loan services to those otherwise not served by Haitian banks. The organization also engages in training and infrastructure development.

Haiti Reborn/Quixote Center, P.O. Box 5206, Hyattsville, Md. 20782, 301-699-0042, haiti@quixote.org, www.quixote.org/haiti. Haiti Reborn raises funds and builds support for community-based and grassroots development work in Haiti, specifically reforestation initiatives and popular education programs. At the same time, it raises awareness about the current economic, social, and political situation in Haiti.

Kay Fanm, Women's House, 11 Rue Armand Holly, Port-au-Prince, Haiti, (509)245-4221. Kay Fanm is a feminist organization struggling to improve women's status by providing a forum to fight social, political, and economic discrimination against women. It also provides legal, health, literacy, and other services to women.

Lambi Fund of Haiti, P.O. Box 18955, Washington, D.C., 20036, (202)833-3713 or (800)606-9657, lambi@igc.org; #94 Ave. Lamartinière, Port-au-Prince, Haiti,(509)245-9445, fonlanbi-ayiti@haitiworld.com. The Lambi Fund supports community organizing and grassroots economic development through giving financial and technical assistance and training to democratically run projects. Special areas of focus are agriculture, reforestation, and women's ventures.

Mouvman Peyizan Nasyonal Kongre Papay (MPNKP), National Peasant Movement of the Congress of Papay, #17 Delmas 39, Port-au-Prince, Haiti, (509)249-2755. A national peasant movement, MPNKP amasses the strength of peasants as a political force and works on specific projects such as soil conservation, reforestation, agricultural production, and artisan production. The Women's Section of MPNKP is a strong, large group.

Partners in Health, 643 Huntington Avenue, 4th Floor, Boston, MA, 02115, (617)432-5256, info@pih.org. Partners in Health works toward a preferential option for the poor in health care, through efforts to improve the health and well-being of communities struggling against poverty. A health and education program in Haiti, and another program with Haitians in Boston, comprise a significant portion of Partners in Health's work.

Plate-forme Haïtienne de Plaidoyer pour un Développement Alternatif (PAPDA), Platform to Advocate Alternative Development in Haiti, #7 Ruelle Rivière, Angle 1ère Ruelle Rivière, Port-au-Prince, Haiti, (509)244-4727, camille.sec-exe@papda.org. This coalition of worker, peasant, women's, religious, professional, and technical assistance groups advocates a new macroeconomic policy for Haiti. The coalition provides research, advocacy, and education services and mobilizes the popular and democratic movement to fight for a just development path in Haiti.

Solidarite Fanm Ayisyen (SOFA), Solidarity Among Haitian Women, 42 Ave. Lamartinière, Port-au-Prince, Haiti, (509)245-8477. This feminist organization is composed of peasant, slum-dwelling, and professional women. It operates throughout the country to promote conscientization, training, education, and health care.

Tèt Kole Ti Peyizan Ayisyen, Heads Together Small Haitian Peasants, Rue Montalais, Port-au-Prince, Haiti, (509)222-4070. This national peasant association is based primarily in the Northwest of Haiti. It organizes peasants to gain political and economic power through advocacy and specific projects, such as credit unions, food banks, and collective animal husbandry.

World Bank Bonds Boycott, c/o Center for Economic Justice, 1830 Connecticut Ave., NW, Washington, DC, 20009, (202) 299-0020, bankboycott@econjustice.net, www.worldbankboycott.org. The World Bank Bonds Boycott is a campaign which gives people leverage over the policies of the World Bank, based on the fact that roughly 80% of World Bank funding comes through the sale of bonds to institutional investors, including those in local communities. In the spirit of the anti-Apartheid disinvestment movement, the World Bank Bonds Boycott urges people to demand accountability over economic policy-making and to get their municipalities, universities, unions, and other institutions to adopt policies against buying those bonds.

BIBLIOGRAPHY

Abu-Lughod, Lila. *Writing Women's Worlds: Bedouin Stories*. Berkeley: University of California Press, 1993.

Agarwal, Bina. *A Field of One's Own: Gender and Land Rights in South Asia*. Cambridge: Cambridge University Press, 1984.

———. "Gender, Resistance and Land: Interlinked Struggles over Resources and Meanings in South Asia." *Journal of Peasant Studies* 22, No. 1 (October 1994).

Allman, Suzanne. *Profil de la femme Haïtienne*. Port-au-Prince: United Nations, 1984.

Americas Watch and National Coalition for Haitian Refugees. *Silencing a People: The Destruction of Civil Society in Haiti*. New York: Human Rights Watch and National Coalition for Haitian Refugees, 1993.

Amnesty International USA. "Justice and Women in Haiti." Unpublished, no date cited.

Anglade, Mireille Neptune. *L'Autre moitié du développement*. Port-au-Prince: Imprimerie Henri Deschamps, 1986.

———, ed. "Une revue des conférences internationales sur la femme." Port-au-Prince: Comité Inter-Agences Femmes et Développement en Haïti, 1995.

Anglade, Mireille Neptune, and Georges Anglade. *Des espaces et des femmes*. Port-au-Prince: United Nations Development Program, 1988.

Aristide, Jean-Bertrand. *In the Parish of the Poor*. Maryknoll, N.Y.: Orbis Books, 1990.

———. "Mesaj Prezidan Aristide lan okazyon jounen 8 Mas la." Washington, D.C.: Ministère de l'Information, de la Culture, et de la Coordination, March 8, 1993.

———. "Women: In Labor for Deliverance." Unpublished, July 1994.

———. "Message du Président Jean-Bertrand Aristide à l'occasion de la Journée Internationale de la Femme." Port-au-Prince, March 8, 1995.

Aristide, Jean-Bertrand, and Beverly Bell. "Epilogue: Stronger Than the Gun." In *Jean-Bertrand Aristide: An Autobiography*, by Jean-Bertrand Aristide. Maryknoll, N.Y.: Orbis Books, 1993.

Auguste, Rose-Anne. "Femmes Haïtienne et la lutte pour la démocratie." Unpublished, December 1996.

Bazin, Danielle Tardieu. "Femmes et secteur informel en Haïti." Port-au-Prince: Forum Libre, 1989.

Bazin, Danielle Tardieu, Danielle Magloire, and Myriam Merlet. "Femmes/population/développement: Organisations féminines privées en Haïti." Port-au-Prince: Fonds des Nations Unies pour les Activités en Matière de Population, 1991.

Behar, Ruth. *Translated Woman*. Boston: Beacon Press, 1993.

Behar, Ruth, and Deborah Gordon, eds. *Women Writing Culture*. Berkeley: University of California Press, 1995.

Belance, Alerte. "Message of a Haitian Survivor on International Women's Day." *Update*, March 8, 1996 (Port-au-Prince).

Belizaire, Garry. "Les femmes Haïtiennes disent non à la violence." *Le Nouvelliste*, March 8, 1993.

Bell, Beverly. *Women Targeted for Attack, Rape in Haiti*. Washington, D.C.: International Liaison Office for President Aristide, April 1994.

———. *Women Targeted in Growing Military Violence in Haiti*. Washington, D.C.: International Liaison Office for President Aristide, May 1994.

———. *Women's Struggles, Women's Hopes*. Washington, D.C.: International Liaison Office for President Aristide, April 1995.

Bello, Bayyinah. "Situation of Women during the 36 Months of the U.S. Coup against the People of Haiti." Flushing, N.Y.: Spiral of Thinkers in Action, 1994.

Benjamin, Medea. *Don't Be Afraid, Gringo: A Honduran Woman Speaks from the Heart*. New York: Harper Perennial, 1987.

Benjamin, Medea, and Andrea Freedman. *Bridging the Global Gap*. Cabin John, Md.: Seven Locks Press, 1989.

Bennett, Olivia, Jo Bexley, and Kitty Warnock, eds. *Arms to Fight, Arms to Protect: Women Speak Out about Conflict*. London: Panos, 1995.

Berggren, Gretchen, Nirmala Murthy, and Stephen J. Williams. "Conjugal Unions among Poor Haitian Women." *Journal of Marriage and the Family* 37, No. 4 (November 1975).

Boff, Leonardo, and Clodovis Boff. *Introducing Liberation Theology*. Maryknoll, N.Y.: Orbis Books, 1994.

Boucard, Francoise, and Myriam Merlet. *Femmes et développement*. Port-au-Prince: Oxfam UKI, 1994.

Brady, Daniele. *From "Women and Development" to "Women and Gender."* Port-au-Prince: UNICEF, 1995.

Braxton, Joanne M. *Black Women Writing Autobiography*. Philadelphia: Temple University Press, 1989.

Brown, Karen McCarthy. *Mama Lola: A Vodou Priestess in Brooklyn*. Berkeley: University of California Press, 1991.

Bruch, Elizabeth. *Another Violence against Women: The Lack of Accountability in Haiti*. Minneapolis: Minnesota Advocates for Human Rights, December 1995.

Bruch, Elizabeth, and Neil Elliott. *No Justice in Sight for Rape Survivors*. Minneapolis: Resource Center of the Americas, February 1996.

Brydon, Lynne, and Sylvia Chant. *Women in the Third World: Gender Issues in Rural and Urban Areas*. New Brunswick, N.J.: Rutgers University Press, 1989.

Bunch, Charlotte, and Roxanna Carrillo. *Gender Violence: A Development and Human Rights Issue*. New Brunswick, N.J.: Center for Women's Global Leadership, 1991.

Cannon, Katie G. *Black Womanist Ethics*. Atlanta: Scholars Press, 1988.

Caritas d'Haiti. "Mesaj Karitas Nasyonal pou Jounen Entènasyonal Fanm." Papay-Hinche, Haiti, March 8, 1986.

Castor, Suzy. *Les femmes haïtiennes aux élections de 1990*. Port-au-Prince: Centre de Recherche et de Formation Economique et Sociale pour le Développement, 1994.

Castor, Suzy, et al. *Théories et pratiques de la lutte des femmes*. Port-au-Prince: Centre de Recherche et de Formation Economique et Sociale pour le Développement, 1987.

Castor, Suzy, Monique Brisson, and Morna McLeod. *Femme: Société et législation*. Port-au-Prince: Centre de Recherche et de Formation Economique et Sociale pour la Développement, 1988.

Center for International Policy. "Mobilizing Resources for Development: A Retrospect on President Aristide's Economic Strategy for Haiti and His Administration's Record with Aid Donors." *International Policy Report*, May 1992.

Centre de Promotion des Femmes Ouvrières (CPFO). "Legal Education and Legal Assistance Program for Haitian Women Factory Workers." Port-au-Prince: CPFO, 1990.

———. *La participation des femmes ouvrières de l'industrie de la sous-traitance en Haïti au mouvement syndical depuis Février 1986*. Port-au-Prince: CPFO, 1988.

Centre Haïtien de Recherches et d'Actions pour la Promotion Féminine. *Violences exercées sur les femmes et les filles en Haïti*. Port-au-Prince: Les Imprimeries Henri Deschamps, 1996.

Chalmers, Camille. "Haiti's Latest Coup: Structural Adjustment and the Struggle for Democracy." *Multinational Monitor*, May 1997.

Chalmers, Camille, and Jonathan Pitts. "Haiti: Responses and Alternatives to Structural Adjustment." London: Catholic Institute for International Relations, June 1997.

Charles, Carolle. "Feminism and Power: Haitian Women Political Struggles in Haiti and the Diaspora, 1930–1990." Unpublished, 1990.

———. "Toward a Redefinition of Citizenship, Democracy, and Civil Society: Haitian Women's Struggles during 1980–1990." Unpublished, 1994.

———. "Gender and Politics in Contemporary Haiti: The Duvalierist State, Transnationalism, and the Emergence of a New Feminism 1980–1990." *Feminist Studies* 21 (Spring 1995).

Clastres, Pierre. *Society against the State*. New York: Zone Books, 1989.

Clifford, James, and George E. Marcus, eds. *Writing Culture: The Poetics and Politics of Ethnography*. Berkeley: University of California Press, 1986.

Collectif Haïtien pour la Protection de l'Environnement et le Développement Alternatif, Multinational Resource Center, and Plate-forme Haïtienne de Plaidoyer pour un Développement Alternatif. "Resolutions from the Colloquium on the Environment." Port-au-Prince, June 1998.

Comaroff, Jean. *Body of Power, Spirit of Resistance*. Chicago: University of Chicago Press, 1985.

Commission Nationale de Verité et de Justice. *Si m pa rele*. Pétionville, Haiti: Commission Nationale de Verité et de Justice, 1995.

Danticat, Edwidge. "We Are Ugly, But We Are Here." *Creole Connection* IV, No. 11, Issue XIII (April–June 1998).

DeWind, Josh, and David Kinley. *Aiding Migration*. Boulder, Colo.: Westview Press, 1989.

Douglass, Frederick, "The Significance of Emancipation in the West Indies." Speech, Canandaigua, New York, August 3, 1857; collected in pamphlet by author. In *The*

Frederick Douglass Papers. Series One: Speeches, Debates, and Interviews. Vol. 3, 1855–1863. Edited by John W. Blassingame. New Haven: Yale University Press, 204.

Etter-Lewis, Gwendolyn, and Michele Foster, eds. *Unrelated Kin: Race and Gender in Women's Personal Narratives.* New York: Routledge, 1996.

Fanm SAJ, Groupe de Femmes Luttant pour la Democratie, and SOFA. "Deklarasyon fanm Ayisyen pou 8 Mas 1994." Port-au-Prince, March 5, 1994.

Farah, Douglas. "U.S. Shares Anti-Drug Data with Haiti's Military." *Washington Post,* October 24, 1993.

Farmer, Paul. *The Uses of Haiti.* Monroe, Maine: Common Courage Press, 1994.

Farmer, Paul, Margaret Connors, and Janie Simmons, eds. *Women, Poverty, and AIDS.* Monroe, Maine: Common Courage Press, 1996.

Fass, Simon. *The Economics of Survival: A Study of Poverty and Planning in Haiti.* Washington, D.C.: U.S. Agency for International Development Bureau of Development Support, 1980.

Fick, Carolyn E. *The Making of Haiti: The Saint Domingue Revolution from Below.* Knoxville, Tenn.: University of Tennessee Press, 1990.

Fonds Haïtien de Développement Economique et Social (FONHADES). *Les femmes dans le secteur informel.* Port-au-Prince: FONHADES, 1995.

Foucault, Alain. *Power and Knowledge.* New York: Pantheon Books, 1980.

———. *A History of Sexuality.* New York: Random House, 1990.

Fox Morning News. "Interview with Senator John Kerry (D-MA)." *Reuters Transcript Report, Fox Morning News,* October 28, 1993.

Freire, Paulo. *Cultural Action for Freedom.* Cambridge: Harvard Educational Review, 1970.

———. *Pedagogy of the Oppressed.* New York: Seabury Press, 1970.

Gallin, Rita, and Ann Ferguson. "Conceptualizing Difference: Gender, Class and Action." *Women and International Development Annual* 12 (1991).

Gaventa, John. *Power and Powerlessness: Quiescence and Rebellion in the Appalachian Valley.* Urbana: University of Illinois Press, 1980.

Gluck, Sherna Berger, and Daphne Patai, eds. *Women's Words: The Feminist Practice of Oral History.* New York: Routledge, 1991.

Golden, Renny. *The Hour of the Poor, the Hour of Women: Salvadoran Women Speak.* New York: Crossroad, 1991.

Gopaul, Roanna. *The Impact of Structural Adjustment on Women.* London: Oxfam UKI, 1994.

Government of Haiti. "Strategy of Social and Economic Reconstruction." Washington, D.C., August 22, 1994.

Gramsci, Antonio. *Selections from the Prison Notebooks.* New York: International Publishers, 1978.

Green, Mary Jean, Karen Gould, Micheline Rice-Maximin, Keith L. Walker, and Jack A. Yeager, eds. *Postcolonial Subjects: Francophone Women Writers.* Minneapolis: University of Minnesota Press, 1996.

Haitian Information Bureau. "Conflict on Woman's Day." *Haiti Info* 1, No. 15 (March 14, 1993).

———. "Women Criticize U.N." *Haiti Info* 2, No. 12 (March 12, 1994).

———. "Haitian Women: Facing Challenges." *Haiti Info* 4, No. 9 (March 9, 1996).

Harbury, Jennifer. *Bridge of Courage.* Monroe, Maine: Common Courage Press, 1995.

hooks, bell. *Yearning: Race, Gender, and Cultural Politics.* Boston: South End Press, 1990.

Hooks, Margaret. *Guatemalan Women Speak*. Washington, D.C.: Ecumenical Program on Central America and the Caribbean (EPICA), 1993.

Human Rights Watch and National Coalition for Haitian Refugees. *Silencing a People: The Destruction of Civil Society in Haiti*. New York: Americas Watch and National Coalition for Haitian Refugees, 1993.

———. *Rape in Haiti: A Weapon of Terror*. New York: Human Rights Watch, 1994.

Inter-American Development Bank. *Economic and Social Progress in Latin America: 1990 Report*. Washington, D.C.: Inter-American Development Bank, 1990.

———. *Haiti: Basic Socio-Economic Data*. Washington, D.C.: Inter-American Development Bank, November 1994.

———. *Women in the Americas: Bridging the Gender Gap*. Washington, D.C.: Inter-American Development Bank, 1995.

International Civilian Mission to Haiti, Organization of American States/United Nations. "Communique de presse." Port-au-Prince, May 19, 1994.

International Monetary Fund. *Country Information*. http://www.imf.org/external/pubs/ft/scr/1999/cr99118.pdf.

James, Erica. "Political Cleansing in Haiti: 1991–1994." Unpublished, January 1996.

Jayawardena, Kumari. *Feminism and Nationalism in the Third World*. London: Zed Books, 1986.

Jean, Monique, Rica Louis, and Olga Benoit. "Rezolisyon SOFA nan okasyon 25 Novanm jounen entènasyonal kont vyolans k ap fèt sou fanm." Port-au-Prince: SOFA, November 25, 1995.

Jean-Jacques, Maryse, Ghislaine Fabien, Edèle Thébaud, and Michèle Larosilliere. *Femme: Organisation et lutte*. Port-au-Prince: Centre de Recherche et de Formation Economique et Sociale pour le Développement, no date cited.

Kabeer, Naila. *Reversed Realities*. London: Verso Books, 1995.

Kay Fanm. "Différentes formes de violence faite aux femmes." *Résistance et démocratie* 2, No. 36 (May 10–20, 1994).

Kifner, John. "Haitians Ask If U.S. Had Ties to Attache." *New York Times*, October 6, 1994.

Lappe, Frances Moore, and Rachel Shurman. *Taking Population Seriously*. San Francisco: Institute for Food and Development Policy, 1990.

Lawless, Robert. *Haiti's Bad Press*. Rochester, Vt.: Schenkman Books, 1992.

Lewis, Faith, and Allen LeBel. *Source Report on Haitian Factory Women: Present Work and Household Conditions, with Recommendations for Development Intervention*. Port-au-Prince: U.S. Agency for International Development Office of Women in Development and U.S. Mission to Haiti, 1994.

Lorde, Audre. "The Master's Tools Will Never Dismantle the Master's House." In *This Bridge Called My Back*, edited by Cherrie Moraga and Gloria Anzaldua. New York: Kitchen Table/Women of Color Press, 1983.

Lukes, Steven, ed. *Power*. New York: New York University Press, 1986.

Macdonald, Mandy. *Women's Rights and Development: Visions and Strategy for the Twenty-First Century*. London: Oxfam UKI, 1995.

Marcelin, Magalie. "Les féministes de l'Amérique Latine au Salvador." *Rencontre* 9 (June–July 1994).

Martineau, Jean-Claude. "Cultural Resistance: Haitian Culture: Basis for Haiti's Development." *Roots* 1, No. 4 (Winter 1996–1997).

Maternowska, Mary Catherine. "Coups d'Etat and Contraceptives: The Forces of Fertility in Haiti." Unpublished, 1996.

McGowan, Lisa. *Democracy Undermined, Economic Justice Denied: Structural Adjustment and the Aid Juggernaut in Haiti.* Washington, D.C.: Development Group for Alternative Policy, January 1997.

Miami Herald. "Files Contend Haiti Ignoring Trafficker." *Miami Herald*, April 4, 1993.

Milfort, Rose Laure. "Nòt pou laprès." Port-au-Prince: Solidarite Fanm Ayisyen, May 17, 1993.

———. "Nòt pou laprès." Port-au-Prince: Solidarite Fanm Ayisyen, April 28, 1994.

Ministère à la Condition Féminine et aux Droits de la Femme. Collection of statements and position papers (no title). Port-au-Prince, 1995.

———. "Message on the Occasion of the Inauguration of the Headquarters of the Ministry on the Status and Rights of Women." Port-au-Prince, 1995.

Mohanty, Chandra. "Under Western Eyes: Feminist Scholarship and Colonial Discourses." *Feminist Review* 30 (Autumn 1988).

Momsen, Janet, ed. *Women and Change in the Caribbean.* London: James Currey, 1993.

Moore, Barrington. *Injustice: The Social Bases of Obedience and Revolt.* White Plains, N.Y.: M. E. Sharpe, 1978.

Mosse, Julie Cleeves. *Half the World, Half a Chance: An Introduction to Gender and Development.* Oxford: Oxfam, 1993.

Mouvman Peyizan Papay/Education and Development Fund. "MPP Women: Committed to Permanent Resistance." *Peasant* 3, No. 1 (February 1986).

Myers, Marcia. "Claiming CIA Ties, Haitian Sues over Detention in U.S." *Baltimore Sun*, December 12, 1995.

Nairn, Allan. "Behind Haiti's Paramilitaries." *Nation*, October 24, 1994.

———. "Haiti under the Gun: How U.S.-Backed Paramilitaries Rule through Fear." *Nation*, 262, No. 2 (January 8–15, 1996).

New England Observers' Delegation. *Courage Washing Misery: Haitians Told Us Their Stories.* Boston: July 1994.

Nordstrom, Carolyn, and JoAnn Martin, eds. *The Paths to Domination, Resistance, and Terror.* Berkeley: University of California Press, 1992.

Occident, Kesta. Message de la conférence des religieux haïtien. "Démocratie: La solution à la crise Haïtienne." Washington, D.C.: Government of Haiti, 1994.

Organisations des Femmes du Sud. "Déclaration adoptée par des organisations des femmes du sud a l'occasion de la Conférence des Femmes pour le Changement." Thailand, February 26–March 2, 1994.

Organization of American States Inter-American Commission on Human Rights. "Communication Respecting the Violations of Human Rights of Haitian Women." Washington, D.C.: Organization of American States, 1994.

Personal Narratives Group. *Interpreting Women's Lives.* Bloomington: Indiana University Press, 1989.

Pharr, Suzanne. "Transformational Organizing." *Ark* (National Organizers Alliance) No. 4 (Winter 1995).

——. "Taking the High Road." *Ms. Magazine* 7, No. 1 (July/August 1996): 65–69.

Phelan, Anna Hamilton. "The Latest Political Weapon in Haiti: Military Rapes of Women and Girls." *Los Angeles Times*, June 5, 1994.

Plate-forme Haïtienne de Plaidoyer pour un Développement Alternatif. "L'Avenir economique d'Haïti." Port-au-Prince: PAPDA, 1995.

——. "Différence entre la justice economique et les politique neo-liberales." Port-au-Prince: PAPDA, 1995.

——. "Economie Haïtienne, le mirage de la croissance." Port-au-Prince: PAPDA, 1999.

——. *Justice Economique.* Port-au Prince: 6, February–June 1998.

——. *Justice Economique.* Port-au Prince: 7, July–September 1998.

——. *Justice Economique.* Port-au Prince: 8, October 1999.

Poulantzas, Nicos. *Political Power and Social Classes.* London: NLB, 1968.

Pressoir, Eveline. *Sexual Discrimination: A Social Construct.* Port-au-Prince: UNICEF, 1995.

——. *Women against Themselves.* Port-au-Prince: UNICEF, 1995.

Puleo, Mev. *The Struggle Is One: Voices and Visions of Liberation.* New York: State University of New York, 1994.

Ramazanoglu, Caroline. *Feminism and the Contradictions of Oppression.* London: Routledge, 1989.

Randall, Margaret. *Sandino's Daughters.* Vancouver: New Star Books, 1981.

——. *Risking a Somersault in the Air: Conversations with Nicaraguan Writers.* San Francisco: Solidarity Publications, 1984.

——. *Sandino's Daughters Revisited.* New Brunswick, N.J.: Rutgers University Press, 1994.

——. *Our Voices, Our Lives: Stories of Women from Central America and the Caribbean.* Monroe, Maine: Common Courage Press, 1995.

Reardon, Geraldine. *Power and Process.* UK and Ireland: Oxfam UKI, 1995.

Roots. "Report on Haitian Women." *Roots* 1, No. 3 (Summer 1995).

Russell, Letty M., Kwok Pui-lan, Ada María Isasi-Díaz, and Katie Geneva Cannon, eds. *Inheriting Our Mothers' Gardens: Feminist Theology in Third World Perspective.* Philadelphia: Westminster Press, 1988.

Sant Enfòmasyon Dokimantsyon ak Rechèch sou Ayiti. "Represyon sou fanm ayisyen: Yon represyon sou tout fas." *Ayiti an pèspektif* 4, No. 3 (March–April 1994).

Schneider, Beth, and Nancy Stoller. *Women Resisting AIDS: Feminist Strategies of Empowerment.* Philadelphia: Temple University Press, 1995.

Scott, James C. *Weapons of the Weak: Everyday Forms of Peasant Resistance.* New Haven: Yale University Press, 1985.

——. *Domination and the Art of Resistance.* New Haven: Yale University Press, 1990.

Sen, Rinku. *We Are the Ones We Are Waiting for: Woman of Color Organizing for Transformation.* Durham, N.C.: United States Urban Rural Mission, 1995.

Smith, Jennie. *When the Hands Are Many: Community Organization and Social Change in Rural Haiti.* Ithaca: Cornell University Press, 2001.

Solidarite Fanm Ayisyen. "Rezolisyon rankont solidarite: Dwa fanm enfas krazezo." Port-au-Prince, March 9, 1993.

Swiss, Shana, and Joan Giller. "Rape as a Crime of War." *Journal of American Medical Association* 270, No. 5 (August 4, 1993).

Sylvain, Madeleine. "The Feminist Movement in Haiti." *Bulletin of the Pan American Union* 72, No. 6 (1939).

Tardif, Francine. "La situation des femmes Haïtiennes." Port-au-Prince: Comité Inter-Agences Femmes et Développement, Système des Nations Unies en Haïti, 1991.

Thébaud, Edèle. *La femme dans l'économie nationale.* Port-au-Prince: UNICEF, 1996.

———. *Gid pou travay ak fanm nan kominote yo.* Port-au-Prince: Comité Inter-Agences Femmes et Développement en Haïti, 1994.

Trouillot, Michel-Rolph. *Haiti State against Nation.* New York: Monthly Review Press, 1990.

———. *Silencing the Past: Power and the Production of History.* Boston: Beacon Press, 1995.

Tula, Maria Teresa, and Lynn Stephen. *Hear My Testimony: Maria Teresa Tula, Human Rights Activist of El Salvador.* Boston: South End Press, 1994.

United Nations Development Program. *The World's Women 1995: Trends and Statistics.* New York: United Nations, 1995.

———. *Human Development Report 1995.* New York: Oxford University Press, 1995.

———. *Human Development Report 1998.* New York: Oxford University Press, 1998.

———. *Report for Cooperation and Development.* New York: Oxford University Press, 1998.

———. *Human Development Report 2000.* http://www.undp.org/hdr2000/english/book/back2.pdf, 2000.

U.S. Department of State. "Declassified State Department Document 79 D." Washington, D.C., 1964.

———. "Memorandum to Latin American Committee 80 B." Washington, D.C., 1964.

U.S. Embassy, Port-au-Prince. "Confidential Cablegram." Port-au-Prince, April 12, 1994.

Verna, Virginia, and Jessica Nicolas. *Le travail féminin en milieu rural.* Port-au-Prince: Comite Haïtien de Coopération avec la CIM, no date cited.

Vicioso, Luisa Sherezada. *In Search of Equal Opportunity.* Port-au-Prince: UNICEF, 1995.

———. *Working with Rather than for Women.* Port-au-Prince: UNICEF, 1995.

Weiner, Tim. "Haitian Ex-Paramilitary Leader Confirms CIA Relationship." *New York Times,* December 3, 1995.

Weisbrot, Mark, et al. *Restoring Democracy to Haiti: A Question of Economic and Ecological Survival.* Washington, D.C.: Institute for Policy Studies, 1994.

Werleigh, Claudette. "Socio-Cultural, Economic, and Political Portrait of Haitian Women." Unpublished, April 1989.

———. "Working for Change in Haiti." *Justice Paper 12,* London: Catholic Institute for International Relations, July 1989.

———. "Press Release." Washington, D.C.: Ministère des Affaires Etrangères, May 25, 1994.

———. "Women and Their Participation in Politics." *Forum libre du jeudi,* no date cited.

Williams, Stephen J., Nirmala Murthy, and Gretchen Berggren, "Conjugal Unions among Poor Haitian Women. *Journal of Marriage and the Family,* 37, No. 4 (November 1975).

World Bank. "Draft of Haiti: The Challenges of Poverty Reduction." Washington, D.C., 1997.

Wright, Scott. *Promised Land: Death and Life in El Salvador.* Maryknoll, N.Y.: Orbis Press, 1994.

Yee, Danny. "Anthropology Informs Political Economy: A Book Review." http://www.anatomy.su.oz.au/danny/book-reviews, 1–4, 1994.

About the Author

For more than twenty years, Beverly Bell has worked to support and strengthen grassroot movements for political and economic rights and gender justice in Latin America, the Caribbean, the United States, and South Africa. Her most extensive work has been with the Haitian democracy and women's movements. Bell currently directs the Center for Economic Justice.